Designing Effective Library Tutorials

D1370031

CHANDOS
INFORMATION PROFESSIONAL SERIES

Series Editor: Ruth Rikowski
(Email: Rikowskigr@aol.com)

Chandos' new series of books is aimed at the busy information professional. They have been specially commissioned to provide the reader with an authoritative view of current thinking. They are designed to provide easy-to-read and (most importantly) practical coverage of topics that are of interest to librarians and other information professionals. If you would like a full listing of current and forthcoming titles, please visit our website, www.chandospublishing.com, email wp@woodheadpublishing.com or telephone +44 (0) 1223 399140.

New authors: we are always pleased to receive ideas for new titles; if you would like to write a book for Chandos, please contact Dr Glyn Jones on gjones@chandospublishing.com or telephone +44 (0) 1993 848726.

Bulk orders: some organisations buy a number of copies of our books. If you are interested in doing this, we would be pleased to discuss a discount. Please email wp@woodheadpublishing.com or telephone +44 (0) 1223 499140.

Designing Effective Library Tutorials

A guide for accommodating multiple learning styles

LORI S. MESTRE

CP

CHANDOS
PUBLISHING

Oxford Cambridge New Delhi

ZA
3075
M47
2012
c.3

Chandos Publishing
Hexagon House
Avenue 4
Station Lane
Witney
Oxford OX28 4BN
UK
Tel: +44 (0) 1993 848726
Email: info@chandospublishing.com
www.chandospublishing.com
www.chandospublishingonline.com

Chandos Publishing is an imprint of Woodhead Publishing Limited

Woodhead Publishing Limited
80 High Street
Sawston
Cambridge CB22 3HJ
UK
Tel: +44 (0) 1223 499140
Fax: +44 (0) 1223 832819
www.woodheadpublishing.com

First published in 2012
06-20-13
ISBN: 978-1-84334-688-3 (print)
ISBN: 978-1-78063-325-1 (online)

Typeset by Domex e-Data Pvt. Ltd., India
Printed in the UK by 4edge Ltd, Hockley, Essex.

Contents

List of figures, tables and charts

Figures

Tables

Chart

Acknowledgements

The idea for this book came as a result of talking with many librarians who were struggling with best ways in which to design learning objects. Many librarians enter the profession without a background in teaching or design strategies, and many have limited technological skills. I thank these librarians for their candor, suggestions, and calls for help with a guide that will help them to create effective, pedagogically sound learning objects for their students.

I thank the students at the University of Illinois who were willing to take part in the usability study of the tutorials and provide their perspectives and suggestions for improving them.

I also thank the University of Illinois for granting me a sabbatical to work on the book and the Research and Publication Committee of the University of Illinois at Urbana-Champaign Library which provided support for the completion of my research and to hire an indexer. Special thanks to Linde Brocato for her careful scrutiny of the manuscript and for her indexing work. Additionally, I appreciate the copy-editing work of Geraldine Lyons.

Finally, to my husband, Jose, I am deeply grateful for the editing suggestions for the book and for your patience.

About the author

Dr. Lori Mestre is an Associate Professor of Library Administration and Head of the Undergraduate Library at the University of Illinois at Urbana-Champaign. In addition to her Master of Arts in Library Science degree, she has a doctorate in Education specializing in language, culture, and curriculum and has devoted the last eighteen years to exploring the intersection between multicultural librarianship, learning styles, and online learning environments that best reflect the diverse needs of students. In addition to numerous articles and presentations related to her research, in 2010 she published a book entitled *Librarians Serving Diverse Populations: Challenges and Opportunities* (ACRL Publications in Librarianship).

Introduction: matching online learning and tutorial design with learning styles – the student perspective

With an ever-growing list of demands placed on faculty and librarians' shoulders, it is not surprising that in today's electronically connected world, more time and energy are being used in the creation and implementation of online web-based tutorials. The creation of learning objects and tutorials can expand the instructional reach and effectiveness of educators and can free up time-intensive responsibilities like classroom instruction, while providing 24/7 access to instructional services for library users. Often these online library tutorials are "linear and basically follow a sequential order" (Bailin and Peña, 2007). Other presentations and structures might be effective for learners, but may be overlooked. This book provides evidence from various research studies and student comments of some of the strategies and best practices for designing learning objects and tutorials to facilitate learning for students with multiple learning styles. In addition to examples, it also provides steps for creating tutorials to match the learning styles of students, based on usability studies of students from multiple cultural groups and with multiple learning styles. Students' perceptions of their experiences using tutorials and learning objects are merged throughout the chapters and form the basis of the creation of best practices for designing these tools to accommodate multiple learning styles.

Numerous processes and software packages are being used to create tutorials to either augment or replace face-to-face instruction. The research studies that will form the foundation of this book (Mestre, 2010, 2012) investigated three types of tutorials: a static web page with screenshots; a video tutorial (produced with Camtasia, a screen casting software); and an interactive Flash-based tutorial. Tutorials can facilitate a teachable moment at the point of need, and can be embedded within course sites, web pages, online guides, online catalogs, or other databases to provide instructions on specific tasks. They can provide asynchronous assistance and students can view them repeatedly in their own time at any hour of the day, which is particularly helpful for students who wish to learn independently. Closed captioning features can assist students who may be non-native English speakers or who have auditory disabilities. Depending upon the interactivity available in these tutorials, they have the potential to engage visual, auditory, and kinesthetic learners, as well as to accommodate students who learn best through observation, listening, or by engaging in hands-on activities. In addition to the results of this research study, this book expands on data, comments, and preferences by students with various learning styles from this and other tutorial research studies. It also suggests best practices for designing tutorials to provide optimal learning experiences for all types of learners. Permission was granted to include the screenshots of representative tutorials and learning objects.

Definitions

Generally, terms will be defined as needed throughout the book. However, the following two terms warrant definition here, since they are immediately and frequently used.

Learning object

A learning object is a reusable instructional resource, usually digital and web based, developed to support learning. Some common examples of learning objects are instructional modules, tutorials, instructional games, blogs, research guides, narrated PowerPoint presentations, podcasts, photographs, images, quizzes, surveys, and videos. Chapter 4 provides a more thorough definition.

Learning style

The term "learning style" is sometimes used interchangeably with terms such as "learning preferences," "thinking styles," "cognitive styles," and "learning modalities." Research on learning styles evolved from psychological research on individual differences, which was widespread in the 1960s and 1970s (Curry, 1987). Learning style research has resulted in the development of more than 70 models and instruments that have been used to understand how individuals approach learning. Fleming (2005) described learning styles as individuals' characteristics and preferred ways of gathering, organizing, and thinking about information. Keefe (1979), working with The National Association of Secondary School Principals (NASSP), described learning styles as "characteristic cognitive, affective, and psychological behaviors that indicated how learners perceived, interacted with, and responded to the learning environment" (p. 4). More definitions, approaches, and theories are described in Chapter 1.

Summary of chapters

Chapter 1 discusses the controversy related to learning styles and provides an overview of the challenges and research that document the potential impact, both negative and positive, that can occur in the learning process when learning styles are taken into consideration.

Chapter 2 provides an overview of learning styles, including definitions, theories, and models.

Chapter 3 explores the intersection of culture, learning styles, and online learning. It summarizes studies exploring how students from different cultures process and retain information and suggests some applications for designing online tools to better reflect cultural needs or expectations. Examples of tutorials and learning objects that provide options for various learning styles are included.

Chapter 4 provides an overview of the benefits of creating or using learning objects and tutorials; categories of tutorials developed; current practices for accessing tutorials; challenges to creating tutorials (online information literacy); and an overview of the role of librarians in creating tutorials.

Chapter 5 details some of the tools and tutorials used by instructors to provide supplemental support to their students, as well as examples of types of tutorials developed, whether web based, podcasts, screencasting, or videos.

Chapter 6 discusses strategies and guidelines for designing learning objects to accommodate various learning styles. The strategies are informed by research related to effective pedagogical strategies in the online medium.

Chapter 7 outlines some pedagogical considerations for generating meaningful content for both the novice and the advanced learner, and presents examples of instructional cognitive theories, and looks at how elements of the theories can be integrated into tutorials.

Chapter 8 discusses the value of providing interactivity and active learning in tutorials as well as examples of exercises and interactivity.

Chapter 9 describes the role assessment plays in tutorial design and includes various assessment strategies that can be used to evaluate the effectiveness of tutorials.

Chapter 10 discusses the purpose and methods of usability testing and provides some examples.

Chapter 11 includes strategies for publicizing and marketing websites and tutorials by working with faculty, using social networking tools, and creating online and print marketing.

Chapter 12 is devoted to resources and examples related to the design of tutorials and learning objects, such as scripts used for usability studies, guidelines for designing tutorials, and descriptions and links to tutorials.

Finally, the appendices provided at the end of the book give examples of scripts used in usability studies, guidelines for creating a Camtasia tutorial, and a sample communication plan.

References

Bailin, A. and Peña, A. (2007) Online library tutorials, narratives, and scripts. *The Journal of Academic Librarianship*, 33(1): 106–17.

Curry, L. (1987) *Integrating Concepts of Cognitive Learning Style: A Review with Attention to Psychometric Standards*. Ottawa, ON: Canadian College of Health Science Executives.

Fleming, N.D. (2005) *Teaching and Learning Styles: VARK Strategies* (2nd edn.). Christchurch, New Zealand: The Digital Print and Copy Center.

Keefe, J.W. (1979) Learning style: an overview. In *NASSP's Student Learning Styles: Diagnosing and Prescribing Program*, pp. 1–17. Reston, VA: NASSP.

Mestre, L.S. (2010) Matching up learning styles with learning objects: what's effective? *Journal of Library Administration*, 50(7–8): 808–82.

Mestre, L.S. (2012) Student preference and results after comparing screencast and static tutorials: a usability study. *Reference Services Review*, 40(2): 258–76.

The learning styles debate: do we need to match up learning styles with presentation styles?

Abstract: This chapter discusses the controversy related to the study of learning styles, and provides an overview of the challenges and research that document the potential impact, both negative and positive, that can occur in the learning process when learning styles are taken into consideration. Some of the criticisms of the study of learning styles revolve around: the lack of a common definition for learning styles; whether the learning style inventories are valid; whether learning styles are measurable; and whether learning style-based instruction results in learning gains. The chapter also examines the debate on whether or not educators should consider learning styles when preparing their courses, and includes solutions/compromises regardless of the controversy for educators interested in using learning style research to modify their instructional efforts.

Key words: learning styles, teaching styles, learning style inventories, teaching methods, cognitive styles.

Introduction

The theory, practice, and validity of learning styles and learning style inventories have generated great interest and controversy for more than thirty years. Issues have surfaced from both the educational psychology field and that of adaptive educational systems regarding the belief that it is possible to attribute a particular learning style to an individual. One of the challenges lies in the fact that it is not possible to accurately attribute a learning style due partly to the complex nature of learning and numerous uncontrollable variables. Debate is also ongoing as to whether or not teachers should consider learning styles when preparing or teaching their courses. This chapter provides an overview of the criticisms and challenges of incorporating learning styles into teaching as well as observations, quotes, and suggestions from educators regarding learning styles to illustrate the multitude of issues. The chapter also contains suggestions for solutions and compromises regardless of the controversy for educators interested in using learning style research to modify their instructional efforts.

Definition of learning styles

The term "learning styles" is sometimes used interchangeably with terms such as "learning preferences," "thinking styles," "cognitive styles," and "learning modalities." Cassidy (2004) noted that researchers have yet to agree on any aspects of learning style, including its definition. Here are some of the commonly used definitions in the literature:

- Dunn (1990, p. 353): a biologically and developmentally determined set of personal characteristics that make the identical instruction effective for some students and ineffective for others and "the way in which individuals begin to concentrate on, process, internalize, and retain new and difficult information."

- Cornett (1983): a consistent pattern of behavior but with a certain range of individual variability.

- Fleming (2001, p.1): refers to individuals' characteristics and preferred ways of gathering, organizing, and thinking about information.

- Gregorc (1997, 1979, p. 19): "distinctive and observable behaviors that provide clues about the mediation abilities of individuals and how their minds relate to the world and, therefore, how they learn."

- James and Gardner (1985, p. 20) suggest that individual learning styles are developed as an outcome of heredity, experience, and current environment, and that a core concept of learning styles is "how people react to their learning environment."

- Keefe (1979, p.4): "a composite of characteristic cognitive, affective and psychological factors that serve as relatively stable indicators of how a learner perceives, interacts with and responds to the learning."

- Kolb (1984): perceived learning as a circular process in which learning was a series of experiences with cognitive additions: concrete experience, reflection and observation, abstract concepts and generalizations, and active experimentation.

- Messick and Associates (1976): information processing habits representing the learner's typical mode of perceiving, thinking, problem solving, and remembering.

The lack of a standard definition for learning style has resulted in learning style models and instruments that are based on different concepts of learning style, and therefore cause variation in the standards of reliability and validity of psychometric instruments (Curry, 1987). Beyond the definitions, learning style theories contend that individuals differ in how they understand the external world through their senses (the sense modality of stimuli). This can impact on how they best absorb, retain, and process new information (Honey and Mumford, 1982; Dunn, 1983, 1993; Kolb, 1984; Curry, 1990; Felder, 1993; Cassidy and Eachus, 2000; Zapalska and Dabb, 2002; Harrison et al., 2003; Fleming, 2005; Pheiffer et al., 2005). Specifically, how well a person absorbs and retains information depends largely on whether the information was received in the person's preferred learning modality. According to learning style theory, a person who is a visual learner needs to see, observe, record, and write to learn best; an auditory learner prefers information that is spoken and heard, as it is in dialog and discussion; and a kinesthetic learner prefers to learn in an environment where material can be touched and he or she can be physically involved with the to-be-learned information. For instance, a "visual learner" is hypothesized to learn optimally with pictorial or other visual stimuli such as diagrams, charts, or maps, whereas an "auditory learner" performs best with spoken stimuli, such as a lecture.

Proliferation of learning style models, inventories, and terms

With more than 70 learning style models and inventories to choose from it can become problematic to accurately describe learning style characteristics. Terms and concepts sometimes overlap and there is no mapping between different models (and no agreed taxonomy). Some of the possible problems that critics see in the application of learning styles involve the potential to categorize students into a specific learning style and simply label them as such. Another potentially problematic area is the stability of learning style (whether an individual's learning style can change over a period of time). Some researchers believe that learning style is a permanent attribute of human cognition, while others believe that it can change over time.

Popescu (2010) devised a Unified Learning Style Model with the hope that it could address some of the identified criticisms related to learning styles. This model synthesizes characteristics from the main models in the literature, providing an integrative taxonomy. More specifically, Popescu's model integrates learning preferences related to perception modality, ways of processing and organizing information, as well as motivational and social aspects. The criticisms described below pre-date the article that discussed the model. Although much of the criticism focuses on the fact that there is not just one model, other criticisms pertain to the need for accurate measures.

Learning gains?

Even though it appears that learning style research is frequently used to assist in course design and teaching practices, not all researchers agree that learning style-based instruction results in learning gains. Studies involving the effectiveness of learning style-based instruction have yielded mixed results, with some researchers concluding that students learn more when presented with material that is matched with their learning style (Claxton and Murrell, 1987; Sims and Sims 1995; Ford and Chen, 2000, 2001) while others have not seen any significant improvements (Stahl, 1999; Pashler et al., 2008). One of the problems with determining the effectiveness of learning styles in an educational setting is that there are many variables to consider, such as learner aptitude/ability, willingness, motivation, personality traits, the learning task and context, prior student knowledge, and the environment (Jonassen and Grabowski, 1993). A review commissioned by the Association for Psychological Science (APS) (Pashler et al., 2008) was unable to uncover any evidence to suggest that tailoring instruction to these preferences actually produces better learning outcomes.

Krätzig and Arbuthnott (2006) observed that learning style questionnaires can provide educators with information about respondents' preferences or self-beliefs and could be useful to them as they modify their instruction to be more familiar to students. However, they caution educators against believing that those modifications might improve their students' learning, although they might help their motivation to learn. Their results show that although categorizing each person as a specific type of learner is easy, individuals' memory efficiency is not limited by sensory modality, nor are people able to learn in the same way in all situations. Instead, most people are likely to be multimodal and multisituational learners, changing learning strategies depending on the context of the to-be-learned material.

Some adaptations to learning styles may lead instructional developers to teach concepts using multiple illustrations. In such practices, the instructional material may illustrate concepts, presumably the complex ones, in different ways, leading learners to form multiple representations. The designer may assume that the multiple illustrations work because learners choose the representation that is most congruent to their learning styles. It is probably more likely that such instruction is effective because the multiple illustrations induce learners to devote more time to these concepts.

The personality traits of each individual student also play an important role in the learning process. Some students are naturally anxious, have a low tolerance for ambiguity, and tend to get frustrated easily, while others are patient and are able to work through ambiguity without getting frustrated.

Are learning styles measurable?

Most researchers and educators agree that individuals have learning preferences, albeit liable to change depending upon the situation and need. Their concern, however, is with the reliability and validity of the inventories and instruments used to identify learning styles, as well as whether or not it is effective to consider learning styles in education (Stahl, 1999; Coffield et al., 2004). Researchers have observed a great deal of variability between many of these instruments. Harrison et al. (2003) argue that many of the available learning style instruments have never been validated.

Criticism of variables influencing responses on the questionnaires

There are numerous learning style inventories and questionnaires designed to test learning preferences through a series of questions. Some researchers conclude that the questions do not typically result in individuals engaging in detailed analysis of their previous experience, such as the recall and categorization of several relevant memories (e.g., Tourangeau et al., 2000). Rather, such questions are typically answered by respondents using information that readily comes to mind in response to the question and then making judgements either on the basis of limited information or using other factors such as the ease with which relevant information came to mind (Sloman, 2002; Krätzig and Arbuthnott, 2006).

Many of the learning style inventories, questionnaires, and instruments are self-reports. In other words, the adult or student fills out a response to a series of questions, and the frequency of responses indicates certain preferences for specific approaches to learning. One of the main criticisms is that learning style research has simply identified learning styles through self-report questionnaires (e.g., Delahoussaye, 2002; Haar et al., 2002; Loo, 2002) without assessing the basic hypothesis underlying the theory. When a person is asked to respond to specific words and questions, the language is interpreted through personal (cultural) experience. Some assessment instruments test a person's strengths, or the ability to do tasks with a certain approach (and by recalling an instance at that particular point in time; memory performance). When strengths are tested and learning style inferred from the results of these instruments, a great deal of variety exists within like-cultural groups.

Additionally, the learning style questionnaires are based upon an assumption that students are motivated to answer them properly and that the students are aware of their preferred way of learning. Social and psychological aspects can also influence students' answers (Graf, 2007). There are many factors which could influence how a participant responds to a question on any given day, including: motivation (Shih and Gamon, 2001), health, emotions, environment (time of day, distractions, the temperature in the room), the familiarity with the topics in the questions, how much sleep they have had, or if they are hungry or thirsty. The amount of time individuals take to consider the question and to recall examples or experiences related to the question could vary tremendously. Also, if participants answer quickly without reflecting on actual experiences, or choose the most recent example that comes to mind, it becomes difficult to know if that one instance is indicative of a particular preference. In addition, the accuracy of self-perceptions is questionable: "self-perceptions can be misleading and the answers are easy to fake if someone is determined to give a misleading impression" (Honey and Mumford, 1982, p. 20, 2006).

Criticism of the reliability and validity of instruments

Another criticism is that dedicated inventories suffer from psychometric weaknesses: some of the instruments used to measure learning styles could not demonstrate internal consistency, test-retest reliability or construct and predictive validity (Coffield et al., 2004). Psychometric instruments can usually be applied only once per student. Questionnaires themselves raise issues, for example that they should fulfill four criteria: construct validity, predictive validity, internal consistency reliability, and test-retest reliability. Construct validity looks at whether the instrument measures the theoretical construct that it claims to measure. Predictive validity looks at whether the range of behavior can be seen to have an impact on task performance. The internal consistency reliability refers to there being a consistency in the results, and attempts to ensure that the items that measure the constructs (concept, model, idea) deliver consistent scores. The test-retest reliability measures the extent to which an individual achieves the same result when performing the questionnaire twice within a specific period. Coffield et al.'s study showed that only three of the 13 learning styles studied came close to these standards. As a result, it is advised that individuals are aware of the limitations when interpreting the results.

Most of these instruments were developed based on college-educated Caucasian reliability and validity samples (Messick and Associates, 1976; Claxton and Murrell, 1987; Hickcox, 1995). So when these instruments are used with diverse populations, the reliability and validity of the instrument might not hold. The increasingly diverse population has prompted researchers to conduct learning style research on various ethnic groups to get a more accurate assessment of how ethnicity factors into the validity and reliability of these instruments. Additional concerns are discussed below.

Criticism of the research designs used to measure learning styles

Pashler et al. (2008) argue that very few studies regarding the effectiveness of learning styles have had an adequate research design, which in their view would be to assign students randomly into one classroom or another, with one teacher modifying the course to match student learning styles and the other teacher continuing with the standard practice. With regard to the few studies which used the controlled environment they contend that the researchers mostly failed to support the hypothesis that teaching styles should match students' learning styles. They assert that no one has ever proved that any particular style of instruction simultaneously helps students who have one learning style while also harming students who have a different learning style. In a given lesson, one instructional technique turns out to be optimal for all groups of students, even though students with certain learning styles may not favor that technique.

Criticisms of tailoring instruction based on learning styles

This section examines some of the criticism related to modifying teaching to accommodate different learning styles. A common objective has been that educators should identify their students' learning styles and then develop teaching methods to fit each student. Many psychologists recommend that the teaching style of the instructor should correspond to the learning style of the student (the "matching hypothesis"). Felder (1993, p. 289), for example, mentions that mismatching can have serious consequences, as students may feel as though: "they are being addressed in an unfamiliar foreign language. They tend to get lower grades than students whose learning styles are better matched to the instructor's teaching style and are less likely to develop an interest in the course material."

Dunn and Griggs (2003) also suggest that teachers adapt the instruction and environmental conditions by allowing learners to work with their strong preferences and to avoid, as far as possible, activities for which learners report having very low preferences. Santo (2001) observed that a major mismatch between the instructor's style and learners' styles can lead to trouble. She gives an example of one such mismatch in a case where a learner preferred independent work and reading, but the instructor preferred group projects. Santo advocates for varying methods, remaining flexible to changing planned activities rather than relying on one method in order to work with students whose learning style might be at odds with a teaching style.

This matching hypothesis means that students' learning style should be similar to the instructional style (Coffield et al., 2004). Smith et al. (2002) also researched this area and found that for each research study supporting the matching hypothesis there is a study rejecting it. Some psychologists support a view that using a variety of teaching styles and providing mismatching materials could help avoid boredom, boost attention, and at the same time prepare students to develop new learning strategies and improve their weaker learning styles (Grasha, 1984; Apter, 2001). Although they may agree that individuals might prefer to learn in some ways more than others, they are concerned that if preferences are reinforced students may fail to learn how to learn in other ways. Some are also concerned that if educators teach in terms of preferred "learning styles" this could limit students' success in solving problems beyond school.

Some researchers who support the use of learning styles insist that the purpose of obtaining learning style information is to help teachers design classes that appeal to a majority of students (Hickcox, 1995; Felder and Brent, 2005). Teachers can encourage collaborative and active learning by augmenting a traditional lecture style with charts, diagrams, pictures, and slides. Felder and Brent (ibid.) advocate another use of learning style information which is to help students understand exactly how they learn so they can try to maximize their learning opportunities by using strategies that work best with their particular learning style. However, supporters of learning styles do not advocate that students should only be taught with instruction matched to their learning styles. In fact, many researchers acknowledge the importance of challenging students to promote flexible thinking by presenting information that is mismatched to their learning style (Messick and Associates, 1976).

There is also concern related to the limitations of traditional face-to-face education, given the unrealistic burden it would place on the teachers to try to change their style to accommodate multiple learning styles. This problem can be alleviated in e-learning systems, which have the built-in potential of offering individualized learning paths to the students, with little overhead for the teachers.

Does knowing a student's learning style make teachers more effective?

There is a common sentiment that to teach students best, teachers need to be aware of and transcend their own learning styles, and figure out the most effective way to present a lesson. Many comments from educators revolve around teachers needing to understand that people learn in different ways and, thus, teachers should use sound pedagogy which would include using a variety of methods to convey and explain material. Sternberg and several colleagues worked intensively on models of learning styles for more than a decade. Their research (Sternberg et al., 1999) found that students who were strongly oriented toward "analytical," "creative," or "practical" intelligence did better if they were taught by instructors who matched their strengths.

Should we match teaching style to the content being taught?

Instead of matching teaching style to learning style, some educators and researchers suggest that it would be better to match instruction to the content being taught (Curwin and Mendler, 1999). They suggest that learning is topic dependent. Some concepts are best taught through hands-on work, some are best taught through lectures, and some are best taught through group discussions. Culinary arts, for example, lends itself primarily to a physical, kinesthetic learning style. Studying ancient history lends itself primarily to a visual, reading learning style. Many would agree that it is advantageous to expose students to as many different teaching and learning styles as possible, but to retain the authenticity of topic by focusing primarily on the method that best illuminates the specific topic at hand. Some classes may require a certain teaching or presentational style, but that does not mean that it should be the only style used.

Pashler et al. (2008) state that educators should not be concerned with determining the composition of learning styles in classrooms (whether or not students are visual, auditory, or kinesthetic learners). Instead, he argues that teachers should worry about matching their instruction to the content they are teaching. Kolb (1984) and Kolb and Kolb (2005) argued for many years that college students are better off if they choose a major that fits their learning style. Their advice to teachers is that they should lead their classes through a full "learning cycle," without regard to their students' particular styles. There may also be practical and ethical problems in sorting people into groups and labeling them. Tracking in education has a bad history.

Students who struggle may be studying in an area that is not their strength or may be unfamiliar with the instructor's approach to presenting the material. An example would be a math major, very right-brained, and quite strong in the preferences for logical, sequential, and visual formats, in a poetry class where the professor's presentation styles are contrary to the math student's styles. If the professor's style is very verbal and intuitive, the math student may struggle if s/he is not good with verbal or auditory communication and cannot see any step-by-step logic to finding metaphors in poetry. This student may have real trouble if s/he cannot mark out the step-by-step process of how to get from words on a page, to image in the brain, to metaphor. It may be that instructors teach to the content and in this case some students will excel with the style, whereas other more sequentially-thinking students may struggle.

What about the accounts of the positive benefits of knowing learning styles?

Regardless of whether or not the matching hypothesis is well supported or not, there are hundreds of studies and personal accounts showing positive effects of matching learning styles to teaching, and even accounts that students do better when instructors are trained in learning-style theory.

One possibility is that the mere act of learning about learning styles prompts teachers to pay more attention to the kinds of instruction they are delivering. An instructor who attends a learning-style seminar might start to offer a broader mixture of lectures, discussions, and laboratory work – and that variety of instruction might turn out to be better for all students, irrespective of any "matching." Most educators would agree that it is advantageous for instructors to be cognizant of how their students learn so they might think about the best instructional methods to use for a lesson. Coffield et al. (2004) acknowledge the benefits of using different learning styles as they may promote self-awareness and metacognition, a lexicon of learning for dialog, as well as being a catalyst for individual, organizational, or even systemic change.

Another concern regarding learning styles is that teachers do not have the time, resources, or ability to test their students and modify their style to accommodate each learner. Some teachers are concerned that there is not enough time to do anything other than what they have always done, given the pressures to spend time on research and publications. Students will have multiple learning styles and depending upon the content, environment, and other variables, their needs may shift.

Solutions and compromises regardless of the controversy

Much research exists that documents differences in learning and teaching styles, along with the impact (both negative and positive) that can occur in the learning process depending upon whether or not material is presented in a way that matches particular learning styles (e.g., Felder and Silverman, 1988; Cristea and Stash, 2006; Lu et al., 2007). Suggestions have been made to offer material (whether face-to-face or online) in a number of ways to allow the student to choose a preferred method.

There seems to be agreement that people take in information in different ways based on a variety of factors (the brain, the environment, conditioning, habit, content area, and presentation style). The controversy seems to lie in the differing opinions about the validity of the inventories and questionnaires used to assess learning styles, and in how to work with the plethora and overlap of learning style models and definitions. The question also remains as to whether we are talking about learning styles, learning preferences, learning strategies, or something totally brain related. What resonates from most of the literature and from individual comments is that it makes sense for teachers to "mix up" their teaching styles and strategies.

Provide supplemental strategies

Most results from learning inventories will reveal that most teachers and students have more than one learning modality. That variable could contribute to or confound experimental findings. Depending on the situation, a multimodal learner could create mental processing based on the need at the time. So, for example, in a lecture, if a learner is both a verbal and a kinesthetic learner, s/he might need to create or envision some hands-on process to better retain the information. Not all learners understand the best ways for them to process the information, so it might help to have instructors offer suggestions for further activities or processing. Often, there are study skills classes and tutoring situations offered at colleges that might help learners understand what they can do to process the information at a deeper level. For some, that might mean recording lectures and listening again to the content. For others, it might mean making bullet points on note cards and reviewing them periodically. Others might need to find supplemental material that is presented either visually (e.g., in the form of a graph) or perhaps via step-by-step sequencing. If instructors provide additional suggestions for learning then the instructor can continue with a preferred teaching style, while at the same time allowing the learner to go more "in-depth" if desired.

The curriculum can also play a role in how well students process the information, regardless of learning style. An instructor can provide students with additional material with which to practice (perhaps presented in varying styles). Sometimes it just helps to see or hear a concept presented differently. One of the benefits of online learning is that there are so many opportunities for instantly updating blogs, wikis, and discussion boards with additional suggestions and ideas. In each week's lesson, instructors could provide a place for "alternate examples," or "supplementary materials." In this section they could include videos or podcasts from YouTube, additional readings or examples, or they could encourage students to create and share materials that have helped them understand the material better. In this way, students can pick and choose the material that will best help them to learn (which may be in their primary or secondary learning style). Instructors can then build on this bank of material each year. This may also take some pressure off the instructor to find extra information.

Reinforcement assignments and activities can provide adaptive strategies for those who do not get the maximum learning from the methods that are available. Cues for instructors to alert them to these students' needs include students asking for help through email, chat, or in office visits. Instructors can provide alternative suggestions to students and then post them online for those students who did not personally contact the instructor. Instructors can consult with others who teach (or taught) the same course and ask for their activities (which may include some hands-on or multimodal explanations) and post those examples online, thus expanding the range of resources for students.

Mix up the instruction

It is most likely that each person has a primary and a secondary learning style. As students mature they may pick up strategies from different learning styles and become more flexible in how they prefer material be presented. They may learn how to incorporate strategies that are useful from the various styles. However, faculty can also be flexible and "mix up" their instruction and strategies, rather than relying on what is most comfortable for them. Since it may not be possible to learn the dominant style of all the students, it is useful to prepare a variety of techniques with which to communicate content and to give students multiple ways to interact with it – through reading, lectures, journaling, by listening to recorded podcasts or watching short screencasts, or offering opportunities for authentic practice (to learn by doing). Faculty can make suggestions to students, with a comment such as: "In order to learn this material, some students found success doing _____ while others did _____."

Conclusion

There is a multitude of learning style models and questionnaires designed to inform educators and other instructors about their students' learning preferences. Some of the researchers suggest that focusing on learning styles as defined by sensory modalities may be a wasted effort. There is concern that the inventories are not as valid as they should be, or that students may believe they have a preferred learning style but in reality may learn or study in ways that are contrary to what is found experimentally or through the inventories. Although categorizing each person as a specific type of learner may be easy, individuals' memory efficiency is not limited by sensory modality, nor are people able to learn in the same way in all situations. Instead, most people are likely to be multimodal and multisituational learners, changing learning strategies depending on the context of the to-be-learned material.

Even though learning style research may lack focus, in terms of a consistent definition for the concept, and may seem to be full of disagreements, still, it has made a significant difference to changing the role of learners in an educational process. Learners are now considered to be active participants in the learning process as opposed to sponges that absorb information. Knowing the learning styles of the students in a class may help the teacher to develop instructional material that can be effective for students with various learning styles. It also helps the students if they understand their own learning styles as this understanding could help them study effectively and efficiently at their present grade level, and in their future learning experiences.

Helping individuals to learn effective memory strategies across all stimulus modalities and contexts, rather than only assessing learning type, may also prove to be beneficial for both the student and the education system. As discussed throughout the learning styles literature, presenting material to students in multiple sensory modalities is undoubtedly beneficial to learning and interest (e.g., Lapp et al., 1999; Morrison et al., 2002).

Learners generally have more than one learning style, but usually possess certain strengths or weaknesses. The underlying thesis of most learning style research is that a person learns more effectively when information is presented in a manner congruent with his/her favored method of acquiring and processing information. The key principle to remember from all of these theories is that it is good practice to provide a mix of teaching and learning activities in order to accommodate diversity. Inclusive learning and teaching is less about accommodating people with particular needs and more about good planning and design for all.

Advocates of learning style models postulate that students learn in different ways. Taking this as a basic premise leads to the implication that higher education faculty should not assume: (1) that all adult students learn in the same way; and (2) that a faculty member's own dispositions and/or preferences for learning are broad enough to accommodate the learning needs of most or all of the students on the course. Rather, because the premise is that adult students learn in different ways, faculty in higher education have a responsibility to expand their repertoire of learning activities to embrace as wide a field of adult student learning styles as possible in order to achieve more effective learning.

Many of the most effective teacher-scholars and many of the most successful students learn to adapt to different modalities. They learn or cultivate multiple modes of teaching and learning and thus accumulate evolving systems for teaching and learning, which they use differently depending on the context.

References

Apter, M.J. (2001) *Motivational Styles in Everyday Life: A Guide to Reversal Theory*. Washington, DC: American Psychological Association.

Cassidy, S. (2004) Learning styles: an overview of theories, models, and measures. *Educational Psychology*, 24: 419–44.

Cassidy, S. and Eachus, P. (2000) Learning style, academic belief systems, self-report student proficiency and academic achievement in higher education. *Educational Psychology*, 20: 307–22.

Claxton, C. and Murrell, P. (1987) *Learning Styles: Implications for Improving Educational Practices*. College Station, TX: Association for the Study of Higher Education.

Coffield, F., Moseley, D., Hall, E. and Ecclestone, K. (2004) *Learning Styles and Pedagogy in Post-16 Learning: A Systematic and Critical Review*. London: Learning and Skills Research Centre.

Cornett, C.E. (1983) *What You Should Know About Teaching and Learning Styles*. Bloomington, IN: Phi Delta Kappa Educational Foundation.

Cristea, A. and Stash, N. (2006) AWELS: Adaptive web-based education and learning styles. *Advanced Learning Technologies, 2006. Sixth International Conference*, pp. 1135–6, 5–7 July. DOI: 10.1109/ICALT.2006.1652660. Available at: *http://ieeexplore.ieee.org/stamp/stamp.jsp?tp=&arnumber=1652 660&isnumber=34637*.

Curry, L. (1987) *Integrating Concepts of Cognitive Learning Style: A Review with Attention to Psychometric Standards*. Ottawa, ON: Canadian College of Health Science Executives.

Curry, L. (1990) A critique of the research on learning styles. *Educational Leadership*, 48(2): 50–6.

Curwin R.L and Mendler A.N. (1999) *Discipline with Dignity* (2nd edn.). Alexandria, VA: ACSD.

Delahoussaye, M. (2002) The perfect learner: an expert debate on learning styles. *Training*, 39(5): 28–36.

Dunn, R. (1983) Learning style and its relationship to exceptionality at both ends of the continuum. *Exceptional Children*, 49: 496–506.

Dunn, R. (1990) Understanding the Dunn and Dunn learning style model and the need for individual diagnosis and prescription. *Reading, Writing, and Learning Disabilities*, 6: 223–47.

Dunn, R. (1993) Learning styles of the multiculturally diverse. *Emergency Librarian*, 20(4): 24–32.

Dunn, R. and Griggs, S. (2003) *Synthesis of the Dunn and Dunn Learning Styles Model Research: Who, What, When, Where and So What – the Dunn and Dunn Learning Styles Model and its Theoretical Cornerstone*. New York: St. John's University.

Felder, R.M. (1993) Reaching the second tier: learning and teaching styles in college science education. *College Science Teaching*, 23(5): 286–90.

Felder, R.M. and Brent, R. (2005) Understanding student differences. *Journal of Engineering Education*, 94(1): 57–72.

Felder R.M. and Silverman L.K. (1988) Learning and teaching styles in engineering education. *Engineering Education*, 78: 674–81.

Fleming, N.D. (2001) *Teaching and Learning Styles: VARK Strategies*. Christchurch, New Zealand: The Digital Print and Copy Center.

Fleming, N.D. (2005) *Teaching and Learning Styles: VARK Strategies* (2nd edn.). Christchurch, New Zealand: The Digital Print and Copy Center.

Ford, N. and Chen, S.Y. (2000) Individual differences, hypermedia navigation, and learning: an empirical study. *Journal of Educational Multimedia and Hypermedia*, 9: 281–312.

Ford, N. and Chen, S.Y. (2001) Matching/mismatching revisited: an empirical study of learning and teaching styles. *British Journal of Educational Technology*, 32: 5–22.

Graf, S. (2007) *Adaptivity in Learning Management Systems Focusing on Learning Styles*. Ph.D. thesis, Vienna University of Technology, Austria.

Grasha, A.F. (1984) Learning styles: the journey from Greenwich Observatory (1796) to the college classroom. *Improving College and University Teaching*, 32(1): 46–53.

Gregorc, A.F. (1979) Learning/teaching styles: their nature and effects. *NASSP Monograph*, (October/November): 19–26.

Gregorc, A.F. (1997) *Relating with Style*. Colombia, CT: Gregorc Associates.

Haar, J., Hall, G., Schoepp, P. and Smith, D.H. (2002) How teachers teach to students with different learning styles. *The Clearing House*, 75(3): 142–5.

Harrison, G., Andrews, J. and Saklofske, D. (2003) Current perspectives on cognitive learning styles. *Education Canada*, 43(2): 44–7.

Hickcox, L.K. (1995) Learning styles: a survey of adult learning style inventory models. In R. Sims and S. Sims (eds.) *The Importance of Learning Styles: Understanding the Implications for Learning, Course Design, and Education* (pp. 25–47). Westport, CT: Greenwood.

Honey, P. and Mumford, A. (1982, 1992) *Manual of Learning Styles*. London: P. Honey.

Honey, P. and Mumford, A. (2006) *The Learning Styles Helper's Guide*. London: P. Honey.

James, W.B. and Gardner, D.L. (1985) Learning styles: implications for distance learning. *New Directions for Adult and Continuing Education*, 67(Fall): 20.

Jonassen, D.H. and Grabowski, B.L. (1993) *Handbook of Individual Differences, Learning, and Instruction*. Hillsdale, NJ: Lawrence Erlbaum Associates.

Keefe, J. (1979) Learning style: an overview. In J.W. Keefe (ed.) *Student Learning Styles: Diagnosing and Prescribing Programs* (pp. 1–17). Reston, VA: National Association of Student Principles.

Kolb, D. (1984) *Experiential Learning: Experience as the Source of Learning and Development*. Englewood Cliffs, NJ: Prentice Hall.

Kolb, A.Y. and Kolb, D.A. (2005) Learning styles and learning spaces: enhancing experiential learning in higher education. *Academy of Management Learning and Education*, 4(2): 193–212.

Krätzig, G.P. and Arbuthnott, K.D. (2006) Perceptual learning style and learning proficiency: a test of the hypothesis. *Journal of Educational Psychology*, 98(1): 238–46. DOI:10.1037/0022-0663.98.1.238.

Lapp, D., Flood, J. and Fisher, D. (1999) Intermediality: how the use of multiple media enhances learning. *The Reading Teacher*, 52: 776–80.

Loo, R. (2002) A meta-analytic examination of Kolb's learning style preferences among business majors. *Journal of Education for Business*, 77: 252–6.

Lu, H., Jia, L., Gong, S.-H. and Clark, B. (2007) The relationship of Kolb Learning Styles, online learning behaviors and learning outcomes. *Journal of Educational Technology & Society*, 10: 187–96.

Messick, S. and Associates (eds.) (1976) *Individuality in Learning*. San Francisco, CA: Jossey-Bass.

Morrison, T.G., Bryan, G. and Chilcoat, G.W. (2002) Using student generated comic books in the classroom. *Journal of Adolescent and Adult Literacy*, 45: 758–67.

Pashler, H., McDaniel, M., Rohrer, D. and Robert Bjork, R. (2008) Learning styles concepts and evidence. *Psychological Science in the Public Interest*, 9(3): 105–19. DOI: 10.1111/j.1539-6053.2009.01038.x.

Pheiffer, G., Holley, D. and Andrew, D. (2005) Developing thoughtful students: using learning styles in an HE context. *Education & Training*, 47(6): 422–31.

Popescu, E. (2010) A Unified Learning Style Model for technology enhanced learning: what, why and how? *International Journal of Distance Education*, 8(3): 65–81. Preprint available at: *http://software.ucv.ro/~epopescu/papers/preprint_JDET.pdf*.

Santo, S.A. (2001) Virtual learning, personality, and learning styles. Doctoral dissertation, University of Virginia. *ProQuest Digital Dissertation Abstracts*. Available at: *http://wwwlib.umi.com/dissertations/gateway*.

Shih, C. and Gamon, J. (2001) Web-based learning: relationships among student motivation, attitude, learning styles, and achievement. *Journal of Agricultural Education*, 42(4): 12–20. Available at: *http://pubs.aged.tamu.edu/jae/pdf/Vol42/42-04-12.pdf*.

Sims, R. and Sims, S. (1995) *The Importance of Learning Styles: Understanding the Implications for Learning, Course Design, and Education*. Westport, CT: Greenwood.

Sloman, S.A. (2002) Two systems of reasoning. In T. Gilovich and D. Griffin (eds.) *Heuristics and Biases: The Psychology of Intuitive Judgement* (pp. 379–96). Cambridge: Cambridge University Press.

Smith, W., Sekar, S. and Townsend, K. (2002) The impact of surface and reflective teaching and learning on student academic success. In M. Valcke and D. Gombeir (eds.) *Learning Styles: Reliability and Validity* (pp. 407–18). *Proceedings of the 7th Annual European Learning Styles Information Network Conference*, 26–28 June. Ghent: University of Ghent.

Stahl, S.A. (1999) Different strokes for different folks: a critique of learning styles. *American Educator*, 23(3): 1–5. Available at: *http://www.aft.org/pdfs/americaneducator/fall1999/DiffStrokes.pdf*.

Sternberg, R., Grigorenko, E.L., Ferrari, M. and Clinkenbeard, P. (1999) A triarchic analysis of an aptitude-treatment interaction. *European Journal of Psychological Assessment*, 15(1): 3–13. DOI: 10.1027//1015-5759.15.1.3.

Tourangeau, R., Rips, L.J. and Rasinski, K. (2000) *The Psychology of Survey Response*. New York: Cambridge University Press.

Zapalska, A.M. and Dabb, H. (2002) Learning styles. *Journal of Teaching in International Business*, 13: 77–97.

2

Overview of learning style theories and learning style results from the Mestre study

Abstract: This chapter provides an overview of learning styles, including definitions, theories, and models. Learning style research has produced many theories and models that have been applied in various settings such as academia and industry to explain how different people approach learning, as well as how they acquire and process information. Each model offers a different perspective on which elements of individual characteristics affect the learning process. The identification, classification, or definition of learning styles varies widely depending on the perspective of the researcher. This chapter also discusses some learning style theories that were relevant to the Mestre (2010) study.

Key words: learning style theories, learning styles, e-learning, tutorials, cognitive style.

Introduction

Learning style research has produced many theories and models that have been applied in various settings such as academia and industry to explain how different people approach learning, as well as how they acquire and process information. Research on learning styles evolved from psychological research on individual differences, which was widespread in the 1960s and 1970s (Curry, 1987), and has resulted in the development of more than 70 models and instruments that have been used to understand how individuals approach learning. All these models offer a different perspective on which elements of individual characteristics affect the learning process. The identification, classification, or definition of learning styles varies widely depending on the perspective of the researcher. This chapter discusses several learning style theories that were relevant to the study that was conducted. It also shows how the students in the Mestre (2010, 2012) studies were assessed after taking two of the learning style inventories that will be described below.

Learning style models and inventories

Common learning style theories and models

There are numerous ways of characterizing styles. Christison (2003) distinguishes between cognitive style (field dependent versus field independent, analytic versus global, reflective versus impulsive), sensory style (visual versus auditory versus tactile versus kinesthetic), and personality styles (tolerance of ambiguity, right brain versus left brain dominance). The following learning style theories and models are only a few of the most frequently used or cited by individuals as they design online learning environments and tutorials and helped inform the study described in this book. For a comparison of similarities between learning style models see Sternberg et al.'s (2008) Styles of learning and thinking matter in instruction and assessment. Hawk and Shaw (2007) review six well-known and widely available learning style instruments offered by Kolb, Gregorc, Felder and Silverman, Fleming, Dunn and Dunn, as well as the Entwistle and Tait Revised Approaches to Studying model. In each review, they describe the learning styles that emerge from each instrument and review the instruments' validity, reliability, and student performance research, where available.

The theories and models that influenced the design of the study that was described in the Introduction to this book (Mestre, 2010) are:

- The Myers-Briggs Type Indicator (Briggs, 1962);
- Dunn and Dunn (1978);
- Kolb's learning style theory (Kolb, 1984);
- Gregorc's Learning/Teaching Style Model (Gregorc and Ward, 1977; Gregorc, 1979, 1985, 1997);
- Gardner's Multiple Intelligences Theory, (Gardner, 1983);
- Felder-Silverman's Learning Style Theory (Felder and Silverman, 1988; Felder, 1993); and
- Fleming's VARK Model (Fleming, 2001).

The Myers-Briggs Type Indicator (MBTI) (Briggs Myers, 1962) is used to determine the personality type of an individual and consists of four dichotomous scales: introvert/extrovert (IE), thinking/feeling (TF), sensing/intuiting (SN), and judging/perception (JP). There are 16 possible personality types that a person can fall into based on the indicators set up by Myers and Briggs; for example, one individual could be ISTJ (introvert, sensor, thinker, and perceiver) while another could be EFSP (extrovert, feeler, sensor, and perceiver).

- Extroverts are outgoing, and try things out before thinking and interacting with people.
- Introverts are reserved and think before trying things out.
- Thinkers use logic to make decisions.
- Feelers make decisions based on personal and humanistic elements.
- Sensors are detail oriented and focus on facts.
- Intuitors are imaginative and concept oriented.
- Judgers are organized and like to plan.
- Perceivers are spontaneous and can adapt to a changing environment.

The Dunn and Dunn learning style model (Dunn and Dunn, 1978, 1989; Dunn et al., 1982; Dunn, 1990) is based on environmental and instructional preferences. The five stimuli are:

- *Environmental:* sound, light, temperature, and classroom design.
- *Emotional:* motivation, responsibility, persistence, and structure.
- *Sociological:* learning alone or in groups, the presence of an authority figure, learning routine patterns.
- *Physiological:* perception, intake, time, and mobility needs.
- *Psychological processing*: global or analytic, hemisphericity, and impulsive or reflective.

This model offers a set of 100 questions covering all five stimuli and their respective elements. Scores range from 20 to 80, with 40 to 60 reflecting a low or balanced preference for the two ends of each of the 20 elements, and 20 to 40 or 60 to 80 reflecting a stronger preference for the indicated polar end.

David Kolb's experiential learning theory (Kolb, 1984; Kolb and Kolb, 2005) looks at learning style as an aspect of cognitive orientation that can influence preference for learning experiences. Kolb views learning as a multistage process that begins with stage 1, when the learner goes through concrete learning experiences. In stage 2, the learner reflects on his/her concrete experience. In stage 3, the learner derives abstract concepts and generalizations. Ultimately, the learner tests these generalizations in new situations using active experimentation in stage 4. Kolb's Experiential Learning Style Inventory describes learning styles on a continuum running from concrete experience, through reflective observation, to abstract conceptualization, and finally active experimentation (ibid.). The learning cycle is also translated into individual learning styles, starting along two axes. The first dimension relates to whether a person is a concrete or an abstract thinker (whether that person thinks in terms of real things and events or is drawn to ideas and theory). The second dimension relates to whether information is processed in an active or a reflective way. The two axes intersect at right angles, forming a four-quadrant field for mapping individual learning styles. See Figure 2.1 below.

The two dimensions combine to form four different learning styles:

- *Diverger*: thinks concretely and processes what is learned reflectively. Needs to be personally engaged in the learning activity (creative, generates alternatives).

- *Converger*: perceives information abstractly and processes it reflectively. Needs to follow detailed sequential steps in a learning activity (practical, likes practical applications, makes decisions).

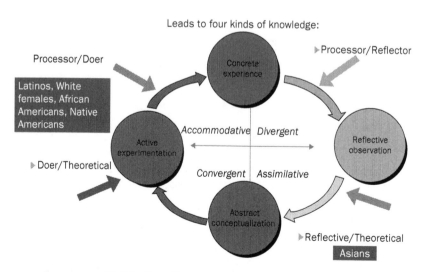

| **Figure 2.1** | Kolb's Four Dimensions, from Kolb (1984). Modified by Mestre (2010) to reflect various cultural considerations |

- *Assimilator*: thinks abstractly and processes new knowledge actively in the company of others. Needs to be involved in pragmatic problem solving in a learning activity (intellectual, defines problems, creates theoretical models).
- *Accommodator*: thinks concretely and processes information actively. Needs to be involved in risk taking, making changes, experimentation, and flexibility (social, takes risks, gets things done).

Honey and Mumford (1982, 1992) applied Kolb's theories in a widely used questionnaire, which describes four different learning styles most often applied to management development:

- *Activists*: respond best to learning situations offering challenges, and enjoy new experiences, excitement, and freedom in their learning. They could describe their preference as "learning by doing something new."
- *Pragmatists*: like relevant learning opportunities with scope for theory and practice – "learning what is useful."
- *Reflectors*: prefer structured learning opportunities, which provide time to step back and observe, reflect, and think about what has happened. They often seek out detail – "learning through reflection."
- *Theorists*: like logical, rational structure, clear aims and the opportunity to question and analyze what they have learned – "learning from theory."

The Gregorc Learning/Teaching Style Model (Gregorc and Ward, 1977; Gregorc, 1979, 1985, 1997) is a model which asserts that individuals have natural predispositions for learning along four bipolar, continuous mind qualities that function as mediators as individuals learn from and act upon their environments. Those mind qualities are:

- abstract and concrete perception
- sequential and random ordering
- deductive and inductive processing and
- separative and associative relationships.

The Gregorc Style Delineator (GSD) provides metrics on the first two qualities, perception and ordering, giving an individual a score from 10 to 40 in each of four learning styles with a maximum of 100 points for all four:

- *Concrete-Sequential* (CS): prefers direct, hands-on experience, desires order and a logical sequence to tasks, and follows directions well.

- *Abstract-Sequential* (AS): likes working with ideas and symbols, is logical and sequential in thinking, and likes to focus on a task without distractions.

- *Abstract-Random* (AR): focuses attention on people and surroundings, prefers discussions and conversations that are wide ranging, and requires time to reflect on experiences.

- *Concrete-Random* (CR): prefers experimentation and risk taking, likes to explore unstructured problems, makes intuitive leaps in solving them, and uses trial and error to work out solutions.

Gregorc describes concrete and abstract as orthogonal to sequential and random. Although the scores indicate the individual's innate dispositions for one, two, three, or all of the styles, individuals can improve their use of the mind qualities for which they do not score highly. For a chart of these combinations and information on the implications related to designing effective instruction based on students' strengths and weaknesses see: *http://web.cortland.edu/andersmd/learning/Gregorc.htm* ('Mind styles – Anthony Gregorc').

Howard Gardner's (1983) theory of multiple intelligences focuses on the importance of individual differences in learning. Gardner drew on research in cognitive psychology to expand the notion of intelligence beyond the traditional focus on linguistic, logical, and mathematical aptitudes, emphasizing multiple modes of thinking. He used biological as well as cultural research to formulate a theory of multiple intelligences which has the following dimensions:

- *Logical-mathematical*: to detect patterns, reason deductively and think logically.

- *Linguistic*: to use language to express oneself and to remember information verbally.

- *Spatial*: to manipulate and create mental images in order to solve problems.

- *Musical*: to recognize and compose musical pitches, tones, and rhythms.

- *Bodily-Kinesthetic*: to coordinate bodily movements.

- *Interpersonal and Intrapersonal*: to understand one's own feelings and intentions and those of others.

According to this theory all intelligences are required and it is important to find ways of supporting and developing all the intelligences, unlike traditional education which has favored logical-mathematical and linguistic intelligence over all else. Everyone has different strengths in each of these, and the level of these intelligences will often determine preferred learning styles.

The Felder-Silverman Learning Style Model (FSLSM) (1988) combines several major learning style models such as the learning style models by Kolb (1984) and Pask (1976), as well as the MBTI (Briggs Myers, 1962). Felder and Soloman developed the Index of Learning Styles (ILS) (Felder and Soloman, 1997; Felder and Spurlin, 2005), which is a 44-item questionnaire for identifying learning styles based on the FSLSM. Although the dimensions themselves are not new, the way in which they are combined and describe the learning styles of students is new. Most other learning style models classify learners into just a few types, whereas Felder and Silverman describe the learning style of a learner in more detail, and provide four values, representing the learners' preference on each learning style dimension expressed by values between +11 and –11. Using the active/reflective dimension as an example, +11 means that a learner has a strong preference for active learning, whereas –11 means that a learner has a strong preference for reflective learning, thereby distinguishing between preferences on four dimensions using this +11 to –11 to indicate the learners' preferences on each dimension.

By using scales rather than types, the strength of learning style preferences can be described, enabling the model to distinguish between strong and weak preferences for a particular learning style. Furthermore, FSLSM is based on the concept of tendencies, indicating that learners with a high preference for certain behavior can also act differently depending on context.

FSLSM has often been used in research related to learning styles in advanced learning technologies. According to Carver et al. (1999), "the Felder Model is most appropriate for hypermedia courseware" (p. 34). Kuljis and Liu (2005) confirmed this by conducting a comparison of learning style models with respect to their application in e-learning and web-based learning systems. FSLSM characterizes each learner according to four dimensions: Active/Reflective, Sensing/Intuitive, Visual/Verbal, and Sequential/Global:

- Active/Reflective
  - *Active* learners learn by trying things out and working together with others;
  - *Reflective* learners learn by thinking things through and reflecting about them, and they prefer to learn alone.

- Sensing/Intuitive
  - *Sensing* learners like to learn from concrete material-like examples, tend to be more practical and are careful with details;
  - *Intuitive* learners prefer to learn from abstract material, such as challenges, and are more innovative.
- Visual/Verbal
  - *Visual* learners remember best what they have seen;
  - *Verbal* learners get more out of words, regardless of whether they are spoken or written.
- Sequential/Global

  - *Sequential* learners learn in linear steps, prefer to follow stepwise paths and prefer to be guided through the learning process;
  - *Global* learners learn in large leaps and prefer a higher degree of freedom in their learning process.

The VARK inventory (Fleming, 2001) is one style that is applicable in the presentation of e-learning content for the organization of a self-paced e-learning course. It uses the three main sensory receivers – Vision, Auditory, and Kinesthetic (movement) – to determine the dominant learning style. Learners use all three to receive information. However, one or more of these receiving styles is normally dominant. This dominant style defines the best way for a person to learn new information by filtering what is to be learned. This style might not always be the same for different tasks. The learner may prefer one style of learning for one task, and a combination of others for another task. Again, a preferred model is to design e-learning to present information using all three styles. This allows all learners, regardless of their preferred style, the opportunity to become involved.

Mestre (2010, 2012) used the Felder and Soloman ILS described above and also used Fleming's VARK learning style inventory (available at: *http://www.vark-learn.com/english/index.asp*) as the two inventories for her study. The VARK inventory adds another dimension to the VAK inventory – Read/Write. This was valuable in the usability studies of tutorials to help understand approaches to the text in tutorials. In this study, three of the 21 students tested with a single learning preference on the Learning Style Inventory, that of a read/write learning style. In the usability study, this preference was evidenced as they first read the text on the page, before looking at the visuals. The only other single learning preference was a kinesthetic learner. The remaining 17 students tested as multimodal learners; however, overall, the percentage of students who scored with a high read/write preference was almost the same as those who scored highly for kinesthetic. These students explained that they looked at the visuals first and only looked at the text if the visuals were not clear. For this study it was very important to gauge the read/write preferences of students, which is one of the reasons why the VARK inventory was used rather than the VAK inventory.

The VARK inventory provides metrics for each of four perceptual modes:

- *Visual* (V): prefer maps, charts, graphs, diagrams, brochures, flow charts, highlighters, different colors, pictures, word pictures, and different spatial arrangements.

- *Aural* (A): like to explain new ideas to others and discuss topics with other students and teachers, use a tape recorder, attend lectures and discussion groups, and use stories and jokes.

- *Read/Write* (R): favor essays, reports, text, manuals, definitions, printed handouts, readings, manuals, web pages, and taking notes, written feedback, multiple-choice questions.

- *Kinesthetic* (K): prefer trial and error and hands-on approaches, doing things in order to understand them, role-playing, demonstrations, laboratories, field trips, recipes and solutions to problems, using the senses, and collections of samples.

The instrument contains 16 multiple-choice questions and participants can choose more than one answer for each question. Although learners are not restricted to only one of four modes, they may show a strong preference for one particular mode. An individual's preference may range from a single mode to all four modes (Fleming, 2001, 2005; Hawk and Shaw, 2007).

Table 2.1 provides families of learning styles (Coffield et al., 2004).

Discussion

In the Mestre study (2010, 2012) students took both the ILS and VARK inventories. There was some overlap in the dimensions assessed with both inventories, as well as unique categories. Table 2.2 lists the similar categories.

Table 2.1 Families of learning styles

Author(s)	Assessment tool	Year introduced
Dunn and Dunn	Learning Style Questionnaire (LSQ) Learning Style Inventory (LSI) Building Excellence Survey (BES)	1979 1975 2003
Gregorc	Gregorc Mind Styles Delineator (MSD)	1977
Cognitive structure		
Riding	Cognitive Styles Analysis (CSA)	1991
Stable personality type		
Apter	Motivational Style Profile (MSP)	1998
Jackson	Learning Style Profiler (LSP)	2002
Myers-Briggs	Myers-Briggs Type Indicator (MBTI)	1962
Flexibly stable learning preferences		
Allison and Hayes	Cognitive Style Index (CSI)	1996
Herrmann	Brain Dominance Instrument (HBDI)	1985
Honey and Mumford	Learning Styles Questionnaire (LSQ)	1982
Felder and Silverman	Index of Learning Styles (ILS)	1996
Kolb	Learning Style Inventory (LSI) LSI Version 3	1976 1999
Learning approaches and strategies		
Entwistle	Approaches to Study Inventory (ASI) Revised Approaches to Study Inventory (RASI) Approaches and Study Skills Inventory for Students (ASSIST)	1979 1995 2000
Sternberg	Thinking Styles	1998
Vermunt	Inventory of Learning Styles (ILS)	1996

Source: from Coffield et al., 2004

Table 2.2 Similar categories in ILS and VARK

ILS	VARK
Active	Kinesthetic
Visual	Visual
Verbal	Aural Read/Write

By comparing how students scored in these similar areas in both inventories it was possible to determine how consistent students were in their preferences. The VARK inventory further broke down the ILS's Verbal category into Aural and Read/Write which was used during the tutorial analysis to understand more clearly whether a student did better with a tutorial with narration or a static web page with text and images. The comparison of student results from both these inventories indicated that results were comparable for the visual and verbal categories. Those preferences were generally similar in the results reported for both inventories. However, there was some discrepancy in the Active category (ILS) and the Kinesthetic category (VARK), especially for the Asian students. Five of the six Asian students tended to be more reflective learners than active learners on the ILS inventory, yet on the VARK inventory they scored in the strong or very strong categories for kinesthetic learners. In discussions with these students during the tutorials' debriefs, it was explained that although the students liked to be actively involved and enjoyed hands-on activities they also wanted time to reflect on the information and use problem-solving techniques.

The ILS inventory also included an assessment of whether a student preferred sequential learning or a more global approach. This was critical in the assessment of tutorials to determine if the tutorials were designed in an effective way for students. Since most tutorials are designed in a sequential, step-by-step manner it was important to understand if students were able to reproduce a search with this method, or if a more global approach would be more effective (such as seeing the whole process at a glance and picking and choosing sections).

The results of these inventories will be discussed further in subsequent chapters pertaining to tutorial design (Chapter 6) and pedagogical considerations (Chapter 7). The next chapter will discuss the relevance of culture and learning styles, and implications for the online environment.

Conclusion

This chapter presented an overview of some of the most commonly used learning style theories and inventories. Some of them overlap with each other in terms of what they measure. Many may measure whether a student prefers material presented visually, aurally, or kinesthetically. Others measure how a student processes information. The Mestre

(2010, 2012) study used two of the common inventories (VARK and ILS) to measure students' preferences. The results helped to understand better how students approach tutorials, including the amount of text, visuals, interaction, extra help, and activities needed in order to process, replicate, and transfer the information in a new situation. The original tutorials were created by librarians with a high read/write preference, whereas only one student in this usability study had a high preference for read/write material. The other students preferred a more multimodal approach. By learning about the preferences of students, and also by observing them in a usability study and debriefing with them after the study, the researchers are now able to modify the tutorials to better match the learning preferences of the students.

References

Briggs, M.I. (1962) *Manual: The Myers-Briggs Type Indicator*. Palo Alto, CA: Consulting Psychologists Press.

Carver, C.A., Howard R.A. and Lane W.D. (1999) Addressing different learning styles through course hypermedia. *IEEE Transactions on Education*, 42: 33–8.

Christison, M.A. (2003) Learning styles and strategies. In D. Nunan (ed.) *Practical English Language Teaching* (pp. 267–88). New York: McGraw Hill.

Coffield, F., Moseley, D., Hall, E. and Ecclestone, K. (2004) *Should We Be Using Learning Styles? What Research Has to Say to Practice*. London: Learning and Skills Research Centre.

Curry, L. (1987) *Integrating Concepts of Cognitive Learning Style: A Review with Attention to Psychometric Standards*. Ottawa, ON: Canadian College of Health Science Executives.

Dunn, R. (1990) Understanding the Dunn and Dunn learning style model and the need for individual diagnosis and prescription. *Reading, Writing, and Learning Disabilities*, 6: 223–47.

Dunn, R. and Dunn, K. (1978) *Teaching Students Through their Individual Learning Styles*. Reston, VA: Reston Publishing Company, Inc.

Dunn, R. and Dunn, K. (1989) *Learning Style Inventory*. Lawrence, KS: Price Systems.

Dunn, R., Dunn, K. and Price, G.E. (1982) *Productivity Environmental Preference Survey*. Lawrence, KS: Price Systems.

Felder, R.M. (1993) Reaching the second tier: learning and teaching styles in college science education. *Journal of College Science Teaching*, 23: 286–90.

Felder, R.M. and Silverman, L.K. (1988) Learning and teaching styles in engineering education. *Engineering Education*, 78: 674–81.

Felder, R.M. and Soloman, B.A. (1997) *Index of Learning Styles Questionnaire*. Available at: *http://www.engr.ncsu.edu/learningstyles/ilsweb.html*.

Felder, R.M. and Spurlin, J. (2005) Applications, reliability and validity of the index of learning styles. *International Journal of Engineering Education*, 21(1): 103–12.

Fleming, N.D. (2001, 2005) *Teaching and Learning Styles: VARK Strategies*. Christchurch, New Zealand: The Digital Print and Copy Center.

Gardner, H. (1983) *Frames of Mind: The Theory of Multiple Intelligences*. New York: Basic Books.

Gregorc, A.F. (1979) Learning/teaching styles: their nature and effects. *NASSP Monograph*, (October/November): 19–26.

Gregorc, A.F. (1985) *Inside Styles: Beyond the Basics*. Maynard, MA: Gabriel Systems.

Gregorc, A.F. and Ward, H.B. (1977) A new definition for individual: implications for learning and teaching. *NASSP Bulletin*, 401(6): 20–3.

Gregorc, D.F. (1997) *Relating with Style*. Columbia, CT: Gregorc Associates.

Hawk, T.F. and Shaw, A.J. (2007) Using learning style instruments to enhance student learning. *Decision Sciences Journal of Innovative Education*, 5(1): 1–19. DOI:10.1111/j.1540-4609.2007.00125.x.

Honey, P. and Mumford, A. (1982, 1992) *The Manual of Learning Styles*. Maidenhead, UK: Peter Honey.

Kolb, D. (1984) *Experiential Learning: Experience as the Source of Learning and Development*. Englewood Cliffs, NJ: Prentice-Hall.

Kolb, A.Y. and Kolb, D.A. (2005) Learning styles and learning spaces: enhancing experiential learning in higher education. *Academy of Management Learning and Education*, 4(2): 193–212.

Kuljis, J. and Liu, F. (2005) A comparison of learning style theories on the suitability for elearning. In M.H. Hamza (ed.) *Proceedings of the IASTED Conference on Web Technologies, Applications, and Services* (pp. 191–7). Calgary, AB: ACTA Press.

Mestre, L.S. (2010) Matching up learning styles with learning objects: what's effective? *Journal of Library Administration*, 50(7–8): 808–29.

Mestre, L.S. (2012) Student preference and results after comparing screencast and static tutorials: a usability study. *Reference Services Review*, 40(2): 258–76.

Pask, G. (1976) Styles and strategies of learning. *British Journal of Educational Psychology*, 46: 128–48.

Sternberg, R.J., Grigorenko, E.L. and Zhang, L.(2008) Styles of learning and thinking matter in instruction and assessment. *Perspectives on Psychological Science*, 3(6): 486–506. DOI: 10.1111/j.1745-6924.2008.00095.x.

3

The intersection of culture and learning styles

Abstract: For decades, researchers have analyzed how students from different cultures process and retain information. Even acknowledging that there are diverse learning styles within each ethnic and racial group, researchers report that certain cultural groups maintain similar learning style characteristics. This chapter explores the intersection of culture, learning styles, and online learning. It summarizes studies exploring how students from different cultures process and retain information and suggests some applications for designing online tools to better reflect cultural needs or expectations. Examples of tutorials and learning objects that provide options for various learning styles are included.

Key words: cultural learning styles, e-learning, tutorials, online learning, cognitive style.

Introduction

As discussed in the previous two chapters, most educators can talk about learning differences, whether these are called learning styles, cognitive styles, psychological type, or multiple intelligences. They generally agree that learners bring their own individual approach, talents, and interests to the learning situation. There is no one preferred learning style that works for all students or even for any one particular ethnic or cultural group. In fact, different measurement methods assess different dimensions of learning styles and address such factors as instructional practices, information processing, social interaction tendencies, and the influence of personality. "Researchers have clearly established that there is no single or dual learning style for the members of any cultural, national, racial, or religious group" (Dunn, 1997, pp. 74–5).

Generally, there are concerns about linking culture and learning styles. Although people connected by culture may exhibit a characteristic pattern of style preferences, one cannot conclude that all members of the group have the same style traits, nor that their style preferences necessarily reflect how they learn best. The notion that it is possible to generalize about the learning styles of an entire ethnic or racial group could be seen as labeling, pigeon-holing and stereotyping students. Skeptics of a culture-focused approach contend that methods that would be useful to specific cultures would also benefit all students and advocate an instructional approach that considers cultural propensities but also greatly varies instructional methods for all students.

However, it is known that an individual learner's culture, family background, and socioeconomic level affect his or her learning. The context in which someone grows and develops has an important impact on learning. Culture and learning are connected in important ways. Early life experiences and the values of a person's culture affect both the expectations and the processes of learning. These beliefs, principles, and theories have an important impact on the opportunities for success for every student and should have an impact on how online instruction is designed.

For decades, researchers have analyzed how students from different cultures process and retain information. Even acknowledging that there are diverse learning styles within each ethnic and racial group, researchers report that certain cultural groups maintain similar learning style characteristics (Dunn, 1993; Dunn and Griggs, 1995, 2000; Irvine and York, 1995; R. Jacobson, 2000; Mestre, 2000; Neuman and Bekerman 2000; M. Jacobson, 2001; Honigsfeld and Dunn, 2003; Cifuentes and Ozel, 2006; Allison and Rehm, 2007).

Some examples of the relevance of culture and learning styles

Instructional style preferences can differ among cultures. It is important to take into consideration cultural resources before applying education theories in practice. Some students may be used to a quiet environment and a formal design while working independently whereas others may prefer sound (music) and working collaboratively. Some groups are accustomed to listening to the instructor lecture and others are used to learning material in a variety of ways, including kinesthetically. Some of this may be due to habit, exposure, practice, or even upbringing. It should be noted that "being used to an approach" does not necessarily mean that the individual learns best with that approach. It may be that students adapt to a particular environment or style, but may learn better in another.

Another model that has relevance to cultural considerations in learning is Witkin's notion of field dependence/field independence, measured by the Embedded Figure Test, or the Group Embedded Figure Test (GEFT) (Witkin, 1962; Witkin et al., 1977). Field independent individuals tend to be highly motivated, independent, and nonsocial people who think logically/analytically and are not influenced by their surroundings. On the other hand, field dependent individuals are very much affected by their environment, have difficulty extracting important information from their surroundings, have a short attention span, and tend to make decisions based on human factors rather than logic. In many classroom situations modifications and variations may not be available, so students "get used to" a particular approach. This may be especially true for students from non-mainstream cultures. These attributes may carry over to the online environment. Some of the research studies on certain cultural groups that offered suggestions for some of these preferences are examined below.

Native Americans

One study involving Native American students on a biology course at a community college was performed with a focus on improving the curriculum and the teacher–student learning process (Haukoos and Satterfield, 1986). Data were gathered from a group of 20 native students and 20 nonnative students. The native students were found to be visual linguistic in their behavior and preferred not to express themselves orally, while the nonnative students were mostly auditory linguistic and preferred to express themselves orally. Based on the results of the study, the course for Native American students was modified to accommodate their visual linguistic tendencies (including more slides and graphics) and to find ways to help them express themselves through discussions, questions, and small-group study. These changes had a tremendous impact in terms of improving group interactions. The course completion rate also improved, and more students ended up pursuing advanced degrees.

According to Philips (1983), "learning styles" for Native Americans were directly linked to a set of cultural norms that include observation, careful listening, supervised participation, and individualized self-correction or testing. Educational practices that emphasize meaning and process over product, that use cooperative work, that capitalize on oral language, and that integrate subject areas were also found to be valued. These features are compatible with Native American students' preference for communal learning and personal meaning, use of time, and holistic world-view (Kasten, 1992).

African Americans

Some of the reported findings suggest that "many African-American students are more engaged in a classroom that encourages interpersonal interaction, multiple activities, and multiple modality preferences than in quiet classrooms in which students are supposed to pay attention to only one thing at a time" (Shade, 1989). Shade distinguishes between two different cognitive styles: analytical and synergetic. Her primary thesis is that schools are designed for an "analytical style" of learning while most African American students (and she extrapolates to minority students including Latino or Native American) tend to function in a "synergetic style." Analytical learners are competitive and independent, and they focus well on impersonal tasks. They learn well though print, focus best on one task at a time, and work in a step-by-step sequence. Synergetic learners, on the other hand, prefer to work cooperatively rather than independently; they do not block out their peers, but rather they attempt to integrate personal relationships into learning tasks. Synergetic learners are stimulated by multiple activities and become bored when only one thing is happening. They often prefer kinesthetic and tactile involvement as well as discussion. Similar findings are suggested for Latino students.

Asian students

Some educational systems (especially Asian) are very teacher centered in that the teacher lectures and the students are passive recipients; see Kirkbride and Tang, 1992; Chan, 1999; Neuman and Bekerman, 2000; Wong, 2004. These researchers found that Chinese students preferred didactic and teacher-centered styles of teaching and would show great respect for the wisdom and knowledge of their teachers; these same students might struggle when they encountered a teacher who used a constructivist or student-centered approach. Chinese students are generally quiet in class and were taught not to question or challenge their teachers. Teachers are regarded as having the authority and knowledge to teach and students readily accepted the information given by teachers. A Chinese student may therefore be less likely to express his/her opinion, unless asked to do so. Chinese children learned well through concrete examples. They usually did better in concrete subjects but were weaker in abstract thinking and lacked creativity and originality (Salili, 1996, p. 100). Chan (1999) claimed that Chinese students were assessed mainly by examination (factual knowledge), with little emphasis on solving practical problems.

In a study carried out in Australia (Wong, 2004), 78 first-year to fourth-year Asian international undergraduate students participated in a survey to determine teaching and program quality in higher education from the students' perspective. The three main difficulties highlighted by Asian international students were: different learning styles, cultural barriers, and language problems. When the Asian international students surveyed began their study in Australia, initially more of them (33 percent) preferred the lecture style because they came from a background of teacher-centered learning, but as they moved into their third and fourth year of study this preference seemed to shift. This was evidenced by the fact that only 23 percent of the third- and fourth-year students preferred this style of teaching and learning. As students became more immersed in the programs, their preferred style of teaching and learning evolved into one that was student centered (with more discussion, independent learning, and critical thinking) despite their previous educational and cultural background.

The above study illustrates some of the experiences and views of Asian students who left their native educational system and then had to adapt to a new system. In the debriefing with the Asian students in this study, the students indicated similar desires to have information given to them in order to be able to answer a question based on that information, rather than exploring some alternative. They relied on a standard process that they could look to for getting information and expected it to be applied throughout. Once they understood a procedure they were confused if there was any variation.

Education scholar Geneva Gay (2000) argues that the nexus of cultural influence is a student's "learning style," shaping the way in which students receive and process information most effectively. By understanding cultural characteristics of different ethnic, racial, and social groups, it is hoped that educators will see the need to develop instructional practices that are more responsive to cultural pluralism. Some of the cultural characteristics to consider are communication styles, thinking styles, value systems, socialization processes, relational patterns, and performance styles (Gay, 2003; St. Amant, 2007; Pagan, 2009; Yang et al., 2010). All of these may influence a student's receptivity to various styles of teaching, presentation modes, and design of online materials.

Cultural styles in the online environment

Other research studies showed that there are ethnic cultural differences in asynchronous web-based conferences (Liang and McQueen, 1999; Kim and Bonk, 2002). For example, in one study, learners from Europe (Finland) demonstrated a higher level of reflection in behaviors such as posting summaries than did American and Asian (Korean) learners (Kim and Bonk, 2002) who were more action-oriented. Liang and McQueen (1999) reported that American students are peer-oriented and are more likely to interact with peers, while Asian students rely more on the instructor's directions in an online environment. Thus, Asian students' participation and communication in online environments is heavily influenced by the instructor's involvement and clear directions, while American students take more initiatives. In the study carried out for this book, although students were instructed not to ask questions of the researcher in the room, four of the seven Asian students did ask for clarifying information and directions. None of the other participants in the study asked for clarification.

Graff et al. (2004) found that individual differences in cognitive styles vary principally according to nationality. Studies of cross-cultural usability have gained attention by linking culture and web use (Bourges-Waldegg and Scrivener, 1998; Kim and Allen, 2002; Faiola and Matei, 2005), and cross-cultural studies from a behavioral perspective have also proven relevant to these topics of research (Honold, 2000; Marcus and Gould, 2000; Zahedi et al., 2001; Chau et al., 2002; Preece and Maloney-Krichmar, 2005; Faiola and Macdorman, 2008). Mestre reviewed learning style research for diverse groups (Mestre, 2006) and looked at how that information could be used in the design of online tutorials. If designed appropriately, tutorials and learning objects can provide various options for diverse learning and cognitive styles through presenting information in multiple ways.

As previously mentioned, Mestre (2010, 2012) used two learning style inventories to assess how students from various cultures and learning styles approached online tutorials. The Index of Learning Style Inventory from North Carolina State University (NCSU) was one of the two inventories. This categorizes learners as: Active/Reflective learners; Sensing/Intuitive learners; Visual/Verbal learners; and Sequential/Global learners. The definitions of the categories below were chosen from those on the website (*http://www.engr.ncsu.edu/learningstyles/ilsweb.html* and *http://www4.ncsu.edu/unity/lockers/users/f/felder/public/ILSdir/styles.htm.*) because they speak to the many elements one should consider when designing learning objects for various learning styles.

Active/Reflective learners

- Active learners (including Latinos, African Americans, and Native Americans) tend to retain and understand information best by doing something active with it – discussing or applying it or explaining it to others. "Let's try it out and see how it works" is an active learner's phrase. They also tend to like group work more than reflective learners. Sitting through lectures without getting to do anything physical other than taking notes is hard for most learning types, but particularly hard for active learners.

- Reflective learners (including Asian Americans) prefer to think about the material quietly first. "Let's think it through first" is the reflective learner's response. They tend to prefer working alone.

Sensing/Intuitive learners

- Sensing learners tend to like learning facts, whereas intuitive learners often prefer discovering possibilities and relationships. Sensing learners often like solving problems using well-established methods and dislike complications and surprises. Sensors don't like courses that have no apparent connection to the real world.

- Intuitive learners like innovation and dislike repetition. Intuitors don't like "plug-and-chug" courses that involve a lot of memorization and routine calculations.

Visual/Verbal learners

- Visual learners remember best what they see in pictures, diagrams, flow charts, time lines, films, and demonstrations.

- Verbal learners get more out of words, both written and spoken explanations.

Sequential/Global learners

- Sequential learners tend to gain understanding in linear steps, with each step following on logically from the previous one, and tend to follow logical step-by-step paths to find solutions.

- Global learners tend to learn in large jumps, absorbing material almost randomly without seeing connections, and then suddenly "getting it."

These students may be able to solve complex problems quickly or put things together in novel ways once they have grasped the big picture, but they may have difficulty explaining how they did it.

Global and analytical learners

Cultural differences based on whether a student has a "global" or "analytical" learning style have also been explored. It was possible to categorize most of the students in the study carried out for this book as being one type or the other, even if their results from the learning style inventory were not so clearly categorized.

Global learners are those who learn better from an approach emphasizing an overview of the topics, and from holistic forms of thinking that emphasize the interconnectedness between cognition and affect (Hao, 2004). Global learners are generally image oriented, cooperative, learn by experience, depend on insight and intuition, prefer indirect expressions, value the subjective, and avoid standing out. Japanese learners have been associated with having a global learning style, while learners from Europe, North America, Australia, and New Zealand have been associated with an analytical learning style.

Analytical learners generally learn by reasoning. They value the objective and the rational, are text oriented, prefer direct expressions, like to compete, and assert themselves. See Table 3.1 for a comparison of the two learning styles.

Table 3.1   Global vs. analytical learning styles

Global learning style	Analytical learning style
Learns by experience	Learns by reasoning
Image oriented	Text oriented
Depends on insight and intuition	Depends on logic and reasoning
Cooperative, collective	Competitive, individualistic
Subjective and poetic	Objective and rational
Avoids standing out	Asserts self
Prefers indirect expression	Prefers direct expression

Source: Adapted from Shunichiro Ito (2005) Cultural inclinations in learning styles, Gakuin College, Tokyo, Japan

In the Mestre study (2010, 2012), when comparing whether a student was a sequential or a global learner (in the ILS inventory) more students indicated a higher tendency toward sequential preferences than global preferences, and this was distributed across ethnicities. During the actual tutorial assessments students were instructed to "talk aloud" as they progressed through the pre-tests, post-tests, and when navigating through the tutorials. Through the analysis of these conversations, the Asian students had clear expectations for an analytical approach, whereas all of the other students exhibited tendencies consistent with global learners.

The term "global learner" has also been attributed to "Millennials" (those born since 1982). This assumes it is possible to clump all students (based on age) into one group. The preferences mentioned below are also relevant for interactive tutorials.

A study by Oblinger and Oblinger (2005) discussed the learning characteristics of those who are termed Millennials. Their characteristics are said to be:

- the ability to multitask rather than single task;
- a preference to learn from pictures, sound, and video rather than text; and
- a preference for interactive and networked activities rather than independent and individual study.

Disadvantages of the above include:

- a shorter attention span or choosing not to pay attention;
- a lack of reflection;
- relatively poor text literacy; and
- a cavalier attitude to the quality of sources.

Raines and Arnsparger (2010) listed these characteristics:

- skilled at teamwork;
- techno savvy;
- a preference for structure;
- a desire for entertainment and excitement; and
- biased toward experiential activities.

One of the original goals for the Mestre (2010) study, which used Millennial students, was to ascertain if there were any commonalities in learning styles between the ethnic groups that participated in the tutorial usability study. For the 21 students in the study (two African Americans, eight Anglo Americans, seven Asian Americans, and four Hispanic Americans), neither the results from the VARK inventory nor the ILS inventory indicated any common tendency toward any particular dimension based on ethnicity. However, certain similarities were noticed during the usability test related to how students approached the various tutorials and their expectations, especially for the Asian Americans. All but one of the seven Asian American students were the most analytical and had a preference for a systematic, clear, sequential approach with additional information to help as needed. The other students preferred an approach that would allow them to see within the picture what they needed to do and to jump quickly through the page to find the answer they needed.

Of the 21 participants in the usability study, 17 could be classified as global learners. They noted that they first looked at the images and only read the text if the steps were not clear from the images. All of the students, when going through the web-based tutorial with screen captures, were very adept at opening another web page and working along with the tutorial. Their facility in manipulating multiple pages and activities at one time was very apparent. They all commented that they liked the interactivity and liked being engaged with the process.

The next section will provide a few examples of some of the cultural considerations that may influence approaches to learning in the online environment.

Culturally responsive instruction

There are various definitions for being "culturally responsive." Culturally responsive, standards-based instruction (CRSBI), for example, is a teaching style that validates and incorporates students' cultural background, ethnic history, and current societal interests into daily, standards-based instruction. It addresses socioemotional needs and uses ethnically and culturally diverse material (Banks, 1991; Gay, 2000). Ladson-Billings (1994) states that it is a pedagogy that empowers students intellectually, socially, emotionally, and politically by using cultural and historical references to convey knowledge, impart skills, and change attitudes. Culturally responsive teachers are also sensitive to the linguistic and behavioral skill gaps. This same pedagogy should be applied to the online environment.

Providing relevant examples

Making examples culturally relevant to all students, rather than solely to the majority, should be a goal in the design of learning objects. Gay (2000) discusses the importance of using the students' past experiences and knowledge (whether cultural or frames of reference) in examples used to help make their learning more relevant and effective. As educators become more aware of specific examples that resonate with students, those examples could be incorporated into any redesign of learning objects and exercises. Even a relatively simple act of displaying images representative of students' cultural backgrounds can help students feel accepted and better engaged.

Environments that are positive and affirming are important to students (Banks, 1991, 2006; Ladson-Billings, 1994; Wlodkowski and Ginsberg, 1995; Nieto and Rolón, 1997; Gay, 2000, 2002; Sleeter, 2001; LeCompte and McCray, 2002; Clayton, 2003; Mestre, 2004, 2009; Robins et al., 2006; Davis, 2007). There are many ways in which to make examples real and relevant to students, such as using authors, sources, or topics with which specific cultures associate (e.g., a relevant African American, Latino, Asian American, or member of the gay community). Sheets (2005) points out that competent teachers acknowledge the connection between culture and learning. Agosto (2007) also addresses the importance for educators of evaluating and integrating multicultural resources into their curricula. By incorporating the students' historical knowledge and analysis into learning objects, students may feel as though they are validated and that their culture is relevant to the learning experience. They may also be more engaged and motivated to succeed if their cultural knowledge and learning styles are acknowledged.

It is also important to understand how culture influences cognitive and social development and know how to apply these understandings in the design of learning objects. Students should be given multiple and consistent opportunities to practice higher-level thinking skills if they are to develop as advanced critical thinkers. Cultural adaptations may be needed with diverse learners because students acquire and display knowledge in different ways. It is also important to remember that all students come with some prior knowledge on which they can build. Again, making the task relevant to their everyday practical experience will help students be successful in recognizing patterns and classifying and categorizing terms and tasks. Providing opportunities for students to view reality through numerous perspectives helps them understand, evaluate, question, and challenge the issues.

During usability testing of learning objects the researcher will need to remember that a student might not understand or verbalize a particular difficulty. For example, if the participant was viewing a database and the researcher asks, "What do you think I would need to do in order to retrieve these items?" the student first might ask, "What do you mean by retrieve?" Alternatively, if the student does understand the concept s/he would talk aloud and might say, "Well, I've already checked the items that I want. I guess I would look for some button that says 'get the articles or open ... .'" The chances are that the database will not have those particular terms, which then provides useful information that will help in the redesign of a tutorial to better explain what the student will actually encounter in the database.

Suggestions for accommodating various cultural and learning styles

The same pedagogically sound approach of "mixing up" instructional strategies, as suggested in Chapter 1, should apply here as well. Educators can incorporate a variety of strategies that could benefit students, regardless of the cultural make-up of the class. This is especially important in the online environment since it is usually not possible to know the strengths or cognitive styles of students. Faculty should take into consideration the individual cultural differences among students, and use that knowledge to improve instructional planning and delivery.

Application to tutorials

Betty (2008) described efforts to standardize several tutorials in order to make them intuitive to users. She concluded that using consistent features, such as standardized language and color schemes, may help minimize confusion among end-users, especially in sections that prompted user interaction. The tutorials also used common introductions and endings and short 10–15-second video clip introductions featuring members of the library faculty. Close captioning of audio and slide notes were also used in order to increase accessibility.

Watson (2004) provides examples of the benefits of combining audio and visual components into tutorials. In addition to step-by-step instructions (great for sequential learners due to the chunking of information), he explains that voice narration provides positive feedback through communication cues in the narration. The step-by-step instructions and the narration help reduce cognitive load as students are guided through the information. He concludes that students are able to learn better with the combined visual and audio components.

Costello et al. (2004) offer an example of the value of differentiating instruction within the online environment to address the specific learning styles of students from the X and Y generations. Generational learning styles can sharply define the methods for delivering instruction. For the Internet generation these preferences include: instruction focused on short, concise practical bits of information; a tendency to rely on familiar resources; a predilection towards active, kinesthetic learning utilizing innovative technology; an excessive reliance on Internet resources when conducting research; and an expectation that educational experiences will be individualized through personal contact and feedback from instructors.

Educators who understand learning and cultural differences will strive for intentional variety in instruction, curriculum, classroom management, and assessment. If a learning experience is adjusted to accommodate diverse styles, students will be able to use their strengths to achieve success. Some approaches which can be helpful are:

- Organizing material in a non-linear, open-ended format, with a clear table of contents.
- Scaffolding instruction so that learners can choose the material they need.
- Allowing students to control their progress, while providing step-by-step instructions as needed.
- Incorporating interactivity throughout, including exercises that require responses and choices.
- Providing opportunities for learning in context.
- Making situations, scenarios, and examples relevant and "personal" to students (allowing them to choose from several options).
- Including ways to view the material through multiple modalities (visual, aural, kinesthetic).
- Limiting the amount of text, but providing additional opportunities for more examples, theories, information for those who want it.
- Including feedback, assistance, pacing, sequencing, and different levels of difficulty. This would require much more programming in order to allow students to advance in different ways, depending upon their choices.

Suggestions

The following were derived from suggestions from the students in the Mestre (2010) usability study that was described in the Introduction to this book.

Include scenarios that require students to think about and relate to their real-world experience. The plagiarism tutorial used in this study included four characters who were facing a real-life scenario. Students needed to choose a character with whom they might identify and help that character through the process. The Hispanic students in the study commented on the importance of finding relevance in tutorials and working together to help someone solve a task. They remarked that having a task to work through that was applicable to them helped them to engage with the information that was presented. They felt empathy for the character when the wrong response sent the character to a fire pit. Some of the students chose the Hispanic-looking character, some chose the character closest to their own area of study, and one chose a character because of the color of their clothes and because there was a cat. However, one student (identified as Asian) did not see why she had to choose a character because she did not see how it would help her learn the information.

Organize learning objects sequentially where the user can proceed one step at a time and allow students to choose sections. If students are using a learning object for something other than a one-shot experience, they may need to refer back to it as they go through the actual process. All but one of the students in the study needed to refer back to the tutorial for guidance. The Camtasia tutorial was problematic in that there were no chapter markers to let students jump to a particular section. None of the students attempted to consult the Camtasia tutorial, whereas all but one student did refer back to the static web page with screen captures to remind them of the process. The more recent versions of screencast software do allow for chapter markers so it is possible to provide an index on the left for students to jump to various sections. A good navigation structure and a table of contents with jumping-off points is very useful, regardless of the type of tutorial.

Design the learning object with sound design principles based on multimedia learning. Although all but three students in the study scored in the upper regions for at least two learning styles, they all commented that the most effective tutorial or learning object would be one that had visuals that flowed along with voice narration. They wanted to see text represented within the image or in a pop-up that appeared from time to time to highlight a particular point. They mentioned that students are in a hurry so they don't want to waste time reading a lot of information. They want to glance at it quickly and get to the task at hand. The visuals that included arrows, highlights, or that drew attention to a particular aspect were especially effective. During the post-test, students would verbally recall a particular feature that had been highlighted in the image or in a pop-up. Only one student read the captioning at the bottom of the Camtasia tutorial. In the static tutorials with screenshots, none of the students read the text unless the image wasn't adequately clear. Even if a student normally has a preferred learning style, that doesn't necessarily mean that information has to be geared to just that format. If multiple styles are represented a student can focus on their preferred style (visual or aural) and use the other cues to supplement the information. Or, they can choose to ignore the other modes.

Include interactivy. Interactivity was equally important. The students who were able to recreate the steps and find articles were those who had done the search alongside the static tutorial. After interacting with the plagiarism tutorial, students indicated that being able to choose options helped them to focus on the task at hand. Even though they had many suggestions for improving the interactivy of the tutorial, they did like the "game-like" quality and knowing that there might be consequences if they chose the wrong response. In the online environment educators have the opportunity to design materials that can engage students' visual, aural, and critical-thinking abilities. In this study, measured by the VARK learning style questionnaire, most students were multimodal learners, so providing ways to accommodate many styles should help them to be successful. What seems to be missing in the online environment (as compared with the face-to-face) is the ability for a hands-on component, so educators should think of ways to intersperse active learning into their objects in order to help students learn the intended information.

Solicit feedback. Students also wanted to receive feedback after choosing a response, and wanted to engage the mind (using critical thinking) rather than just passively view a video object. Learning objects that require the user to be interactive – by rolling a mouse over an object to gain further information, by choosing a response, or in the use of drag and drop – engage the mind. Students in this study were able to repeat steps from the tutorial when there had been interactivity during the tutorial process.

Allow the student to choose the learning mode s/he prefers. Various tutorials do allow students to choose whether or not they prefer to view a static tutorial with screenshots, a video tutorial, or a learning object with sound or with captions. A study to ascertain which mode students choose (matching their learning style) would be illustrative. Would students choose something like a Camtasia tutorial because they might think it would be more enjoyable, even though their learning style might be more closely matched to a static tutorial where they need to work alongside the tutorial? Because educators know they also need to provide captioning or a script along with their visual and auditory learning objects, there is great flexibility for the learner to choose a format that best complements their learning style. When designing screencast learning objects it might be good design practice to ascertain whether a learner could get equal information if they listenened, or read, or just visually said the information. If not, then alternate versions should be made available. In this study, the Camtasia tutorial provided inputs for the aural, read/write and visual styles. Students varied in what they focused on, but, because the tutorials had been designed to convey the relevant information whether looking, listening, or reading, the students were equally able to explain what they needed to do. The difficulty, however, was that there was no interactivity built into the tutorial so actually going back to recreate the task was problematic. Integrating interactivity within learning objects appears to be the element that is missing in many tutorials. Adding a quiz "check-in" question periodically in the tutorial may help with the retention of information.

Chapter 6 provides a much more detailed discussion of suggestions for designing tutorials to accommodate multiple learning styles. Those suggestions are based on student feedback, comments from the Mestre (2010) usability study, and other research studies.

Conclusion

Studies related to learner preferences in an online environment continue to document the potential for providing strategies to enhance learning as a very individualized process. Bennett (1986, p. 116) warns that ignoring the effects of culture and learning style affects all students:

> If classroom expectations are limited by our own cultural orientations, we impede successful learners guided by another cultural orientation. If we only teach according to the ways we ourselves learn best, we are also likely to thwart successful learners who may share our cultural background but whose learning styles deviate from our own.

Regardless of cultural influence, students approach learning with many different strategies, habits, expertise, and expectations. One of the best methods for designers is to use many different instructional methods to reach all students. Different instructional methods are better at tapping into the different neural systems (recognition, strategic, and affective), and successful teaching and learning requires the interaction of these three systems. It is also important to use multiple methods of demonstrating understanding of essential course content, including flexibility and opportunities for student choice. Specific examples related to designing learning objects and tutorials are covered in Chapters 6 to 8.

References

Agosto, D.E. (2007) Building a multicultural school library: issues and challenges. *Teacher Librarian: The Journal for School Library Professionals*, 34(3): 27–31.

Allison, B.N. and Rehm, M.L. (2007) Teaching strategies for diverse learners in FCS classrooms. *Journal of Family & Consumer Sciences*, 99(2): 8–10.

Banks, J. (1991) A curriculum for empowerment, action, and change. In C.E. Sleeter (ed.) *Empowerment through Multicultural Education* (pp. 125–41). Albany, NY: State University of New York Press.

Banks, J.A. (2006) *Cultural Diversity and Education: Foundations, Curriculum, and Teaching*. Seattle, WA: Pearson Education, Inc.

Bennett, C. (1986) *Comprehensive Multicultural Education, Theory and Practice*. Boston, MA: Allyn and Bacon.

Betty, P. (2008) Creation, management, and assessment of library screencasts: the Regis libraries animated tutorials project. *Journal of Library Administration*, 48(3–4): 295–315.

Bourges-Waldegg, P. and Scrivener, S.A.R. (1998) Applying and testing an approach to design for culturally diverse user groups. *Interacting with Computers*, 9(3): 287–310.

Chan, S. (1999) The Chinese learner – a question of style. *Education & Training*, 41(6/7): 294–305.

Chau, P.Y.K., Cole, M., Massey, A.P., Montoya-Weiss, M. and O'Keefe, R.M. (2002) Cultural differences in the online behavior of consumers. *Communications of the ACM*, 45(10): 138–43.

Cifuentes, C. and Ozel, S. (2006) Resources for attending to the needs of multicultural learners. *Knowledge Quest: Journal of the American Association of School Librarians*, 35(2): 14–21.

Clayton, J.B. (2003) *One Classroom, Many Worlds: Teaching and Learning in the Cross-cultural Classroom*. Portsmouth, NH: Heinemann.

Costello, B., Lenholt, R. and Stryker, J. (2004) Using Blackboard in library instruction: addressing the learning styles of Generations X and Y. *The Journal of Academic Librarianship*, 30(6): 452–60. DOI:10.1016/j.acalib.2004.07.003.

Davis, J.R. (2007) Making a difference: how teachers can positively affect racial identity and acceptance in America. *Social Studies*, 98(5): 209–16.

Dunn, R. (1993) Learning styles of the multiculturally diverse. *Emergency Librarian*, 20(4): 24–32.

Dunn, R. (1997) The goals and track record of multicultural education. *Educational Leadership*, 54(7): 74–7.

Dunn, R. (2000) Capitalizing on college students' learning styles. In R. Dunn and S.A. Griggs (eds.) *Practical Approaches to Using Learning Styles in Higher Education* (pp. 3–18). Westport, CT: Bergin & Garvey.

Dunn, R. and Griggs, S. (1995) *Multiculturalism and Learning Style: Teaching and Counseling Adolescents*. Westport, CT: Praeger.

Dunn, R. and Griggs, S. (2000) *Practical Approaches to Using Learning Styles in Higher Education*. Westport, CT: Bergin & Garvey.

Faiola, A. and Macdorman, K.F. (2008) The influence of holistic and analytic cognitive styles on online information design: toward a communication theory of cultural cognitive design. *Information, Communication & Society*, 11(3): 348–74.

Faiola, A. and Matei, S.A. (2005) Cultural cognitive style and web design: beyond a behavioral inquiry into computer-mediated communication. *Journal of Computer-mediated Communication*, 11(1): 375–94. DOI:10.1111/j.1083-6101.2006.00018.x.

Gay, G. (2000) *Culturally Responsive Teaching: Theory, Research, and Practice*. New York: Teacher's College Press.

Gay, G. (2002) Culturally responsive teaching in special education for ethnically diverse students: setting the stage. *International Journal of Qualitative Studies in Education (QSE)*, 15(6): 613–29.

Gay, G. (2003) Culture and communication in the classroom. In L.A. Samovar and R. E Porter (eds.) *Intercultural Communication: A Reader* (pp. 320–38). Belmont, CA: Thomson Wadsworth.

Graff, M., Davies, J. and McNorton, M. (2004) Cognitive style and cross cultural differences in internet use and computer attitudes. *European Journal of Open, Distance and E-Learning*. Available at: *http://www.eurodl.org/index.php?p=archives&year=2004&halfyear=2*.

Hao, Y.-W. (2004) Students' attitudes toward interaction in online learning: exploring the relationship between attitudes, learning styles, and course satisfaction. Unpublished doctoral dissertation. Austin, TX: University of Texas at Austin.

Haukoos, G. and Satterfield, R. (1986) Learning styles of minority students (Native Americans) and their application in developing a culturally sensitive science classrooms. *Community/Junior College Quarterly*, 10(3): 193–201.

Honigsfeld, A. and Dunn, R. (2003) High school male and female learning-style similarities and differences in diverse nations. *The Journal of Educational Research*, 96(4): 195–20.

Honold, P. (2000) Culture and context: an empirical study for the development of a framework for the elicitation of cultural influence in product usage. *International Journal of Human–Computer Interaction*, 12(3–4): 327–45.

Irvine, J. and York, D. (1995) Learning styles and culturally diverse students: a literature review. In J. Banks and C.A. McGee (eds.) *Handbook of Research on Multicultural Education* (pp. 484–97). New York: Macmillan.

Ito, S. (2005) Cultural inclinations in learning styles. Cross cultural communication online: Perspectives from around the globe. Presented by the Webheads Community at Networking. Available at: *http://users.chariot.net.au/~michael/ccc/pres.htm*.

Jacobson, M.H. (2001) Primer on learning styles: reaching every student. *Seattle Law Review*, 25(139): 139–77.

Jacobson, R.R. (2000) *Differences Between Traditional and Nontraditional Students on the Motivated Strategies for Learning Questionnaire*. Auburn, AL: Auburn University.

Kasten, W. (1992) Bridging the horizon: American Indian beliefs and whole language learning. *Anthropology and Education Quarterly*, 23: 108–19.

Kim, K.-J. and Bonk, C.J. (2002) Cross-cultural comparisons of online collaboration. *Journal of Computer-Mediated Communication*, 8(1). DOI:10.1111/j.1083-6101.2002.tb00163.x.

Kim, K.S. and Allen, B. (2002) Cognitive and task influences on web searching behavior. *Journal of the American Society for Information Science and Technology*, 2: 109–19.

Kirkbride, P.S. and Tang, S.F.Y. (1992) Management development in the Nanyang Chinese societies of South-east Asia. *The Journal of Management Development*, 11(2): 54–66.

Ladson-Billings, G. (1994) *The Dreamkeepers: Successful Teachers of African American Children*. San Francisco, CA: Jossey-Bass.

LeCompte, K.N. and Davis McCray, A. (2002) Complex conversations with teacher candidates: perspectives of whiteness and culturally responsive teaching. *Curriculum & Teaching Dialogue*, 4(1): 25–35.

Liang, A. and McQueen, R.J. (1999) Computer assisted adult interactive learning in a multi-cultural environment. *Adult Learning*, 11(1): 26–9.

Marcus, A. and Gould, E.W. (2000) Crosscurrents: cultural dimensions and global web user interface design. *Interactions*, 2(4): 32–46.

Mestre, L.S. (2000) Latinos, libraries and electronic resources. Unpublished doctoral dissertation. Amherst, MA: University of Massachusetts.

Mestre, L.S. (2004) Culturally relevant instruction for Latinos. *Academic Exchange*, 8(1): 46–51.

Mestre, L.S. (2006) Accommodating diverse learning styles in an online environment. *Reference & User Services Quarterly*, 47(2): 27–32.

Mestre, L.S. (2009) Culturally responsive instruction for school librarians. *Teacher Librarian*, 36(3): 8–12.

Mestre, L.S. (2010) Matching up learning styles with learning objects: what's effective? *Journal of Library Administration*, 50(7–8): 808–82.

Mestre, L.S. (2012) Student preference and results after comparing screencast and static tutorials: a usability study. *Reference Services Review*, 40(2): 258–76.

Neuman, Y. and Bekerman, Z. (2000) Cultural resources and the gap between educational theory and practice. *Teachers College Record*, 103(3): 471–84.

Nieto, S. and Rolón, C. (1997) Preparation and professional development of teachers: a perspective from two Latinas. In Jacqueline J. Irvine (ed.) *Critical Knowledge for Diverse Teachers and Learners*. Washington, DC: AACTE Publications.

Oblinger, D. and Oblinger, J. (2005) Is it age or IT: first steps toward understanding the net generation. In D. Oblinger and J. Oblinger (eds.) *Educating the Net Generation*. Available at: *http://www.educause.edu/educatingthenetgen*.

Pagan, L. (2009) Teaching for diversity and globalization in online and web-based learning environments. Paper presented at the 5th International Conference on Multimedia and ICT in Education, April 22–4, 2009, Lisbon.

Philips, S. (1983) *The Invisible Culture: Communication in Classroom and on the Warm Springs Indian Reservation*. New York: Longman, Inc.

Preece, J. and Maloney-Krichmar, D. (2005) Online communities: design, theory, and practice. *Journal of Computer-Mediated Communication*, 10(4). Available at: *http://jcmc.indiana.edu/vol10/issue4/preece.html*.

Raines, C. and Arnsparger, A. (2010) Millennials at work. Available at: *http://www.generationsatwork.com/articles_millennials_at_work.php* (retrieved July 14, 2012).

Robins, K.N., Lindsey, R.B., Lindsey, D.B. and Terrell, R.D. (2006) *Culturally Proficient Instruction: A Guide for People Who Teach* (2nd edn.). Thousand Oaks, CA: Corwin Press.

Salili, F. (1996) Accepting personal responsibility for learning. In D.A. Watkins and J.B. Biggs (eds.) *The Chinese Learner: Cultural Psychological and Contextual Influences* (pp. 86–105). Hong Kong: CERC.

Shade, B.J. (ed.) (1989) *Culture, Style, and the Educative Process*. Springfield, IL: Charles C. Thomas.

Sheets, R.H. (2005) *Diversity Pedagogy: Examining the Role of Culture in the Teaching-Learning Process*. Boston, MA: Pearson/Allyn & Bacon.

Sleeter, C.E. (2001) Preparing teachers for culturally diverse schools: research and the overwhelming presence of whiteness. *Journal of Teacher Education*, 52(2): 94–106.

St. Amant, K. (2007) *Linguistic and Cultural Online Communication Issues in the Global Age*. Hershey, PA: Information Science Reference.

Watson, J. (2004) Going beyond screen captures: integrating video screen recording into your library instruction program. *Feliciter*, 50(2): 66–7.

Witkin, H.A. (1962) *Psychological Differentiation: Studies of Development.* Chichester: Wiley.

Witkin, H.A., Moore, C.A., Goodenough, D.R. and Cox, P.W. (1977) Field-dependent and field-independent cognitive styles and their educational implications. *Review of Educational Research*, 47(1): 1–64.

Wlodkowski, R.J. and Ginsberg, M.G. (1995) A framework for culturally responsive teaching. *Educational Leadership*, 53(1): 17–21.

Wong, J.K.K. (2004) Are the learning styles of Asian international students culturally or contextually based? *International Education Journal*, 4(4): 154–66.

Yang, D., Olesova, L. and Richardson, J.C. (2010) Impact of cultural differences on students' participation, communication, and learning in an online environment. *Journal of Educational Computing Research*, 43(2): 165–82.

Zahedi, F., van Pelt, W.V. and Song, J. (2001) A conceptual framework for international web design. *IEEE Transactions on Professional Communication*, 44(2): 83–103.

The need for learning object development

Abstract: Web-based instruction and tutorials can easily include a variety of learning objects so that instruction can be flexible, interactive, and student centered. The development of reusable learning objects can help expand the repository of material that educators and librarians can access, embed, or modify for their instructional use. These objects can play a supporting role in active learning strategies in instruction, as well as in supporting student-centered learning environments. This chapter provides an overview of: the benefits of creating or using learning objects and tutorials; categories of tutorials developed; current practices for accessing tutorials; challenges to creating tutorials (online information literacy); and the librarian's role in creating tutorials. Several studies are also summarized which assess students' perceptions of using learning objects and relying on the online environment to receive their instruction.

Key words: learning objects, online learning, tutorials, e-learning, instructional design.

Introduction

As discussed in Chapter 1, students approach learning in various ways, but with virtually every student now expected to acquire information online it becomes even more imperative to develop learning tools that are available to assist them when they need the extra support. The range of online tools available to port content can be a challenge for instructors. In addition to creating content on their own web pages, online course management systems, wikis, blogs, videos, and podcasts, they also need to consider methods that will display correctly on mobile devices. This chapter will provide an overview of: the benefits of creating or using learning objects and tutorials; categories of tutorials developed; current practices for accessing tutorials; challenges to creating tutorials (online information literacy); the librarian's role in creating tutorials; and student perceptions of learning objects. Chapter 5 provides an overview of some of the tools used by instructors to provide supplemental support to their students, as well as examples of types of tutorials developed, whether web based, podcasts, screencasting, or videos.

Learning objects, web-based instruction, and tutorials

Web-based instruction and tutorials can easily include a variety of learning objects so that instruction can be flexible, interactive, and student centered. As previously explained, in this book the term "learning object" will be used to describe a reusable instructional resource, usually digital and web based, that is developed to support learning. Educators and librarians create and use many types of learning objects to deliver instruction. Learning objects can encompass text-based learning modules and lessons as well as animated and streamed video presentations. Examples of smaller reusable digital resources include full- and short-text documents, figures, digital images or photos, live data feeds, live or prerecorded video or audio snippets, animations, and smaller web-delivered applications. An example of a larger reusable digital resource includes a set of web pages that combine text, images, and other media or applications to deliver course modules.

Wiley (2000, p. 3) outlines the basic concept of learning objects as "small (relative to the size of an entire course) instructional components that can be reused a number of times in different learning contexts." Some common examples of learning objects are instructional modules, tutorials, instructional games, blogs, research guides, narrated PowerPoint presentations, podcasts, photos, images, quizzes, surveys, and videos. Jackson and Mogg (2007) describe an Information Literacy Resource Bank at Cardiff University in the United Kingdom as a collection containing "bite-size" interactive tasks, images, diagrams, cartoons, and short tutorials for use by both librarians and faculty as a means of promoting the embedding of information literacy into the curriculum.

Core characteristics of learning objects include efficiency, e.g., cost and time saving (Mardis and Ury, 2008), reusability, interoperability, durability, and accessibility (Keown, 2007). Other features are considered to be the facilitation of competency-based learning, increased value of content, and customization (Longmire, 2000; Holmes, 2003). Learning objects could be course based but also remedial, facilitating "a just-in-case, just-in-time, just-for-you approach" (Holmes, 2003, pp. 1–9).

Providing an engaging environment for students "to learn in as opposed to one to learn from" reflects the underlying principles associated with the design and implementation of learning objects. Mardis and Ury (2008) describe the use of learning objects for library instruction to introduce content, gauge prior knowledge, reinforce understanding, assess learning, save development time, and personalize the curriculum. They can also be used to scaffold student learning.

The development of learning objects incorporating Web 2.0 tools greatly enhances the ability of librarians to interactively engage students in learning activities designed to introduce, provide practice in, and eventually demonstrate mastery of, information literacy skills. Because learning objects are reusable, granular, and contextually adaptable, they can be conveniently packaged and readily retrieved from any number of instruction delivery platforms or access points and thereby greatly extend the reach of library instruction.

The remainder of this chapter will discuss some of the benefits and challenges of commonly used and developed learning objects (such as tutorials, podcasts, and videos). Tutorials range from those with interactive elements aimed to cover advanced information literacy concepts for a broad audience (Blummer, 2007), to simpler screencasts with the goal of answering "point of need" questions and problems, thereby offering assistance with a specific information literacy task (Kerns, 2007).

Benefits of learning objects

Librarians value the face-to-face time they have with students as they help them through the research process. However, it is not possible to meet with every class or every student for an hour-long introduction to the way library materials are stored, accessed, searched, or evaluated. Making use of an online environment provides librarians with the opportunity to teach information literacy skills, research strategies, and effective evaluation of information to large numbers of students without having to be physically present to do so. The development of tutorials by librarians allows them to illustrate some of the explanations and examples students might need to get started with the research process. As librarians work with faculty members they can co-create specific tutorials that will benefit students in a particular content area. Faculty can then embed those tutorials (video tutorials, podcasts, web pages, etc.) in their course content area so that they are readily available to students. Tutorials have a great potential to reach a far greater number of students (if linked through course pages and in other visible places that students would see). This therefore enables libraries to reach segments of the user population who neither sign up for classes nor have the opportunity to participate in course-related instruction. These tools allow libraries to reach a traditionally underserved population of library users, namely, remote users.

Online instruction also suits many of our students, who spend increasing amounts of time online. These students are used to multimedia environments and to figuring things out online for themselves (Lippincott, 2005). They tend to value the convenience provided by technology, and expect to be engaged by their environments (Oblinger, 2008). For these students, traditional in-person classroom instruction sessions, which tend not to be connected to their time and place of need, may not be as effective any more (Ladner et al., 2004).

Tutorials for teaching faculty

The 2010 Sloan Survey (Allen and Seaman, 2010) reported a 21 percent growth rate for online enrollments which far exceeds the 2 percent growth in the overall higher education student population. Sixty-three percent of all reporting institutions said that online learning was a critical part of their institution's long-term strategy, a small increase from 59 percent in 2009. Nearly 30 percent of higher education students now take at least one course online.

Even if faculty members conduct classes in a face-to-face situation, they frequently also make their materials available online, whether through a course management system or web environment. Blogs, wikis, chat forums, and discussion boards are commonplace in online instruction and they encourage interaction between students and faculty. Often, though, students need additional support tools to supplement what they are (or are not) learning in class. In addition to providing lectures (either through a podcast, script, or video), many instructors look for learning objects that will illustrate various processes discussed in class. They search repositories and video repositories (such as YouTube and Google Video) to find objects they can either embed in their site or provide a link to. These may be clips that illustrate the steps required for a certain process, an experiment, comparisons, or anything to make the content "come alive" for students. Some faculty make and post their own video clips. Again, these could range from showing the layout of an art studio to recording a lecture or experiment. These learning objects allow for the incorporation of a number of elements that it might not be possible to cover in the regular class session (whether in a face-to-face or online session). These tools can include illustrations, step-by-step processes, concept training, lectures, strategies, links to additional examples, humor, game-like examples, and exercises.

Librarians are also creating learning objects to support faculty and students. These include enhanced learning guides, podcasts, screencasts, videos, and tutorials to help illustrate the research process and library facilities. Academic librarians recognize that in order to provide good support for students they need to be proactive in embedding library instruction in venues and platforms that students and faculty commonly use, for they may never make it to the library web page to find them. Once a tutorial, video, or web page is created librarians can push them out via web page links to faculty or embed them in faculty web pages and course content modules. Librarians are also working with campus technologists and faculty to create application programming interfaces (APIs) to help students navigate the library resources. These extend beyond optimizing a web page for a mobile device. Some of the APIs developed can work as way-finding guides to help students locate books on a library shelf, or to recommend materials (such as library databases or journal articles or other resources) based on where they are in a call number area of the library. These can then be offered to students and downloaded through iTunes U, the iTunes store, or similar places.

Online instruction can offer a more individualized approach that allows each student to work at his or her own pace. It can be designed to meet the needs of students with various skill levels, and can enable students to repeat or skip sections according to their own needs. For international students, online instruction and tutorials may seem more approachable than a reference desk. Even if some students take longer than others to complete the program, every student has the opportunity to learn the same information.

Data gathering and assessment are other potential benefits of online instruction. Tutorials and web pages can be used to gather information such as right and wrong answers, patterns, completion times and rates, and other information to help in modifying the tutorial, web page, module, or program. Similarly, students can get immediate feedback on their responses, next steps to help them based on their responses, and links to relevant review sessions.

Although it requires intensive resource commitment to create an effective tutorial or learning object, the benefit is that educators can then spend less time on basic instruction and instead devote their time to more complex instruction or face-to-face consultations. A base level of information literacy competency can be assumed after the implementation of a tutorial, enabling in-person information literacy instruction to focus on more complex topics.

Challenges of creating learning objects

Similar to previous web page design, faculty must address such issues as: formatting and layout, navigation, loading speed, and technical quality (Scholz et al., 1996; Dewald, 1999a and b; Weston et al., 1999). They must also face the challenge of moving beyond the tendency to simply "lecture" or reproduce into the tutorial a replica of what they would say or do in a face-to-face session (Dabbour, 1997; Dewald et al., 2000). Another challenge is to incorporate the proper active learning and interactive characteristics so that students are not solely passive learners but are active participants (Allen, 1995; Dabbour, 1997; Dewald, 1999a and b; Mestre, 2010).

In addition to the investment of time, expertise, and resources to create learning objects and training materials (Kruse and Keil, 2000), there is also the requirement to keep the object up-to-date. With library tutorials, a common occurrence is that database vendors change their interface or one vendor buys another vendor, thus necessitating a redesign. Additional updating challenges are often triggered by the redesign of web pages which causes changes in navigation, and by changes in course management systems. Maintenance of this sort is fairly typical, worthwhile, and not unexpected, albeit time-consuming.

Another major challenge that can be encountered is portability across devices. Students should be able to view a learning object or tutorial on any computer or device, so creating a tutorial that ports well is critical. Often, designers will create multiple versions of a tutorial so that students can choose the version which best suits their system. They may have a web-based version, a PDF, a video screencast, a podcast, options for downloading with QuickTime or streamed through a server or YouTube, for example. Even so, the processing speeds of a particular computer can still be frustrating if there is lag time in loading.

Investments in software and/or hardware, in developers and programmers, and in usability studies will also be needed. These all require substantial preparation time. Students may need to download plug-ins in order to be able to view or interact with a program. Although some plug-ins, like those needed to view videos (such as Flash or QuickTime) are commonplace, some programs require additional plug-ins which could cause problems for students not using their own computer, as administrative permission to download the plug-ins may be required. It is preferable for faculty/designers to use only programs that can be accessed by public computers without extra plug-ins.

One of the main benefits of online learning is also one of its greatest challenges; namely, designing effective interactive exercises. Although exercises encourage participation and allow for active learning, they are usually limited in their ability and are rarely designed to use higher-order thinking skills. Typically, the exercises only require lower-order thinking skills, such as remembering and comprehending.

Overview of the faculty's or librarian's role in creating tutorials

Often, librarians work with faculty to determine what type of online support or instruction would benefit their students. Library guides are abundant and can be tailored to individual classes. With products such as LibGuides, an online product with templates from Springshare (*http://www.springshare.com/libguides/*), librarians can provide specific citations or links to resources to get a student started on a topic (e.g., searching the library catalog, journal databases, documents, web pages, or other materials). Faculty can embed or link to these in their course management systems and libraries can create searchable indexes for them. Even within these guides a librarian can embed tutorials or learning objects to further explain the research process. Figure 4.1 is an example of a LibGuide from the University of Illinois.

The LibGuide in Figure 4.1 may seem crowded for some learners. However, it is an example of the variety of boxes and flexibility that is available. Videos, quizzes, widgets, and audio can be embedded, making this a popular resource for tutorials. Although library guides may be the most

Figure 4.1   LibGuide for learning objects at the University of Illinois

Source: *http://uiuc.libguides.com/learningobjects*

common learning object developed, librarians are often actively engaged in the creation of other tools, such as tutorials, podcasts, mobile apps, and videos. Yang (2009) examined a total of 372 online information literacy tutorials from the library websites of academic institutions. The findings indicate that about 33 percent of the surveyed libraries have developed their own online tutorials. About 11 percent have links to online tutorials created by other libraries or database vendors. Most of the tutorials assessed were designed to explain how to access and use a specific database (40 percent). In addition to helping students who generally want to know how to use a database, librarians can point patrons to a specific database tutorial to get them going and to explain the basics of the structure of the database and operational procedures and then work with them on more specific search strategies or complex issues.

General and introductory tutorials were found in 32 percent of the pages evaluated. General and introductory tutorials are not tied to any particular subject area but could be very broadly useful (to help patrons understand how to check out a book, renew a book, etc.).

Tutorials for subject research for particular classes or for particular majors accounted for 14 percent of the surveyed tutorials. LibGuides is now being used by many librarians in lieu of a tutorial. For example, see the listing of LibGuides by subject at the University of Illinois: *http://uiuc.libguides.com/index.php*. These can contain resources, step-by-step instructions, and also can embed how-to videos, tutorials, and images (see Figure 4.2).

Other categories of tutorials assessed in the study include those on library-related concepts, procedures, or policies (9 percent), and tutorials on an application or software (5 percent). To create their online tutorials, academic librarians have used a variety of approaches. As libraries can develop the same tutorials with several technologies, one tutorial may take on multiple formats. For instance, a library might create the same

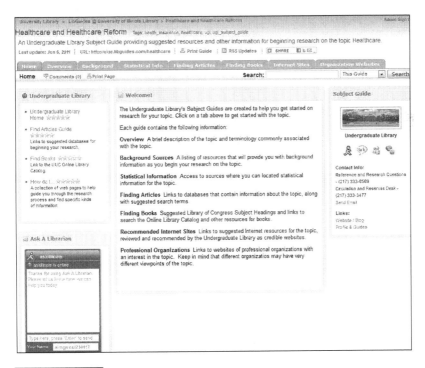

Figure 4.2   LibGuide example from the University of Illinois

tutorials in PDF, HTML, MP3, MP4, QuickTime, streaming, and Microsoft PowerPoint, thereby offering a choice for users. Examples of tutorials can be found in the next chapter.

Access to existing tutorials

There are vast numbers of learning objects available in repositories that are designed for some of the various styles of learning and teaching. They include: visual learning, writing skills, critical thinking, time-revealed scenarios, case studies, and empirical observation. These can be redesigned for other purposes, applications, subjects, and courses with little or no additional programming.

One of the most common ways in which instructors enhance learning is through learning objects and tutorials. Often they can find a link on video sites such as YouTube or Google Videos that illustrates a concept, approach, or method. Sites like MERLOT, ANTS, PRIMO, etc. (defined below) serve as repositories of tutorials that are available for download. Some allow modification of content by providing the files as well.

The PRIMO project (Peer-Reviewed Instructional Materials Online), created by ACRL's Instruction Section (ALA/ACRL, 2004–12), is an excellent peer-reviewed resource that facilitates the goal of collaborative curriculum development. PRIMO's mission is focused on collecting instructional materials related to "discovering, accessing and evaluating information in networked environments" (*http://www.ala.org/apps/primo/ public/search.cfm*) The scope is narrower than gathering instructional materials for information literacy, yet much of the content does address information literacy issues. A similar project is MERLOT (Multimedia Educational Resource for Learning and Online Teaching) (MERLOT, 1997–2012). This project also utilizes a peer-review process, but it has a broader scope than PRIMO, including many field-specific educational materials that are not directly related to information literacy (*http://www. merlot.org*). ANTS (Animated Tutorial Sharing) (ANTS, 2005–12) is an open-source tutorial sharing project. It includes a repository and guidelines for depositing and sharing tutorials (*http://ants.wetpaint.com/*). These three projects represent valuable models for collaboration.

Another resource available includes a set of 39 re-programmable learning object templates representing several modalities of teaching and learning by Talon/nPower Learning Object Suite (*http://www.envisagenow. com/solutions_elearning.html*). It includes the following tools:

- *The intelligent paragraph tool.* The intelligent paragraph tool provides the student with a problem in which content, data, and interactive demonstration may be embedded. The student explores the information and is then asked to respond to a question or create a short piece of creative writing. The student is provided with a series of statements that are right, wrong, or do not pertain to the topic area. The student must not only pick the appropriate statements for the statement database, but also place them in the correct order, creating a meaningful essay. The student receives intelligent feedback on the answer and a grade if the instructor wishes.

- *The click and drag tool.* Many students learn best by visualizing content and developing a visual map of the specific material. The click and drag problem may contain an image of the content with labels that the student can learn by clicking on the sites in the diagram. After the student has developed mastery s/he can take a computer-graded test in which s/he must drag the correct labels to the correct sites in the diagram. This template might also be used to organize written material and create summaries of content. A student may organize content by clicking text items and dragging them to appropriate answer boxes. This template was used in this project as a tool for organizing written or spoken speeches.

- *The time-revealed scenario tool.* The time-revealed scenario tool allows a student to work through a problem by making decisions based on content mastery and briefings in a time-layered approach. Each time layer represents a stage in a process that occurs over a period of time, and is driven by the decisions of the student. The student is first presented with a problem and information that allows him/her to make a decision on the best course of action to solve the problem. The selection triggers the next time layer of the problem and provides an updated situation for the student to examine. The student is then asked to make another decision to push toward a solution of the initial problem. There can be numerous outcomes depending on the decisions made by the student at each stage of the problem. The outcomes represent a spectrum of correct and incorrect strategies.

- *Evaluation tool.* The evaluation tool allows students to evaluate a situation, performance, or text and compare their evaluations to that of their instructor. Intelligent feedback is provided to the students in order to help them understand where their evaluations differed from the correct evaluation and what aspects of the content they should review.

Students' perceptions of learning objects

Online instruction suits many students who spend increasing amounts of time online. These students are used to multimedia environments and to figuring things out online for themselves (Lippincott, 2005). They tend to value the convenience provided by technology, and expect to be engaged by their environments (Oblinger, 2008). For these students, traditional in-person classroom instruction sessions, which tend not to be connected to their time and place of need, may not be as effective anymore (Ladner et al., 2004). Next, several studies are summarized that assess students' perceptions in using learning objects and relying on the online environment to get their instruction.

Harkins and Rodrigues (2011) investigated graduate students' perceptions of an online tutorial that was to be completed independently as a required part of the course, to identify advantages and challenges. The following comments are representative of the students' perceptions of the online tutorial:

> "Showing the step by step helped and to be able to go through it again and again."

> "I liked the verbal step-by-step instructions to accompany the visuals."

> "The effective use of online resources."

> "It can be easy to do at home."

> "I liked the visual aids of the cursor and the highlighted sections on the screen."

One of the findings of the study was that there was interest in combining both face-to-face instruction and online instruction. Participants commented that, "Both the presentation format and the one-on-one support were helpful," and, "A guided (in-person) tour was best and complementary to the online tutorial," as well as, "Actually going through the process with [the librarian] made the most sense to me, but having gone through the initial online tutorial first was a good preparation for [the librarian's] tutorial." Online tutorials can be effective supplements to other methods of delivering library instruction.

Another study carried out by Song et al. (2004) aimed to gain insights into learners' perceptions of online learning. Seventy-six graduate students were surveyed to identify helpful components and perceived challenges based on their online learning experiences. The results of the study indicated that most learners agreed that course design, learner motivation, time management, understanding instructional goals, and familiarity with online technologies impact the success of an online learning experience. Participants identified technical problems, a perceived lack of a sense of community, time constraints, and difficulties in understanding the objectives of the online courses as challenges. Although this book is focused more on the learning objects that can be developed to augment online learning, the issues mentioned above are relevant, even if they only pertain to the broad scope of online learning. The concerns that students voiced above pertaining to design, instructional goals, motivation (is the object engaging?), time management (is it worth their investment of time to go through the object?), and familiarity with online technologies are still concerns for learning objects.

In a qualitative study, Petrides (2002) interviewed learners to obtain their perspectives on web-based learning. The research context was a one-semester regularly scheduled class in a higher education setting using web-based technology (LearningSpace) as a supplement. When interviewed, some participants indicated that they tended to think more deeply about the subject areas when responding in writing as compared with giving verbal responses. They explained that they were able to continually reflect upon each other's reflections because of the public and permanent display of the discussion postings on the web. As one participant noted: "There is something that forces you to think more deeply about subject areas when you have to respond in writing" (ibid., p. 72). Another participant reiterated this sentiment, indicating that online technology allowed more reflection than what might occur for some individuals in face-to-face classroom discussions. Vonderwell (2003) and Chizmar and Walbert (1999) also found that participants indicated that the asynchronous environment allowed them to reflect and write carefully about their ideas. Most learning objects are self-contained units and do not afford the opportunities to write and reflect. There are options that can be included to allow students to write responses; however, usually they are only viewed by the instructor (if the coding sends responses to some database or email account). In order to allow for peer reflection and postings, links to discussion boards could be provided with directions for students to post responses on the boards, thus providing the required reflective experience.

In a study carried out by Silver and Nickel (2007), 216 psychology students participated in an online tutorial session and 70 students participated in a class library session. The tutorial proved to be as effective as classroom instruction, as there were no statistically significant differences in the quiz scores between the students in the tutorial and classroom groups. The challenges students encountered with the tutorials were mostly due to technological problems, including connectivity problems. Students suggested improvements to the pace of the tutorial, to the sizes for images, and to fonts, and requested increased interactivity. As a result the tutorial was revised.

Other student perceptions of a library tutorial were captured in a study by Michel (2001). One student cited "the quickness and simplicity of using it," and another stated that "the Highlander Guide provides a fair amount of information to a student without being consumed by too much information." In terms of feedback regarding its least helpful aspect, some students listed "confusing" or "frustrating," or referred to the inclusion of unnecessary information. One student said the tutorial provided "too much information not exactly relating to topic." Students requested that it be made clearer or less confusing. One student said that there were too many ways to get to too many things; another wanted more updating. Student feedback also suggested that the wording or navigation used in the tutorial might be confusing; perhaps these issues can be resolved in future revisions. These types of comments are common during usability studies. As mentioned above, good design is critical to providing a successful and effective tutorial. If the designer does not ask for student feedback there is a risk that the tutorial will be designed to satisfy the style of the designer, rather than the intended audience. However, when revising tutorials, although it is important to revise according to the needs of the students, it is also important to consider that what might be effective for one student may not be effective for another. Gaining feedback and perspectives from a wide range of students can be beneficial; sometimes simple changes help motivate and enhance student learning. Directly soliciting user comments in the tutorial gives students an opportunity to voice opinions on and suggestions for issues critical to them. The tutorial should make feedback solicitation inviting and feedback should be forwarded to the design and development team. Indirect feedback from users is also very useful for review and revision. Collecting in-depth tutorial site statistics is a good way to help the librarian gain knowledge about the user and the tutorial. Further discussion of assessment and usability studies can be found in Chapters 9 and 10.

Personalization

Another concern of librarians and faculty in replacing face-to-face instruction with tutorials or other learning objects is the loss of the "personal touch" of classroom presentations. In the case of library instruction, for some students, the library visit and classroom interaction with librarians may allay some fears and hesitancy about the library. The key, then, is to incorporate some of the same personalization into the learning object. Some libraries do this by embedding a video clip of a tour of the library and an online map to help students "explore" the environment even before they get there. Another strategy that is used is to include a personal video introduction from the librarian that faculty can embed in their website and in their course management system so that students can recognize "their" librarian and feel as though they've already met them. An example of this is a video clip which featured the librarian for Library and Information Studies at the University of Illinois (*http://www.library.illinois.edu/lsx/learn/Library_Welcomes_You_To_GSLIS.html*; and see Figure 4.3).

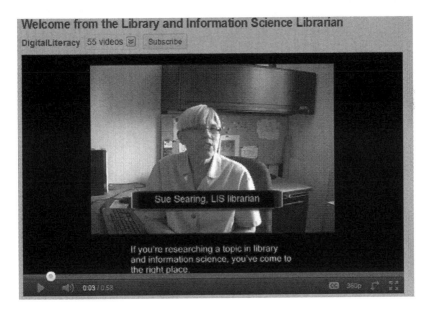

Figure 4.3   Video introduction from the University of Illinois

Source: http://www.youtube.com/watch?v=yv8I28duBjo. Welcome from the Library and Information Science Librarian

These introductions are especially important since there is no longer a dedicated library for those resources.

More personalization can be provided by adding a real-time reference service link, be it chat, IM (Ask a librarian), or video reference to the web page, learning object, or tutorial. This enables the student to immediately obtain seemingly undivided attention from librarians for question answering and guidance to more information. Some tutorials or programs can track learning progress, routes, and scores on exercises and tests within the tutorial. Students particularly like the option of doing a pre-test or answering a question and then being able to avoid certain parts of the tutorial. In the study carried out for this book, several students commented that they already knew some of the information that was being presented and would have preferred an option to skip selected parts. Other students, however, were looking for additional segments to explain certain concepts further.

Even if it is not possible to create individualized tutorials, it is possible to create multiple options for students from which they can choose. In addition to being able to work through a tutorial at a faster or slower pace, successful tutorials include fundamental design elements that provide for students' varying learning styles. One way to accomplish this is through a "branching" design that allows students to choose both the order in which they wish to proceed and the level of difficulty (Dewald, 1999a; Fourie, 2001). This enables students who require more practice to receive it, while those students who have grasped a particular concept can confirm the fact and move on. Some tutorials also provide for guided exploration in which a logical sequence is suggested (Cox and Housewright, 2001) or they use a decision-tree-based structure that mimics the research process (Kaplowitz and Contini, 1998). These options allow for multiple pathways through the tutorial, ensuring the flexibility that accommodates users at many levels. The ability to navigate their own pathways through a tutorial and to access it from a distance also increases the ability of students to receive instruction at their point and time of need. This both aids in the assimilation of knowledge (Dewald, 1999b) and allows the learning experience to be self-directed. Several scholars, including librarian scholars, have emphasized the importance of self-directed learning in teaching critical thinking skills to adult learners (Knowles, 1980, 1990; Gailbraith, 1991; Currie, 2000).

Relevance

Another effective strategy, along with personalization, is relevance. By providing relevance to students and including material and examples that they are familiar with, the students may be better able to build on their knowledge and connect the new information to it. Since people understand and remember more easily if they can connect new information with something familiar to them, building connections with what learners already know is a key strategy for effective learning. This can be done by using comparisons or analogies to other tools with which they may already be familiar, such as Google, iTunes, or another database.

Use of multimedia

Multimedia, screencasts, and other types of animated media put high demands on short-term memory, since a lot of information (text, graphics, audio, motion) needs to be processed simultaneously (Mayer, 2003; Betrancourt, 2005; Moreno and Mayer 2007). This means that it can be difficult for people to process information effectively from multimedia. Studies have shown that instruction using static graphics and visuals, such as labeled screenshots, can be as effective or more effective for learning since it places fewer demands on our short-term memory (Clark and Lyons, 2004), leading to better understanding and retention. Mestre (2010) found that students were much more able to complete a desired task after viewing a static web tutorial with screenshots than they were after viewing a screencast tutorial. In fact, only two of the 21 participants in the Mestre study were able to recreate the necessary steps after watching the screencast tutorial, while 20 of the 21 students could recreate the process after the static tutorial.

Since multimedia is inherently more difficult for learners to process, it should only be used as an instructional tool when it is helpful for learning. The first and most important question to ask when designing screencasts or streaming video tutorials is whether the multimedia is needed at all, or whether the instruction could be delivered just as effectively in some other way. Multimedia is potentially useful in many situations, such as showing processes in action or adding opportunities for student interaction with the material in a realistic setting (Betrancourt, 2005). If it isn't necessary, however, avoid delivering a multimedia tutorial or screencast. Or, in addition to creating a multimedia resource, create and make available for learners alternate formats so that they can choose their preferred method.

Point of need

During the Mestre (2010) study, students started their tutorial assessments at the tutorial page, rather than at the page that indexed all of the tutorials. Because the tutorial was open in another window students could refer back to it as they did the post-test. However, when students were asked if they could figure out where they would go to find the tutorial again, not one student could go from the library website to find the tutorial. Not many library websites have a link for "tutorials" on the first page. Students do not often go to a web page looking for a tutorial. It is most likely that they need help when they are in the middle of a task and will look around (on that page) for some help. Video tutorials should be linked at the point of need. It would be beneficial to link tutorials in several locations, such as in a "Get help" section, and with icons (such as a video icon) on the "Databases" page, within databases, and on any pages with subjects related to the tutorial. When students got "stuck" in the post-tests completed for this study, they were asked what they would do in a "real situation." Not one student in this study said that they would look for a tutorial; instead, they would go back to the front page to look or try again, or click on the "Ask a librarian" link. One of the concerns is whether the librarians, themselves, are familiar with the variety of tutorials that may have been developed by other librarians. Thus, having the tutorials linked from multiple places, and connected to pages on which difficulties are anticipated, is important.

Conclusion

The development of reusable learning objects can help expand the repository of material that educators and librarians can access, embed, or modify for their instructional use. These objects can play a supporting role in active learning strategies in instruction, as well as in supporting student-centered learning environments. If incorporated into web pages, course systems, and tutorials, students have the flexibility to choose the objects that will assist them at the level of instruction they need (novice, expert), as well as to choose the mode of learning (if objects include visual clips, hands-on activities, problem-solving techniques, exploration, etc.). Because learning objects can be small chunks (or packages) of information, educators can choose individual objects or link them together to create a larger object.

This chapter described some of the learning objects, mainly the types of tutorials, used in libraries. Some libraries have staff who are able to produce high-quality Flash objects, yet such objects can be difficult to maintain if the expertise leaves the library. Alternatively, most librarians are now proficient enough in creating web pages and can augment those pages by embedding or linking to learning objects. Examples were provided of some pages that link further demos, definitions, pop-up windows, and even hands-on opportunities. With the availability of Common Gateway Interface (CGI) scripts (especially borrowing from other librarians and educators) librarians can paste code into their web page source to enhance interactivity. Regardless of the type of technology used to create learning objects and tutorials, it is important to consider the design, pedagogy, and student input when creating them. These topics will be explored in the following chapters.

References

ALA/ACRL Instruction Session (2004–12). *PRIMO: Peer-Reviewed Instructional Materials Online*. Database available at: *http://www.ala.org/apps/primo/public/search.cfm*.

Allen, E.E. (1995) Active learning and teaching: improving post-secondary library instruction. *Reference Librarian*, 51/52: 89–103.

Allen, I.E. and Seaman, J. (2010) *Learning on Demand: Online Education in the United States, 2009*. Sloan Consortium: Babson Survey Research Group. Available at: *http://sloanconsortium.org/publications/survey/pdf/learningon demand.pdf*.

ANTS (2005–12) *ANTS: Animated Tutorial Sharing. Libraries working together to create open source library tutorials*. Available at: *http://ants.wetpaint.com*.

Betrancourt, M. (2005) The animation and interactivity principles in multimedia learning. In R.E. Mayer (ed.) *Cambridge Handbook of Multimedia Learning* (pp. 287–96). Cambridge: Cambridge University Press.

Blummer, B. (2007) Assessing patron learning from an online library tutorial. *Community & Junior College Libraries*, 14(2): 121–38. DOI:10.1300/02763 910802139397.

Chizmar, J.F. and Walbert, M.S. (1999) Web-based learning environments guided by principles of good teaching practice. *Journal of Economic Education*, 30(3): 248–64.

Clark, R.C. and Lyons, C. (2004) *Graphics for Learning: Proven Guidelines for Planning, Designing, and Evaluating Visuals in Training Materials*. San Francisco, CA: Pfeiffer/Wiley.

Cox, S. and Housewright, E. (2001) Teaching from the web: constructing a library learning environment where connections can be made. *Library Trends*, 50(1): 28–46.

Currie, C.L. (2000) Facilitating adult learning: the role of the academic librarian. *Reference Librarian*, 69/70: 219–231.

Dabbour, K.S. (1997) Applying active learning methods to the design of library instruction for a freshman seminar. *College and Research Libraries*, 58(4): 299–308.

Dewald, N.H. (1999a) Transporting good library instruction practices into the web environment: an analysis of online tutorials. *The Journal of Academic Librarianship*, 25(1): 26–31.

Dewald, N.H. (1999b) Web-based library instruction: what is good pedagogy? *Information Technology and Libraries*, 18(1): 26–31.

Dewald, N., Scholz-Crane, A., Booth, A. and Levine, C. (2000) Information literacy at a distance: instructional design issues. *Journal of Academic Librarianship*, 26(1): 33–44.

Fourie, I. (2001) The use of CAI for distance teaching in the formulation of search strategies. *Library Trends*, 50(1): 110–29.

Gailbraith, M.W. (1991) *Facilitating Adult Learning: A Transitional Process*. Malabar, FL: Robert E. Krieger.

Harkins, M.J. and Rodrigues, D.B. (2011) Where to start?: considerations for faculty and librarians in delivering information literacy instruction for graduate students. *Practical Academic Librarianship: The International Journal of the SLA Academic Division*, 1(1): 28–50.

Holmes, J. (2003) Online learning objects: helping faculty teach information literacy (and more). *Public Services Quarterly*, 1: 1–9.

Jackson, C. and Mogg, R. (2007) The information literacy resource bank: re-purposing the wheel. *Journal of Information Literacy*, 1: 49–53.

Kaplowitz, J. and Contini, J. (1998) Computer-assisted instruction: is it an option for bibliographic instruction in large undergraduate survey classes? *College & Research Libraries*, 59(1): 19–27.

Keown, R. (2007) Learning objects: what are they and why should we use them in distance education? *Distance Learning*, 4: 73–7.

Kerns, S.C. (2007) Technological tools for library user education. *Medical Reference Services Quarterly*, 26(3): 105–14. DOI:10.1300/J115v26n03_08.

Knowles, M. (1980) *The Modern Practice of Adult Education: From Pedagogy to Andragogy*. New York: Cambridge Books.

Knowles, M. (1990) *The Adult Learner: A Neglected Species* (4th edn.). Houston, TX: Gulf Publishing.

Kruse, K. and Keil, J. (2000) *Technology-Based Training*. San Francisco, CA: Jossey-Bass.

Ladner, B., Beagle, D., Steele, J.R. and Steele, L. (2004) Rethinking online instruction: from content transmission to cognitive immersion. *Reference and User Services Quarterly*, 43(4): 329–37.

Lippincott, J.K. (2005) Net generation students and libraries. *EDUCAUSE Review*, 40(2): 56–66.

Longmire, W. (2000) A primer on learning objects. Available at: *http://vcampus. uom.ac.mu/orizons/html/Res270704/LOR-RLO/Longmire-RLO-primer.doc* (retrieved July 2012).

Mardis, L. and Ury, C.J. (2008) Innovation – an LO library: reuse of learning objects. *Reference Services Review*, 36: 389–413.

Mayer, R.E. (2003) The promise of multimedia learning: using the same instructional design methods across different media. *Learning and Instruction*, 13(2): 125–39.

MERLOT (1997–2012) *MERLOT: Multimedia Educational Resource for Learning and Online Teaching*. Available at: *http://www.merlot.org*.

Mestre, L.S. (2010) Matching up learning styles with learning objects: what's effective? *Journal of Library Administration*, 50(7–8): 808–29.

Michel, S. (2001) What do they really think? Assessing student and faculty perspectives of a web-based tutorial to library research. *College & Research Libraries*, 62(4): 317–32.

Moreno, R. and Mayer, R. (2007) Interactive multimodal learning environments: special issue on interactive learning environments: contemporary issues and trends. *Educational Psychology Review*, 19(3): 309–26. DOI:10.1007/s10648-007-9047-2.

Oblinger, D. (2008) Growing up with Google: what it means to education. *Emerging Technologies for Learning*, 3: 11–29. Available at: *http://partners. becta.org.uk/index.php?section¼rh&rid¼13768*.

Petrides, L.A. (2002) Web-based technologies for distributed (or distance) learning: creating learning-centered educational experiences in the higher education classroom. *International Journal of Instructional Media*, 29(1): 69–77.

Scholz, A.M., Kerr, R.C. and Brown, S.K. (1996) PLUTO: interactive instruction on the web. *College and Research Libraries News*, 57(6): 346–9.

Silver, S.L. and Nickel, L.T. (2007) Are online tutorials effective? A comparison of online and classroom library instruction methods. *Research Strategies*, 20: 389–96.

Song, L., Singleton, E.S., Hill, J.R. and Myung, H.K. (2004) Improving online learning: student perceptions of useful and challenging characteristics. *Internet and Higher Education*, 7: 59–70.

Vonderwell, S. (2003) An examination of asynchronous communication experiences and perspectives of students in an online course: a case study. *Internet and Higher Education*, 6: 77–90.

Weston, C., Gandell, T., McAlpine, L. and Finkelstein, A. (1999) Designing instruction for the context of online learning. *Internet and Higher Education*, 2(1): 35–44.

Wiley, D.A. (2000) Connecting learning objects to instructional design theory: a definition, a metaphor, and a taxonomy. *Learning Technology*, 2830(435): 1–35. DOI:10.1002/stab.200710001.

Yang, S. (2009) Information literacy online tutorials: an introduction to rationale and technological tools in tutorial creation. *Electronic Library*, 27(4): 684–93.

Current practice: categories and features of library tutorials

Abstract: Generally, educators, and especially librarians, design tutorials that reflect the local practices of their library and institution. Their practice is varied in terms of the types of tutorials they create. The design and software used to create tutorials also varies, but typically falls into several categories: web-based tutorials using screenshots; narrated PowerPoints; tutorials used with screencasting software; podcasting; and videos. This chapter will provide an overview of these categories, including an overview of the advantages and disadvantages of each, as well as student perspectives on them. The chapter will also detail some of the tools and tutorials used by instructors to provide supplemental support to their students, as well as examples of types of tutorials developed, whether web based, podcasts, screencasts, or videos.

Key words: online learning, tutorials, online instruction, learning objects, screencasting, instructional design.

Introduction

As more library materials become available online, the need for flexible, portable, asynchronous library instruction increases. A review of the various learning objects used in online learning for supplemental training revealed that tutorials are one of the predominant objects used. The production and dissemination of remote instruction can occur in many ways. One of the easiest ways to add supplemental training is to use pre-packaged tutorials. Pre-packaged tutorials combine contents and computer programming into one package. Generally, they are created by the IT department of an academic institution and later made available to others as an open source program. They have to be downloaded and installed as a package. It takes some technical expertise to customize them for local needs and to install them on a server. There are some good pre-packaged tutorials available on the Internet as well as repositories, such as MERLOT (*http://www.merlot.org/merlot/index.htm*), ANTS (*http://ants. wetpaint.com/*), and PRIMO (*http://www.ala.org/apps/primo/public/ search.cfm*), where educators can either link to tutorials and learning objects or even download and modify them. The resources chapter in this book provides more information on tutorials and repositories.

A number of multimedia software applications can be used to incorporate visual, verbal, and kinesthetic learning into online instruction. The integration of video-based simulations allows learners to control the sequence and pace of the instructional material in a way that benefits them. Some individuals may learn better when they can control the pace of presentations (Mayer, 2006). Many multimedia software applications have been utilized in developing interactive multimedia tutorials as online supplements, and each offers a unique benefit to users.

Generally, educators, and especially librarians, design tutorials that reflect the local practices of their library and institution. Their practice is varied in terms of the types of tutorials they create. The design and software used to create tutorials also varies, but typically falls into several categories: web based tutorials using screenshots; narrated PowerPoints; tutorials used with screencasting software; podcasting; and videos. An overview of each design – and its advantages and disadvantages – follows.

Web-based tutorials with screenshots

Academic libraries have used online instruction for many years, but until recently there were limited options for non-programmers interested in creating learning objects for online instruction. Libraries have tended mainly to produce tutorials using a series of web pages, sometimes with interactive features. Web-based tutorials are the predominant tool used by faculty and librarians to provide step-by-step instructions or directions for accomplishing some task or process. These range from instructions on how to create an account in a web resource to developing content to put online. Web pages are generally quick to create and can be linked to or embedded into various other formats easily, making them very versatile. Because good screenshot capture programs are now available, images can be incorporated to show concepts visually. Students tend to be more at home with images than text, rely heavily on graphics to interpret web pages, and often learn best by doing (Lippincott, 2005; Oblinger, 2008). Adding screenshot images offers students a visual so they can quickly compare what they are doing to ensure the accuracy of their steps.

Methods used

Standard web authoring

Web authoring continues to become easier for faculty and librarians. It is rare that hand coding is used now thanks to the integration of WYSIWYG (What You See Is What You Get) editors used in course content management systems and web content management systems. The ability to create basic web pages with bullets, headers, and some font and color choices is available, as is the ability to insert images and screenshots. However, to perform more complex functions it is usually necessary to toggle to the html editor to do some hand coding. Figure 5.1 is a screenshot of a static web page using screenshots. The pins (red on

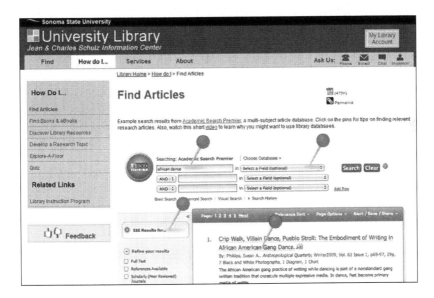

Figure 5.1   Static web page with screenshots from Sonoma State University

Source: http://library.sonoma.edu/howdoi/#collapse3. (It is requested that it be noted that the quiz was a legacy from an earlier web page, and that SSU is still developing an assessment for these tutorials; thus, please disregard the quiz.)

the actual page) provide additional information if clicked. The pages have a consistent table of contents on the left-hand side and an option to watch a video in the text.

Online user guides

Pathfinders, research guides, and handouts (both in print and online) are frequently used by librarians to help students understand the library and research process and to locate and use resources. LibGuides, by Springshare, is an online option with templates that incorporates the WYSIWYG editor, with the ability to customize the page to add in video clips, screenshots, widgets, RSS (Really Simple Syndication) feeds, etc. Some libraries moved from web pages to LibGuides to present not only their library but also material, resources, and "how-tos" more dynamically. Figure 5.2 is an example of a LibGuide from the University of Illinois that provides resources for locating and using learning objects. In addition to providing linked resources, video clips of particular resources are embedded.

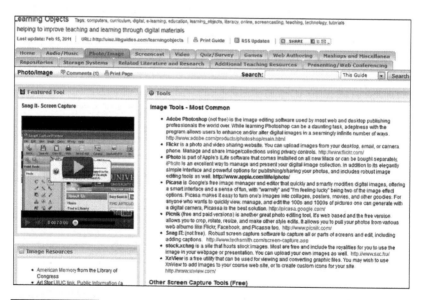

Figure 5.2   Learning object LibGuide from the University of Illinois

Source: http://uiuc.libguides.com/content.php?pid=64638&sid=477614

Some librarians use these online guides as tutorials. The screenshot in Figure 5.3 is of a LibGuide that details how to search the PubMed database. It includes tabs at the top to access the pages that explain how to accomplish a task, and links (on the right-hand side) to screencasting video clips of particular steps and features, so that the student can pick and choose what they want to watch.

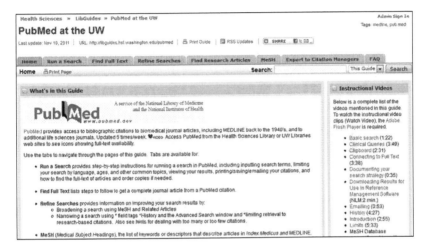

Figure 5.3 LibGuide used as a tutorial from the University of Washington Health Sciences Library

Source: http://libguides.hsl.washington.edu/pubmed

Another example of tutorials that are embedded in LibGuides is taken from the University of Wisconsin Milwaukee Libraries (see Figure 5.4). Each page of a module includes skills, theory, three videos, and a glossary.

Screenshot methods

Prior to the emergence of screencasting software, Suarez (2002) explored the use of the image editor Fireworks, the HTML editor Dreamweaver, and the Dreamweaver learning extension CourseBuilder, to create web interfaces for library instruction. Today, there are many methods that are used to capture screen images, both commercial and open source. Commercial products (such as Snagit) tend to offer robust options for manipulating the images, as well as for generating crisper images. The images in this book were created with a free version of Gadwin PrintScreen. See the resources chapter (Chapter 12) for more information.

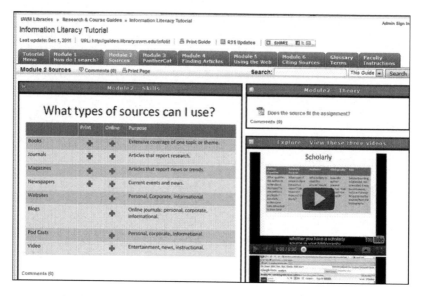

Figure 5.4 Screencast tutorials with screenshots from the University of Wisconsin Milwaukee

Source: http://guides.library.uwm.edu/content.php?pid=121422&sid=1220742. Information Literacy Tutorial by Board of Regents of the University of Wisconsin System is licensed under a Creative Commons Attribution-NonCommercial 3.0 Unported License. Based on work at guides.library.uwm.edu

HTML-only tutorials

HTML-only tutorials can be created by amateurs using tools like Microsoft FrontPage, Claris, or Hotdog, or website development tools like Adobe GoLive, MS Visual InterDev, or Dreamweaver. The list below offers some examples of information literacy tutorials created in HTML:

- UC Berkeley Library – Finding information on the Internet: a tutorial (*http://www.lib.berkeley.edu/TeachingLib/Guides/Internet/FindInfo.html*).

- Cornell University Library – Guide to library research at Cornell: seven steps to effective library research (*http://olinuris.library.cornell.edu/ref/research/tutorial.html*).

- University Library, California State, LA – Research survival guide (*http://www.calstatela.edu/library/tutorial/toc.html*). This includes a standard navigation and table of contents at the bottom, images, and pop-ups for more information.

- University System of Georgia – Online library learning center (*http://www.usg.edu/galileo/skills/*).

Tutorials created in HTML are generally easy to maintain and offer students the opportunity to quickly skim through and find the information they need (if there is a good navigation system). Screenshots and pop-up windows can be added to offer additional visuals and "how-tos." However, HTML alone, without extra coding, is not capable of animation and interactivity, features that are helpful in engaging students in e-learning. HTML-only tutorials are often reproductions of printed teaching materials. These tutorials may be well designed and some may have layouts that are stunningly beautiful, but, due to their lack of actions, such tutorials can be boring and tedious, especially if they are not best suited to the needs of the new digital savvy Generation M. According to Armstrong and Georgas (2006), a game-like nature and interactivity are the key factors in the success of an online tutorial. Therefore, HTML by itself is not ideal in creating tutorials. An HTML tutorial can be greatly enhanced by including some coding or scripts (CGI, Flash, or Java) to add interactivity.

HTML with CGI, Flash, and Java scripts

A CGI script is a small program written in a language such as Perl, Tcl, C, or Cpp C++, and it functions as the glue between HTML pages and other programs on the web server (Course Technology, 2008). Some CGI scripts perform the function of transferring data between HTML pages and a web application. Some are used to enhance and make HTML-coded pages interactive, dynamic, and lively. With CGI scripting, screencasting software can allow the introduction of a second activity without leaving the instruction module, such as incorporating drop-down menus, games, and puzzles.

Below is a list of some examples of online tutorials written in HTML with CGI scripts. The tutorials created by Fairfield University's Media Center were used as part of the game developed and scripted by Fairfield University's DiMenna-Nyselius Library.

- Fairfield University: library scene – Fairfield edition (*http://faculty. fairfield.edu/mediacenter/library/scene/index.html*) with animated characters in the same frame as live people. Includes interactive challenges (see Figures 5.5 to 5.8).

- Rider information literacy search skills tutorial (*http://abaris.rider. edu/tutorial1*).

Figure 5.5 Video of graphic characters with live people interacting – from Fairfield University

Figure 5.6 Option to play a game based on the video – from Fairfield University

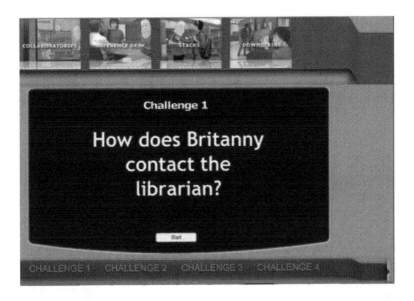

Figure 5.7 Challenges for a tutorial – from Fairfield University

Figure 5.8 Choices for questions – from Fairfield University

- University of North Carolina at Chapel Hill, library research tutorial (*http://www.lib.unc.edu/instruct/tutorial/*).

- American University library's information literacy tutorial (*www.library.american.edu/tutorial/index.html*).

- California State University Los Angeles: navigating the sea of information (Flash and Java) (*http://www.calstatela.edu/library/tutorial/new/*).

- Colorado State University library tutorials (using Flash) (*http://lib.colostate.edu/tutorials/*).

- Healey Library information literacy tutorial (*http://www.lib.umb.edu/newtutorial/*).

- Minneapolis Community & Technical College library tutorial (*http://www.minneapolis.edu/Library/tutorials/infolit/*).

Interactive examples

With various Flash elements, scripts, and Photoshop it is possible to create more interactivity, like drag and drop features, choices, and movement. The web-based tutorial shown in Figure 5.9 from the

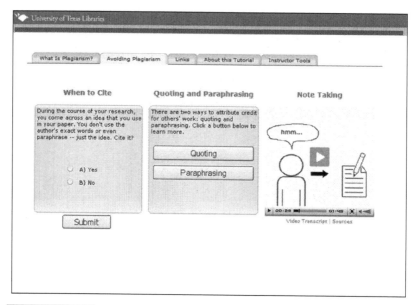

Figure 5.9   Plagiarism tutorial from the University of Texas Libraries

Source: http://www.lib.utexas.edu/services/instruction/learningmodules/plagiarism/avoid.html

University of Texas incorporates interactivity through scripting on the web page and also embeds a screencast or narrated PowerPoint tutorial on the right.

Other examples include:

- Goblin Threat, Lycoming College (Snowden online tutorials): uses Flash to create an interactive game tutorial (*http://www.lycoming. edu/library/instruction/plagiarismgame.html*). Other tutorials in this series include: *http://www.lycoming.edu/library/instruction/tutorials/ index.aspx*.
- Cite it Right, University of Texas at San Antonio: uses video, screencasting, Flash, Photoshop (*http://lib.utsa.edu/Instruction/ citeitright/index.html*).
- Te Punga – Voyager tutorial, the University of Auckland, New Zealand (*http://www.cad.auckland.ac.nz/index.php?p=tepunga*). This is designed to be like a graphic novel, with hands-on simulations.

Many websites provide free CGI scripts written by anonymous programmers for downloading. They are accompanied by live demos and simple instructions for amateurs. The scripts are generally organized into categories by function. One can find CGI scripts that perform almost any function on the web. For instance, some websites contain scripts of interactive quizzes that can be incorporated into the online tutorials for end-session exams. Other scripts include search engines, pop-up windows, flying banners, twinkling stars, etc. You don't have to know how to write CGI scripts in order to deploy them into tutorials. Most CGI scripts do not need server access or installation. A list of resources for librarians to get free CGI scripts on the Internet is included in Chapter 12 of this book.

Narrated PowerPoints

PowerPoint presentations are frequently used as tutorials. Faculty and librarians are familiar with many of the features available to create visually appealing products. Narration and text can also be added to make them accessible to various styles. However, in spite of their informative and well-written contents, these tutorials are not very interactive or game-like. Some designers create their tutorials in PowerPoint and then record them using screencasting software like Camtasia or Captivate in order to add in additional features and interactivity. The following are examples of converted PowerPoints:

- Introduction to the undergraduate library: the undergraduate library at the University of Illinois has an ongoing PowerPoint presentation that loops throughout the day to provide tips and highlights for the week. The presentation is viewed on large digital displays in the library. Figure 5.10 is an example of one of these presentations that was then converted through Camtasia (adding narration and captioning). It was then possible to stream it to the web.

- Cite a source: how and why you should do it (*http://www.library. illinois.edu/learn/videos/cite_source/cite_source.html*). This was originally created using PowerPoint and then uploaded into Camtasia. Call-outs, captioning, narration, and additional features were then added. Other features that could be added include hotspots that link out to other web pages, video clips, music, quizzes, and tables of content.

- Many more examples of academic PowerPoints, and presentations made with Prezi, are available from *http://www.slideshare.net/*.

Introduction to the UGL: November 3, 2009: http://www.youtube.com/watch?v=NzIl5ichELA

Figure 5.10 Narrated PowerPoint from the University of Illinois

Tutorials created with screencasting software

Many educators, and especially librarians, have invested in the production of Flash tutorials to add multimedia, improved graphics, and interactivity to their online instruction. Creating Flash applications has traditionally required specialist knowledge and skill, and has a steep learning curve for beginners. Tools are now available that make the creation of Flash multimedia much easier. In particular, screencast software programs have become readily available. These programs record actions on the computer screen and produce multimedia Flash videos. They are relatively cheap, or even free, fairly easy to learn, even for beginners, and require little technical knowledge, putting online multimedia creation within the reach of most educators. These tools are widely used for creating online tutorials and demos to use in online instruction.

Online screencasting provides demonstrations that are both aural and visual. Students say that they feel as though they are doing the searches along with the tutorial because they can see words being typed into boxes and can follow the process step by step. Williams (2010, p. 157) stresses that "screencasting gives a viable opportunity to effectively demonstrate the more specific steps in information literacy skills such as databases, search tools and how to make proper citations."

Tempelman-Kluit (2006) found that streaming media tutorials like screencasts have the potential to be more effective than static web tutorials. However, the use of the tool itself does not guarantee success. As with any instruction, planning, content development, sound pedagogy, assessment, and use of best practices is critical to success. These issues are discussed in more detail in Chapters 6, 7, and 8. There are several repositories that educators can access to get examples of screencasting tutorials, including the ANTS project, which is a repository of shared tutorials covering topics in information literacy and different subscription databases. MERLOT is another repository of tutorials available to educators. Some of the tutorials can be downloaded and modified. For additional information please refer to Chapter 12.

Methods used

Some tutorial software packages are designed for technological amateurs and are capable of true interactivity. Several of the more popular commercial screencasting software products are:

- Adobe Captivate at *http://www.adobe.com/products/captivate/*.
- Camtasia Studio at *http://www.techsmith.com/*.
- Demo Builder at *http://www.demo-builder.com/index.html*.
- SWiSH Max at *http://www.swishzone.com/*.
- ViewletBuilder at *http://www.qarbon.com/*.

These products offer free demo versions of the software, from the company websites. As an alternative, those on a budget may wish to try freeware screencasting software such as CamStudio, Jing or Wink (see Chapter 12 for more information). While limited in the number of features they possess, they do provide basic functionality, interaction, audio, and a simple intuitive interface. Documentation and links to the software can be found at the project websites.

Examples

The following list highlights some of the libraries that have used tutorial software to create online library instruction:

- Babson College (Camtasia) tutorials linked from LibGuides: *http://libguides.babson.edu/tutorials*.
- Bentley Library research guides (Captivate) tutorials linked from LibGuides: *http://libguides.bentley.edu/librarytutorials*.
- Collins Hill High School Media Center (Screencast-O-Matic): *http://www.chhsmediacenter.com/tutorials.html*.
- Houston Community College Libraries (Jing), hosted on Screencast. com: *http://library.hccs.edu/learn_how/tutorials.php*.
- Pennsylvania State University (ViewBuilder/Flash) minute modules: *http://www.libraries.psu.edu/content/dam/psul/up/lls/audiovideo/MM_Newspaper_Nov08.swf*.
- University of Illinois at Urbana-Champaign (Camtasia): *http://www.library.illinois.edu/learn/ondemand/*.
- University of Nebraska Medical Center (View Builder): *http://webmedia.unmc.edu/library/medline/medlinebasic_viewlet_swf.html*.
- University of Washington University Libraries (Captivate): *http://guides.lib.washington.edu/howdoi*.
- Washington State University (ViewletCam): *http://www.wsulibs.wsu.edu/electric/search/category_results.asp?loc=tutorials&cat=Instructional+Viewlets*.

Advantages of screencasting

Screencasting is ideal for remote instruction but can also be used for training, assessment, and usability testing. Faculty can provide students with additional resources that they can view repeatedly and at their leisure. By viewing instructional screencasts, students can learn how to successfully complete a multi-step research process, such as a series of tasks. With so many students and faculty now utilizing the library via the library website, screencasting provides a great opportunity to meet students and users at the point of need.

Screencast software removes the need for external recording equipment, instead internally capturing events on the computer monitor as they occur. Almost any use of a personal computer can be recorded, edited, and published as a Shockwave Flash (.swf) movie with accompanying audio narration using screencasting software.

Disadvantages of screencasting

Multimedia, screencasts, and other types of animated media put high demands on short-term memory since a lot of information (text, graphics, audio, motion) needs to be processed simultaneously (Betrancourt, 2005). This means that it can be difficult for people to process information effectively from multimedia. Studies have shown that instruction using static graphics and visuals, like labeled screenshots, can be as effective, or more effective, for learning since it places fewer demands on our short-term memory (Clark and Lyons, 2004), leading to better understanding and retention. Mestre (2010) found that 20 of the 21 students who participated in a usability study were better able to recreate a library search after receiving a tutorial from a static web page with screenshots than after viewing a screencasting tutorial.

Since multimedia is inherently more difficult for learners to process, it should only be used as an instructional tool when it is helpful for learning. The first and most important question to ask when designing screencasts or streaming video tutorials is whether the multimedia is needed at all, or whether the instruction could be delivered just as effectively some other way. Multimedia is potentially useful in many situations, such as showing processes in action or adding opportunities for student interaction with the material in a realistic setting (Betrancourt, 2005). If it isn't necessary, however, it is best to avoid doing a multimedia tutorial or screencast.

Flash (screencast) tutorials are best if the teaching is to be divided into short episodes, each one lasting no more than 1–2 minutes, especially if the episodes are passive and students are not required to participate. In order to view a tutorial in Flash format, you will need a Flash plug-in for your browser. The Flash plug-in can be downloaded for free from the Adobe Flash Player Download Center at *http://www.adobe.com/products/flashplayer/*. Most Internet users have already got Flash on their computers. Tutorials in Flash sometimes are referred to as videos because they look like videos. When viewed on the Internet, they load effortlessly into a browser like regular web pages.

Podcasting/vodcasting

Podcasting is a particular form of information and communications technology (ICT) and its use in higher education refers to the production of digital audio or video files that are made available to students via an intranet or Internet. A podcast is an audio file that can be downloaded and listened to either on an iPod or MP3 player, as well as on a computer, laptop, iPad, etc. The converted file size makes podcasts very appropriate for mobile devices. Faculty lectures are routinely podcasted, as are video podcasts (vidcasts, videocasts, vodcasts). Video podcasts are essentially videos or screencasts that have been converted to a podcast format (such as MP3 or MP4). They are very useful for demonstrating steps in a research process, such as how to use software or databases, etc. They can also be useful for revision and assessment, providing visual images that stimulate factual recall and highlight knowledge gaps (Copley, 2007; Evans, 2008; Lazzari, 2009; Hill and Nelson, 2011).

Because almost every student has some type of mobile device, it is important for educators to remember to convert their online objects to a format that can be easily accessed on these devices. Software programs (and screencast software such as Camtasia and Captivate) offer options for converting videos, screencasts, and other projects to the MP3 or MP4 format so that they can be viewed more easily on mobile devices. With the podcast format, students can listen to the material multiple times, and listen to or view the content anywhere (with headphones) while walking, on the bus, between classes, etc.

As with screencasting tutorials, teaching is best done in 1–2-minute segments that can be more easily downloaded to mobile devices. After creating a tutorial in a program such as Camtasia or Captivate, it is easy then to convert it to MP4 format for mobile devices. As with other tutorials or videos, transcripts will still need to be made available to students who request them (because of accessibility needs or just for easier access or review). Examples of podcasts include:

- Maag Library of Youngstown State University: *http://www.maag.ysu. edu/help/Tutorials/Mp3_Librarytour/*.

- University of Illinois at Urbana-Champaign: *http://www.library. illinois.edu/diglit/podcast/index.html*.

- WMV videos – Pace University Library: *http://www.pace.edu/page. cfm?doc_id¼29301*.

- Washington State University libraries at: *http://www.wsulibs.wsu. edu/electric/trainingmods/researchprocess-podcast.html*.

Figure 5.11 is an example of an enhanced podcast that was created using GarageBand.

Scholarly Versus Popular Articles- Enhanced Podcast

Facilitated by the UIUC Digital Learning Unit for the FSI (Faculty Summer Institute at UIUC)

Figure 5.11   Enhanced podcast from the University of Illinois

Source: http://www.library.illinois.edu/diglit/podcast/index.html

Advantages of podcasting

In addition to the increased flexibility of viewing or listening to the podcasts on mobile devices, laptops, or computers, students comment that podcasts add variety to the teaching and learning experience of a course. They can extend resources beyond lecture material and textbooks, and further facilitate understanding. The following are comments from students (in personal conversations with the author) regarding the use of podcasts as additional resources in classes.

"Some things are quite abstract ... just reading about them or hearing about them, but to see them was quite good. It puts them in the context of the environment."

"Seeing the environments the lecture material is based on – helped visually to understand the context. It is easy to feel detached from the environments we learn about on the course, especially having not been there. The podcasts helped the understanding of the environments."

"The podcasts added variety to the teaching and learning experience on the course, extending resources beyond lecture material and textbooks, and further facilitating understanding."

"... useful having another means of learning information ... different way rather than just looking at a book and reading back through my notes. I found it was effective doing it some other way."

"They supported the lecture notes and added more detail, so verified parts that I didn't fully understand."

"I found that being able to see 'real-life' images etc. and listen to processes being talked about was far more beneficial than still images and text from books."

Disadvantages of podcasting

If viewed on mobile devices, images may be very small, bandwidth may be slow, and the audio may not be synced with the video. They are also passive in nature.

Mobile applications

Even though it is possible to convert learning objects for mobile devices, there is an increasing resource pool of applications specifically made for mobile devices. Here are some that have been made for libraries:

- Infopoint: location-based tour of the main and undergraduate libraries at the University of Illinois (*http://sif.grainger.uiuc.edu/tour*). At various places in the library there is a cell-phone sign and a number to call to get the information from that stop.

- Library helper: allows the user to type in a call number of a book in the undergraduate library and a map is displayed with the shelf number of the book (*http://market.android.com/details?id=uiuc.library.helper*).

- Video mobile tour of the undergraduate library at the University of Illinois (*http://search.itunes.apple.com/WebObjects/MZContentLink. woa/wa/link?path=apps%2fugl4eva*).

Videos

Video clips provide excellent opportunities to illustrate or showcase something, as well as to incorporate "real" people. Some of the benefits of incorporating video into a website or course site include:

- The ability to capture a lecture, training, or instruction session for others to view later. Video extends the message to a wider audience.

- The ability to show a live demonstration or "how to do" something that requires movement.

- The ability to build rapport with an audience. A personal video clip or introduction can provide a personal connection.

- The ability to promote or market services. Videos can also provide an overview, introduction, or announcements for a course or service. The screenshot in Figure 5.12 includes two images of videos created to showcase services within the undergraduate library at the University of Illinois.

- The ability to highlight a particular area of expertise or strength. Figure 5.13 introduces the Gaming Center at the undergraduate library at the University of Illinois.

- The ability to capture and preserve exhibits or displays.

Videos Created at the Undergraduate Library

Videos Created at the Undergraduate Library

Here you will find various videos created to showcase the services, collections and facilities of the Undergraduate Library.

Undergraduate Library Information
Snapshot Day at the Undergraduate Library

Library Instruction UGL Intro Rap Video

Introduction to the UGL: November 3, 2009:
http://www.youtube.com/watch?v=NzII5ichELA

- YouTube: http://www.youtube.com/watch?v=rhY0gYKOT8
- MP4: http://www.library.illinois.edu/ugl/av/UGL_Rap.m4v
- For Mobile Devices: http://www.library.illinois.edu/ugl/av/UGL_rap_mobile.m4v

Figure 5.12 Videos from the undergraduate library, University of Illinois

Source: http://www.library.illinois.edu/ugl/about/videos.html

The Gaming Collection at the UGL: October 20, 2009
http://www.youtube.com/watch?v=ucRV6KHmCOk

Figure 5.13 Gaming collection video, University of Illinois

Videos can capture attention and can be more entertaining than simply reading or viewing screenshots. After viewing videos, students may be more likely to further explore the website for additional information. Capturing and editing videos is now a very simple process even when using a camera phone or a low-end camera and some basic editing software that comes as standard on PCs and Macs. Although low-end equipment can produce acceptable videos, higher-end equipment gives more professional results, which reflects well on the institution.

Methods used

- *Cameras.* Although high-performance cameras may be preferred for campus-wide video production, faculty, librarians, and students are having success with low-end cameras, such as the point and shoot cameras that also incorporate video use. If the goal is to create a simple video shot for uploading it may be best to try out a few options. Various departments, technology centers, media production facilities, or the library may have cameras that can be loaned out.

- *Video editing tools.* Macs and PCs usually come with a user-friendly video editing tool such as iMovie or Windows Movie Maker. These are free and allow for basic video editing. However, for more professional editing it may be worth investing in a product like Final Cut Pro or Adobe Premiere. These products are not free and take a bit of practice to master. However, expert guidance on how to use these products effectively is often available on college campuses. Examples of movies created with Windows Media can be found at: *http://libguides.pace.edu/videos.*

- *Streaming.* Many individuals take advantage of uploading videos and tutorials to free services like YouTube. Some quality can be lost in these uploads and there is a size limit. If an institution has a streaming server it then allows for various viewing modes and sizes. Another type of streaming is WMV (Windows Media Video), a format developed by Microsoft Windows for Internet streaming. WMV videos need a media player program in order to be viewed. There are many media player programs, including Windows Media Player, RealPlayer, PowerDVD, and more. WMV format is not a very common format in tutorial creation (but these are videos with audio and animation).

Montages

Another type of multimedia option is to create montages of pictures, video, narration, and music. Although these may not necessarily be used as tutorials, they are learning objects that can be used to showcase elements. They are geared toward the novice and essentially they require the user to upload photos and play with the features to create a mashup video (which is essentially a mixture or blend of songs, images, sounds, video clips, and text). Figures 5.14 and 5.15 are examples of montages created to highlight exhibits at the undergraduate library at the University of Illinois and are available at: *http://uiuc.libguides.com/exhibit*. They were created using One True Media. This software allows for the incorporation of a variety of features which elevate the pictures to a more dynamic presentation. There is a free version or a low-cost premium account that allows the user

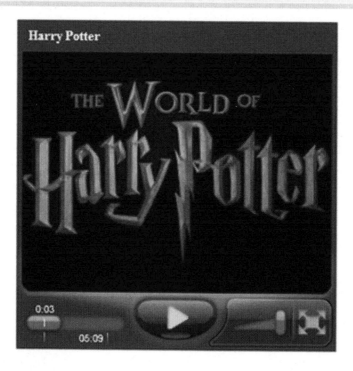

Figure 5.14   Harry Potter exhibit montage, University of Illinois

Figure 5.15 Black History Month exhibit, University of Illinois

to upload and combine media and provides a vast selection of templates, transitions, and music to augment the montage.

Figure 5.16 is a type of mashup video created at the University of Illinois for library instruction using a low-end camera, Audacity, and iMovie for editing. There are a number of ways to access the video: YouTube (*http://www.youtube.com/watch?v=rhY0gYKOT8*); MP4 (*http://www.library.illinois.edu/ugl/av/UGL_Rap.m4v*); and for mobile devices: *http://www.library.illinois.edu/ugl/av/UGL_rap_mobile.m4v*.

Methods used

There are a number of tools that can be used to create montages. Many offer free and prime accounts. There are, of course, limitations on the

Figure 5.16 UGL rap video for instruction, University of Illinois

space size and features that are allowed with a free account. However, the free accounts provide an opportunity to play with the product and to get a sense of the capabilities. Some examples are:

- Animoto: *http://animoto.com/intro/animoto/19b?gclid=COCfxdSa3 KwCFTABQAodhhGWxw.*
- Kizoa: *http://www.kizoa.com/.*
- One True Media: *http://www.onetruemedia.com/.*
- Photobucket: *http://photobucket.com/.*
- Smilebox: *http://www.smilebox.com/slideshows.html?partner=google &campaign=search_slideshow&gclid=CK_8mIWa3KwCFQrGK godNELOrg.*

Conclusion

In the best-case scenario, faculty and librarians can combine all the technologies covered in this chapter into one tutorial so that students can read, watch animation, and have fun at the same time. The best tutorial is always a combination of good content, logically connected links with clear verbal explanations, and animated, interactive demonstrations. HTML, CGI scripts, and tutorial software should all play a part in creating an effective tutorial. Effective tutorials should blend learning with fun. An example of a site that provides options for various types of technologies is the PubMed tutorial site for the U.S. National Library of Medicine (*http://www.nlm.nih.gov/bsd/disted/pubmedtutorial/index.html*). The basic structure of the tutorial is a web page with screenshots, but with options such as "Show me" which then highlight that portion of the step under discussion. There is also a quick-tour page that provides a list of all of the tutorials, including screencasts of the various elements discussed in the static web page, as well as webcasts and handouts (*http://www.nlm.nih.gov/bsd/disted/pubmed.html#qt*).

Most of the technologies covered in this chapter are accessible to the novice with a little practice. However, to produce an effective tutorial requires a lot of planning, good design, and pedagogical principles – these topics are discussed in more detail in Chapters 6 to 8.

References

Armstrong, A. and Georgas, H. (2006) Using interactive technology to teach information literacy concepts to undergraduate students. *Reference Services Review*, 34(4): 491–7.

Betrancourt, M. (2005) The animation and interactivity principles in multimedia learning. In R.E Mayer (ed.) *Cambridge Handbook of Multimedia Learning* (pp. 287–96). Cambridge: Cambridge University Press.

Clark, R.C. and Lyons, C. (2004) *Graphics for Learning: Proven Guidelines for Planning, Designing and Evaluating Visuals in Training Materials*. San Francisco, CA: Pfeiffer/Wiley.

Copley, J. (2007) Audio and video podcasts of lectures for campus-based students: production and evaluation of student use. *Innovations in Education and Teaching International*, 44: 387–99.

Course Technology (2008) *IT Glossary: Programming*. Available at: *http://www.course.com/Careers/glossary/programming.cfm#cgi*.

Evans, C. (2008) The effectiveness of m-learning in the form of podcast revision lectures in higher education. *Computers & Education*, 50: 491–8.

Hill, J.L. and Nelson, A. (2011) New technology, new pedagogy? Employing video podcasts in learning and teaching about exotic ecosystems. *Environmental Education Research*, 17(3): 393–408.

Lazzari, M. (2009) Creative use of podcasting in higher education and its effect on competitive agency. *Computers & Education*, 52: 27–34.

Lippincott, J.K. (2005) Net generation students and libraries. *EDUCAUSE Review*, 40(2): 56–66.

Mayer, R.E. (2003) The promise of multimedia learning: using the same instructional design methods across different media. *Learning and Instruction*, 13(2): 125–39.

Mayer, R.E. (2006) Ten research-based principles of multimedia learning. In H.F. O'Neil and R.S. Perez (eds.) *Web-based Learning: Theory, Research, and Practice* (pp. 371–90). Mahwah, NJ: Lawrence Erlbaum Associates.

Mestre, L.S. (2010) Matching up learning styles with learning objects: what's effective? *Journal of Library Administration*, 50(7–8): 808–29.

Oblinger, D. (2008) Growing up with Google: what it means to education. *Emerging Technologies for Learning*, 3: 11–29. Available at: *http://partners. becta.org.uk/ index.php?section ¼ rh&rid ¼ 13768*.

Suarez, D. (2002) Designing the web interface for library instruction tutorials using Dreamweaver, Fireworks, and Coursebuilder. *Information Technology & Libraries*, 21(3): 129.

Tempelman-Kluit, N. (2006) Multimedia learning theories and online instruction. *College & Research Libraries*, 67(4): 364–9.

Williams, S. (2010) New tools for online information literacy instruction. *The Reference Librarian*, 51(2): 148–62. DOI:10.1080/02763870903579802.

Effective design of learning objects

Abstract: Good design is critical to the success of a learning object. It is important to know and follow standards and conventions. Throughout the design process, from the brainstorming of ideas to the launching of the product, there needs to be iterative assessment to determine if the users are approaching, using, and understanding the object as intended. This chapter discusses strategies and guidelines for designing learning objects to accommodate various learning styles. The strategies are informed by research related to effective pedagogical strategies in the online medium. Also included are examples of ways to design objects for both novices and experts while considering consistency in language, organization, navigation, and actions, and ways to avoid cognitive overload.

Key words: learning objects, instructional design, learning styles, pedagogy, learner engagement, learner-centered design.

Introduction

Learning objects can be effective supplements to, and possibly replacements for, some traditional face-to-face instruction. When designed well with appropriate multimedia they can assist students or faculty at any time of day or night, at their own pace, to focus on learning a specific skill or developing an overall knowledge of a particular aspect. Whether the learning object is a component of an online course, a web page, or functions as a tutorial, students need an interface that has a high degree of usability, facilitates human performance, and makes good use of students' time while minimizing errors (Rosson and Carroll, 2002). In e-learning, the focus should be on learner-centered design. E-learning applications are targeted at learner groups that are heterogeneous, with different computing backgrounds, learning styles, levels of experience, and motivation; hence, the application should be able to address differences in the usability needs of learners. The application interface should be well structured so that it provides easy and efficient navigational methods as well as customization of content to suit learners' requirements. Students should not need to spend substantial amounts of time figuring out how to use the application.

The interface should be intuitive, so that even novice users can begin meaningful interaction immediately. Students should be able to see their options, understand how to achieve their goals, and understand how to accomplish desired tasks. This chapter will discuss strategies and guidelines for the effective design of learning objects that may accommodate various learning styles. The strategies are informed by research related to effective pedagogical strategies in the online medium. A more in-depth discussion of pedagogical considerations can be found in Chapter 7. Chapter 8 discusses designing for interactivity and Chapter 9 includes considerations for creating content for learning objects.

Involving the stakeholders

Before creating any tutorials, discussions with stakeholders and the target audience should occur. These could be within areas of the library, as well as with faculty in subject area departments to discuss what library resources and services should be covered in the tutorials. Other relevant tutorials, learning objects, and websites should be explored to examine appropriate content, technologies, design, activities, and pedagogies to include. Faculty and student collaboration for both curriculum-integrated and individual tutorials created by librarians helps to ensure that the appropriate content, exercises, and technologies are incorporated. Faculty involvement and support is not only critical in the designing of tutorials, but also later on during the promotion and assessment of the tutorials. It can also help encourage faculty to integrate (or recommend) these tutorials in their courses.

In asynchronous online instruction, there is less opportunity to interact with students, and it is not possible to make immediate corrections when things are not going well. Therefore, it is important to learn about the students in advance and use this knowledge to plan the design of tutorials. The first phase in most instructional design models involves analyzing the learners. This could be part of a usability study (Chapters 10 and 11 detail options in assessment and usability studies). However, some of the preparation for "knowing your students" can be accomplished by talking with faculty in the subject area of the tutorial and in doing a pilot testing of several students. Pilot testing is a good way to analyze the target audience for characteristics and pre-existing knowledge.

Some basic questions that Carliner (2002) suggested for analyzing an audience are:

- Who are the learners I am targeting?
- What are their demographic characteristics?
- What related skills and knowledge do they already have, and what gaps are there?
- How familiar are they with technology, and what access to technology do they have?
- What is their motivation?
- How interested are they in the content?
- What influences affect them and their learning?

When analyzing the audience, it is valuable to track what skills they already possess so that the tutorials can build on this knowledge. After compiling and analyzing these data, the tutorial should be created to match the characteristics, skills, and needs of the students. More suggestions will be provided in this chapter for designing both for beginners and those with advanced skills.

Designing for quality instruction

Just as with web pages, it is vital to create learning objects with the same sound design elements, including following established conventions and best practices. Below are some suggestions that this author has found useful from various usability studies, as well as some suggestions from Steve Krug's book, *Don't Make Me Think: A Common Sense Approach To Web Usability* (2005). Krug's basic motto for designing web pages (which can apply to any learning object) is to make them obvious and self-explanatory so that users do not need to think. Quality instruction is concerned with content and teaching strategies. A theoretical model applicable to the development of learning objects is that of Dick et al. (2000). This model reflects a systematic approach to instructional design based on nine components:

- identification of instructional goal(s);
- instructional analysis;

- analysis of learners and context;
- articulation of performance objectives;
- development of assessment instruments;
- development of instructional strategies;
- development and selection of instructional materials;
- design and implementation of formative evaluation of instruction; and
- revision of instruction based on evaluation results.

The above model provides step-by-step guidance for creating instructional modules and is easily adaptable to the design and development of learning objects. A modified version of the above, designed by Mestre, also includes additional components such as design, navigation, and pedagogy, could be used from planning through evaluation and redesign. This is provided in the form of a checklist as shown in Table 6.1 below. The designer would fill in the columns as appropriate to the particular tutorial or module:

Table 6.1   Example of a chart for evaluating design

Category	Examples	Audience and date	Notes
Goals	a. b. c. d.		
Analysis of learners	a. b. c. d.		
Design	a. b. c. d.		
Navigation	a. table of contents b. consistent icons c. consistent bar at bottom d.		
Content	a. b. c. d.		

Concise instructions	a. checked for jargon b. checked for clarity c. checked for comprehension d.		
Effective online pedagogy	a. b. c. d.		
Active learning exercises	a. b. c. d.		
Multimedia that enhances	a. use of ____ b. use of ____ c. use of ____ d. use of ____		
Animated interactive demonstrations	a. demonstration ____ b. demonstration ____ c. demonstration ____ d. demonstration ____		
Assessment	a. student focus group b. faculty focus group c. pilot test d. usability studies		
Revisions done			
Other			

Developing goals and the design plan

Clear goals and objectives

The design of a learning object should focus not only on the technological aspects, but also on the goals, objectives, and expectations for the learners. Setting instructional goals as a starting point will help to streamline and focus the content of the learning object and decide what is essential to include and what is not, and will help prevent content-related memory overload. In successful instruction, the content, practice activities, and assessments are all aligned with the instructional goals

(Carliner, 2002). Consider what the learner should be able to do, know, or understand as a result of completing the tutorial or application. It is also important to state explicitly those goals, objectives, or learning outcomes so that the learners know what they will accomplish by spending their time completing the tutorial. Students want to know if it will be worthwhile for them to invest their time in the process. Providing a rationale also helps to make learner expectations realistic.

Somoza-Fernández and Abadal (2009) found that only 37 percent of the 80 tutorials they evaluated indicated educational objectives. They, and others (Dewald, 1999; Cox and Housewright, 2001), emphasize that goals and/or specific learning objectives should be clearly stated so that learners will have a better understanding of what is expected. This is especially important in order to accommodate subject-dependent learners who are using computer aided instruction (Kahtz and Kling, 1999). There are many models and processes that can be used to assist with the creation of goals and objectives, particularly as they link into a larger course infrastructure (Dick et al., 1999).

Good planning: storyboarding

Storyboarding can help to organize and outline the text, images, illustrations, interactive exercises, navigation, and evaluations that you will use in the sequence you visualize. By creating a storyboard – a series of sketches, flowcharts, or a mock-up – others can provide input and suggestions before too much time is invested. Storyboards can be sketched out on paper or on the computer with any program that allows text and images/drawings to be inserted. Sequences and components can be shifted around to help with clarity and purpose. Others can review this prototype to help refine or expand the layout and concepts.

For a screencasting learning object or for a video several storyboards will be needed to depict various sequences. Each one might include details such as:

- The main concept of the sequence.
  - Break up pages into clearly defined areas; this allows students to decide which areas to focus on and which to ignore.
  - Decide where the main content or image will be (in the middle with call-outs on the right side?).
  - Minimize noise: are there contrasts between sections; is there too much text or business? Determine what information is critical for

each page and what information can be put on a second level, perhaps with an indicator to "click here for more information or examples."

- The location of the various types of navigation, index, etc.
  - Be consistent with rules and carry them from one page to the next. Create a theme so that users become familiar with what to expect (table of contents always on the left?).
  - Decide where the navigation elements, choices, or questions will be placed (at the top, bottom, side?) and be consistent.
- Colors to be used on each page.
- Font type, size, and color to be used for various headings, subheadings, and text. Students tend to notice text that is large and bold.
  - Create a clear visual hierarchy. The more important something is the more prominent it should be.
  - Place larger fonts, and bolder, different colors in the middle near the top.
  - Organize similar items logically (or nested underneath the header in a section of the page). This also helps with cognitive load as segmenting/chunking items together helps pre-process the page so the mind doesn't have to organize it.
- The placement of text on the page (being consistent throughout) and if it appears initially or at what point in the sequence.
- Graphics placement and sizes, and if they appear initially or at what point in the sequence.
- Placement of call-out buttons and if they appear initially or at what point in the sequence.
- Interactive exercises and if they appear initially or at what point in the sequence.
- Indications of links that are clickable: even though designers might think that colored links are clickable, it is not always obvious. If users need to work out whether a link is a hyperlink it adds to cognitive workload, which distracts attention. Usability tests can help designers to see if students are clicking on intended links or not. If not, more obvious elements could be included, like a term that says "Enter" or "Click here" or even an arrow pointing to a term "Search." In a study carried out by Mestre (2010), certain students had difficulty when working through an interactive tutorial because they did not know

when they should click on a figure to make something happen nor how to get to the next page. This confusion diverted them from the message that was to be conveyed on that screen.

- Other multimedia inclusions (such as video, audio, animation) and details of where they appear in the sequence.

- Narration that accompanies the sequence (check with students regarding the pace, voice, and voice quality).

It is important not to clutter the page. Students are good at scanning. Most students glance at a new page, scan some text, and usually click on the first link that catches their attention or appears to be what they are looking for. Much of the rest of the information is redundant. In the Mestre (ibid.) study it was noted that when students went through the static web tutorial they quickly scanned the page, looking at the headers and images, and then attempted to do the exercises. When asked why they only scanned the page they said, "We're usually in a hurry," "We only want to get to the thing that will help us get the answer." Students learn to focus on "trigger words." Students from the Bowles-Terry et al. (2010) study also said that students view library tutorials in a utilitarian light and want to get the necessary information and move forward with the information-seeking process.

Chart 6.1 is an example of a piece of storyboarding created by Mestre, to help plan out the ERIC (Education Resources Information Center) database tutorial. These elements would also be included in the script as cues for what to do during the screencasting.

Chart 6.1 **Storyboard planning example**

Storyboard for ERIC database tutorial

Project: <u>Part 1: Searching ERIC</u>   Tutorial: <u>1 of 3 (in the ERIC series)</u>

Date: <u>April 23 2011</u>

Links from: *http://www.library.illinois.edu/learn/ondemand/*

Links to: <u>ERIC tutorial 2; Ask a librarian</u> (*http://www.library. illinois.edu/askus*)

Navigation:

a. Include a table of contents (create chapter markings) so they can jump to each section
b. Navigation bar across the bottom.

Functionality/interactivity

a. Includes a three-question quiz at the end
b. Includes a hotspot to link out to "Ask a librarian" (at end of tutorial)
c. Includes a hotspot to link to ERIC Tutorial 2 (after quiz).

Background: white background

Title clip: use the ERIC with puzzle

Color schemes: main titles in Green color #___; subtitles in Blue color #___; call-out color Blue color #_____

Font: text 36 point Verdana

Audio: use Audacity, volume at:_____ Do narration after capturing

Video: no video clips added in for this segment; use Camtasia to record screens according to script

Fade: 1-second fades

Stills: add in still of "Ask a librarian" at end, with a link to the "Ask a librarian" live widget

Highlighting features: highlight the following (in Yellow):

- Online research resources
- Article indexes and abstracts
- Cambridge Scientific Abstracts

Box features (in Light Blue, width 4): occur with:

- Search tools
- Thesaurus
- Browse thesaurus (box the search area)

Zoom in features: occur when showing:

- Thesaurus option
- Combine search option

(continued)

Chart 6.1   Storyboard planning example *(continued)*

Arrows: use Red, width 4

Call-out bubbles: use "filled rounded rectangle" and "rectangle call-out" and 28 point Veranda font. Occur at:

- .27 on timeline for 5 seconds (I'm searching community colleges OR two-year colleges OR associate degrees), Blue font, shaded border

- 1.36 on timeline for 5 seconds (see the RefWorks tutorial for more information)

Figure 6.1 shows an example provided from *Usability Net* for a hand-drawn storyboard. *Usability Net* is a project funded by the European Union to promote usability and user-centered design (*http://www. usabilitynet.org/home.htm*). This site provides clickable components of a methods table to dig deeper into examples. Storyboards work well when

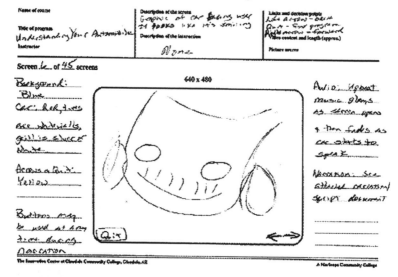

Figure 6.1   Storyboard example from *Usability Net*

Source: http://www.mcli.dist.maricopa.edu/authoring/studio/guidebook/images/ storyboard3.gif

designing web pages to show how each page connects with the previous page and showing consistency in design elements. For screencasting, these elements should be decided upfront with notes placed in the script to alert the person recording the tutorial when to include features such as zooms, highlights, boxes, etc.

Figure 6.2 is an example of a storyboard for branching that would take place depending upon the response to a question.

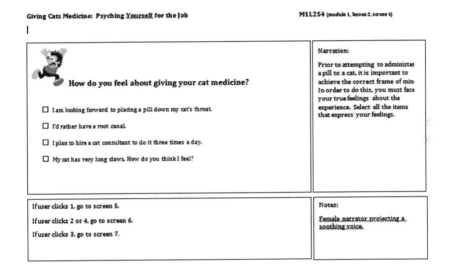

Figure 6.2 Storyboard with branching from *The eLearning Coach*

Source: *http://theelearningcoach.com/downloadsVisual+Storyboard+1*

The list below gives details of certain products that facilitate the storyboarding process; they include step-by-step templates for integrating features and design. There are many other freeware and commercial products available as well.

- Atomic Learning's Free Video StoryBoard Pro (freeware): *http://www. atomiclearning.com/storyboardpro*.

- Storyboard Depot from The eLearning Coach: *http://theelearningcoach. com/resources/storyboard-depot/*.

- StoryBoard Quick (PowerProduction Software to purchase) for film or video production: *http://www.creationengine.com/html/p.lasso?p=10591*. A demo is available here: *http://www.powerproduction.com/quick_mov. html*.

Appendix 4 at the end of this book also includes a PDF document of the Camtasia guidelines used to create the screencasting tutorials at the University of Illinois. These guidelines include suggestions for the settings to be used for all aspects of the tutorial, including fonts, colors, call-outs, and production settings, so that tutorials can be consistently created across library units.

The script

A script can also be used as a storyboard if placeholders are inserted for the various images, exercises, graphics, etc. The script can be evaluated early on by others, including librarians, faculty, and the targeted audience, for clarity and conciseness. It can also be uploaded later in order to provide captioning for the tutorial. We will now look at some of the important aspects to consider when writing the script.

Language and terminology

The language used plays a vital role in whether or not students are able to advance through a learning object and understand the content within. Checking for clarity of terminology, clear instructions, and conciseness of text are key. This can be done once a script has been completed by having a few members of the target audience critique it. Much of the information below was summarized from student comments during the Mestre (2010) usability study.

- *Clarity of terminology.* Care should be taken to ensure that the language is free from jargon that may impede progress for the learner. During testing, users should indicate any term that was unclear to them so that it can be replaced or better defined. The term needs to reflect clearly what the user will see next. Terminology is crucial in terms of making users feel confident that the next page will get them closer to their goal. Will the link take the user to the database search or will it take them to information about the database? Online glossaries and help sections can be included with hyperlinks on terms that need to be defined. Another strategy that can be used is to include a pop-up (or call-out bubble) at points where clarification may be needed. To help with understanding, introduce basic concepts at the beginning of a tutorial, using the same words and images used in the rest of the tutorial (Mayer, 2006). Depending on the tutorial being reviewed, in the Mestre (2010) study for this book students commented on "corny" or "dumbed down" language, or tended to point out excessive use of library jargon or when they needed more explanations of a term. This was observed especially in the static web page and screencast ERIC tutorials which used the term "descriptor" only briefly, so that when the students got to the actual site they didn't completely understand why they needed to change their search to "descriptor." The tutorial was then revised to include additional information to help students understand what was required.

- *Clear instructions.* Instructions and actions to be taken should be self-explanatory and clear.

  - Avoid a lot of introductory text since it will probably be ignored. Large amounts of text on a screen are difficult to read, so text should be succinct, broken up, and arranged for maximum clarity.

  - Keep instructions as brief as possible. Detailed explanations and instructions may confuse or frustrate people who already know something about the subject. For more advanced learners it is important to keep explanations and instructions simple and to a minimum (Kalyuga, 2005). As an example, instead of a long introduction such as: "Imagine you are a junior in college and you need to do a 10-page paper for your class on the topic of ... Now, choose a character from the choices below who will represent you as you go through this ...;" a brief statement might suffice, such as: "Choose a character." In the Mestre (2010) study, 21 students were asked to complete a tutorial that used the first introduction above. Not one person took the time to read the introductory explanation. Instead, they just clicked on the first figure that appealed to them. When asked about their method, the responses included: "Who really wants to read all that stuff?" and "I figured it was like a game so we were supposed to choose a character."

  - Studies also recommend eliminating as much redundancy as possible for more advanced learners; that is, for them, it is usually better to use either graphics only or words only to explain something, rather than both together as for novice learners (Nguyen and Clark, 2005).

- *Conciseness of text.* Students who participated in the Mestre (2010) usability study noticed when pages were too text based. A lot of text makes it hard for students to concentrate and absorb information. Suggestions included introducing different font sizes, more chunking, and less reliance on descriptive paragraphs and long passages of text. Most of the students also wanted the text to be included within the image so that they did not have to glance at two places.

- Omit unnecessary words. By being concise, you make less "noise" on the page and the important information is more prominent. Less text makes the pages shorter and easier to scan without scrolling. In the Mestre study (ibid.) students noted that they focused on words (trigger words) and phrases that would direct them to the main points or to what they needed to do to accomplish a task. They really did not want to know how things work; they just wanted to get enough information to get to the relevant content. As an example, the students just wanted to know which database to use and where to type in terms to get to the results. Having used a database once that gets them information they tend to stick to that database and use it over and over again, even if it isn't the most appropriate resource. Two students insisted on using the JSTOR database because they had used it before and had found a lot of full-text articles, even though it does not provide the most recent publications. It is important to explain *why* a certain concept, strategy, or process is important to students so that they will understand the value of trying something different. In the case of choosing a particular database, it would be instructive to explain *why* they need to check the scope of databases. Although it is important to be concise and only include relevant information, it is also useful to point out critical information in a way that will attract their attention. In this instance a side icon or shape could be included with a message such as seen in Figure 6.3.

Direct attention to important points

Within the script, indicate points at which visual and verbal cues will be inserted during the recording. These cues can be arrows, a new item that pops in, something that is highlighted, or a zoom effect. Verbal cues are effective after a pause in the narration to allow students to process the information. After a pause, give the next direction, e.g., "Choose a character to represent you ... ." Graphics and call-out bubbles can be used selectively to clarify points further, maintaining the student's interest as well.

Figure 6.3 Hot tip example

Directing students' attention to the most important points also reduces extraneous memory load and improves learning. To direct attention, show processes and tasks in context. For example, show a database search screen so that the students know where the search box is located, rather than showing them only the search box out of context. If students do not have context, they may not learn enough to apply what they are learning (Clark and Lyons, 2010). The most important part of the larger screen needs to be highlighted with visual or verbal cues so that students know where to direct their attention. Visual cues might include using an arrow, circle, or grayed-out background to show the important area on the screen, or inserting a title screen between sections to indicate a change in topic. Verbal cues include putting captions on the screen, repeating or summarizing points, using tone and emphasis to indicate important points, or saying explicitly that a particular point is important.

The screenshot of a tutorial in Figure 6.4 illustrates the use of arrows and the fading of non-important content in order to illustrate the citation.

Another technique that can be effective is an occasional pop-up bubble with some important point. These could be consistently labeled "Tip," or "Did you know?" or some other phrase that may indicate to the learner that they should pay special attention. In the Mestre (2010)

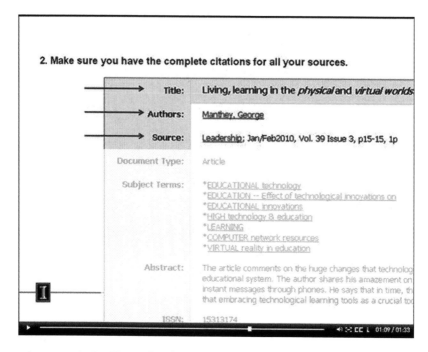

Figure 6.4 Example of directing attention to important elements, University of Illinois

Source: Avoiding Plagiarism tutorial from the University of Illinois *http://www.library. illinois.edu/diglit/tutorials/plagiarism/Plagiarism.html*

study, students unanimously commented during the usability studies that they did focus all of their attention on a pop-up when it appeared in the tutorial. In the design of the tutorial, then, it would be important to introduce a pop-up only when no other new information or narration is occurring on the screen, to reduce overload and to allow the learner to focus on the content of the pop-up.

Length of modules

The length of learning objects and tutorials will vary, depending upon purpose. Preparing a script ahead of time will help to assess where it can be broken into smaller modules. A good strategy, regardless of purpose, is to break up larger tutorials into shorter modules. This allows students to choose the modules that are relevant to their needs. Based on observations during their study, Oehrli et al. (2011) suggest that screencasts should be two minutes or less in length. They conclude that there is a difference between showing students two videos back to back, of approximately two minutes each, and showing one four-minute long video. The script for each video is then conceived differently, with each video addressing a single concept. The viewer can more easily digest shorter screencasts that focus on one concept, which reduces a student's cognitive load for learning. Bowles-Terry et al. (2010) conducted usability testing on video tutorials that were created at the University of Illinois. Although all of the tutorials lasted less than three minutes, they found that many students felt they were too long. They wanted to skip through various parts of the tutorial to find what might be relevant to them. The authors suggest breaking up tutorials into one-minute (or shorter) segments and providing a table of contents so that students can easily scan for content that is relevant. Usability studies with students will help determine how long a segment should be.

Screen pacing and narration

There is no hard and fast rule for how fast or slow one should narrate a video, tutorial, podcast, PowerPoint, Prezi, or other learning object. Some students in the study thought the images went by too quickly and others thought they were not on screen for long enough. Usability testing may help to find a good middle ground. If the reason a student wants the screen to stay up longer is so they can better understand a certain concept, then it may be useful to include a call-out or to explain further. The narration should be clear, crisp, varied, and unhurried.

Navigation and consistency across tutorials

This next section includes suggestions for: internal navigation; providing consistency; designing for different ability levels; and basic design (which includes suggestions for the overall design of a learning object).

Internal navigation

As mentioned above, the design and navigation of tutorials should allow students to see their options easily, understand how to achieve their goals, and know how to accomplish desired tasks. Somoza-Fernández and Abadal (2009) evaluated 180 tutorials to determine how well they met the basic recommendations of usability (browsing and design) of the interface. Only 28 of the tutorials (16 percent) contained a guide on how to browse the tutorial. There are numerous ways to provide consistent internal navigation such as providing a linked table of contents, a site index, a consistent navigation and progress bar, toggle and navigation buttons, and links to live help. These will be described further below.

Linked table of contents

A variety of learner ability levels and learner-chosen objectives can be accommodated when the student is allowed some degree of choice in which learning path to follow. For example, a linked table of contents in a separate frame, or in a set place on the screen (left side or bottom) not only provides a continual overview of the material for the learner, but also allows the user to select the elements and their order. If users choose to leave before completion, the linked contents page allows them to resume at another time without unnecessary repetition. Beginners learn more effectively when provided with structure and guidance, such as when using an outline of the content at the beginning (Nguyen and Clark, 2005; Clark and Lyons, 2010). The outline helps students to create a conceptual framework for their learning, and lets them know what to expect so they can find information better as they progress.

Site index

Another valuable link is to a site index, which also allows users to obtain an overview of the content and to pick and choose the content they want to access. A comprehensive site index allows the student to use the tutorial as a reference for a specific point of need. Providing multiple pathways through the information exploits asynchronous possibilities and allows for a student-controlled and student-directed learning experience (Reece, 2004). Somoza-Fernández and Abadal (2009) found that only 32 of the 180 tutorials evaluated (18 percent) had a site map, which, in most cases, was textual. A list of tutorial topics upfront, with or without indexes (in alphabetical order), could help the viewer decide if the tutorial might offer what s/he needs.

Students in the Mestre (2010) study consistently wanted to see all the components of the tutorial before proceeding. When using the static web page with screenshots, students would scroll down to the bottom of the page to see the various sections before going back to the top to begin the tutorial. If there was a table of contents they would glance at that first. Comments related to this process included:

> First my attention was attracted by the images so I just want to browse through all the images to get a whole picture – see what we are doing here. Then I want to go back and check the text with the images to make sure I get everything right.

> I'd just probably skim through it a little bit and figure out if there are parts that I need that will actually help me with the topic.

Links

Students in the Mestre study (ibid.) consistently commented that it would be best if all key tutorial content could be built directly into page text rather than being introduced through internal linking ("Why can't the information just be included here so I can see it all at once?"). Students also thought that lists of links should be avoided. In this way users would not miss important content ("Too many links;" "I'm not sure what I will get if I click on this;" "Why should I need to click on this?").

Students also thought that there should be less extensive use of external links in particular, since they did not know whether visiting these external links was mandatory or not ("This list of links might be useful if there was a short summary of what I'll get if I click on each one;" "Is the link optional or is it mandatory for me to go to?"). It helps to make it clear to the user whether links are used as examples or whether the external sites themselves do not have to be read in depth.

Progress through the tutorial

Many students in the usability studies mentioned that it would be useful to have some cues for progression through each tutorial module. This could be achieved by using a menu visible at all times showing the table of contents for the module and highlighting the section the user had reached. The length of the learning object should be indicated before a student clicks on the link to begin. Additionally, a progress bar throughout the tutorial lets students know where they are. Somoza-Fernández and Abadal (2009) found that this was an important element that favors autonomous learning. They found that only 37 of the 180 tutorials (21 percent) indicated the time in which the tutorial should be studied (either generally or in sections). Only 11 tutorials (6 percent) included a status bar to help users find their way in the tutorial. Some designers provide chapter markings that are highlighted as students progress through the sections of the tutorials. This can be done easily even in web-based tutorials. If modules and personalization are available, a student may stop at the end of any module and continue next time s/he returns. Learning progress, routes, and evaluation can also be recorded for the student's and tutorial designer's reference. A pre-test of the student's comprehension can also be executed should s/he prefer a customized tutorial.

Moving backwards and forwards

In some of the studies involving tutorial assessment students commented that where interactive image maps or links were used it was sometimes unclear whether to click on a link or use the next button to proceed. Here is an example from the Mestre (2010) study of a student who was trying to figure out what to do and which actions were possible on the interactive tutorial:

> "Oh, at first I thought this was one of those things that you moved." [She starts to summarize what the text says.] "Oh ... you're supposed to say if it is plagiarism?" [Still trying to figure out what she needs to do. She talks through her answer to the question.] "Oh, I'm supposed to click next. I thought once I clicked that button I would be next, like to the next step."

Opening new windows

There should be consistency in how a pop-up window opens. In the tutorials that were surveyed, in some cases when the user clicked on a link a pop-up window appeared. In other cases, a link to an external site would open up in the same window rather than a new window. This caused an inconsistency in navigation and was confusing for users.

Toggle buttons

Videos or narrated tutorials must be captioned in order to be accessible to the hearing impaired, which is an important consideration; indeed to not do so is a violation of Section 508 of the Rehabilitation Act if one is creating tutorials for a university or government organization in the U.S. Therefore, a good design feature would be to include buttons that allow the user to toggle the narration and the captioning on and off. This allows the user to decide whether they want to hear the narration or simply read it (captioning). Visual learners or auditory learners can choose to focus on one channel, which can eliminate overloading the working memory. A script (usually provided in PDF format) should also be included on the web page for individuals to use as desired.

Use of multimedia

It is important to consider whether the use of multimedia is beneficial or not. In the case of the interactive tutorial used for the Mestre (2010) study, one tutorial began with a snoring student. This actually confused the students, who did not know if they were supposed to wait for the next thing to happen or if they should click on something. In that same tutorial, students had some difficulty understanding what the picture had to do with the rest of the information. Another part of the tutorial asked students to choose a character. Although this may help students to invest more in the tutorial, many students did not like how much time it took to read about the characters and most just picked one randomly. One student commented: "If I'm involved that's OK, but if it's just clicking a character that's not helping me."

The comment below is from a female student who eventually chose a male figure because it was the first one:

> Ahhh, I have to go through each person? Oh, OK. This is too much. I have to go through each person to see what they're similar, to what maybe my background is and school, and maybe I can relate to what I have to research ... But, the characters aren't very interactive and it's like I have to look over each one. And if I click on it, it leads to a next page. And I just clicked on Dillon and I think that for each little character it'll ... Yeah, that's really distracting. I don't understand why ... It's like another step ... clicking on each person.

This next student had difficulty because he did not see any instructions as to how to proceed through the tutorial with the various types of multimedia. He made assumptions and finally resorted to trial and error:

Actually, I thought it was going to be interactive the first time I clicked it, cuz I clicked it and nothing happened [the snoring person]. I guess it was kind of a disappointment [chuckle]. So I clicked on it again [after he chose a character] and nothing happened so I clicked on "Next." Now they have two red squares on the bottom where it gives you two choices. I'm assuming you can click on them and I guess you can.

Another student spent 20 seconds staring at the "Choose a character" page before saying: "Am I supposed to click on it? I'm not sure. And where should I go next?"

Suggestions for graphic and multimedia incorporation are further discussed in Chapter 8. In general, though, students like simple, large, clear graphics and images. They do not want call-out bubbles blocking any text. They suggest that the narration should cease when a call-out bubble appears so that the student can focus on the new information. Students do not want cluttered screens.

Link to live help

Dewald (1999) advocated that designers of tutorials should provide a link to a real-time reference service for immediate assistance from, and interaction with, a librarian. Somoza-Fernández and Abadal (2009) found that 31 tutorials of the 180 they evaluated (17.2 percent) offered no possibility of contacting the librarians. The tutorials more often than not included an email option (133 tutorials or 73.9 percent) to allow users to contact a librarian. Another option was to include a form, which occurred in eight (4.4 percent) of the tutorials. Su and Kuo (2010) evaluated 60 tutorials and found that 20 tutorials (33 percent), built by 14 libraries (47 percent of the libraries), provided links to allow students to seek the help of librarians through chat or instant messaging reference services; among which, six libraries (20 percent) served round the clock.

The minimum amount of information that should be provided in any learning object is the inclusion of a contact person and the provision of an email or web link. However, students do appreciate being able to click on a widget or link to get live help while in the midst of the tutorial. These widgets may be to a live chat for "Ask a librarian" services. Faculty can also insert widgets on their web pages or in their course management systems that direct students to Meebo, Google Chat, or other live chat options, so that students can consult with others to have their questions answered, or to get further clarification about an assignment or process. Good practice when using live chat options is to indicate the hours during which the live chat will be monitored.

Consistency within the tutorial

To provide an intuitive interface, standardized language and color schemes should be adopted to minimize confusion among end-users, especially in sections that prompt user interaction. To facilitate branding and product recognition, a common introduction and ending should be developed and used in all learning objects/tutorials. Some points to remember include:

- Make all navigation consistent in the tutorial so that users will know what to expect for the whole tutorial. This should always be in the same area (top, bottom, or left-hand side).

- Use the same font and colors for similar choices, using one color and font for major headings, another color and font for second-level headings, etc.

- Provide an option (table of contents) that is consistently available in the same place so users can jump back and forth. Choose where to position it (persistent navigation) and keep it there
  - Home page
  - Sections/chapters
  - Quizzes.

- Name each page (if creating a web-based tutorial) so users know where they are (this needs to match what was clicked on previously).

- Include breadcrumbs – or a navigation bar – for progress within the tutorial (perhaps by section).

- Indicate when each part is beginning and ending.

- End with a summary to help reinforce the concepts in the student's memory.

Figure 6.5 shows a screenshot of a web-based tutorial from the California State Library that provides guided, yet user-definable, paths, consistent navigation at the top and bottom, and icons to click for additional information (if desired). Each chapter maintains consistent fonts, colors, and navigations.

Figure 6.5 Opening web page for a tutorial from California State Library

Source: http://www.calstatela.edu/library/tutorial/toc.htm

The tutorial in Figure 6.5 is a non-Flash format for users who need most of the information presented in text form: *http://www.calstatela.edu/library/tutorial/toc.htm*. A Flash-based version is available at: *http://www.calstatela.edu/library/tutorial/new/*. Providing alternate formats is important for accommodating users with various types of disabilities and learning needs and to adhere to the ADA (Americans with Disabilities Act).

Consistent internal navigational aids such as buttons, icons, and text links allow users to review material, move between and within sections as needed, and receive additional explanations if desired. The screenshot in Figure 6.6 indicates where the user is (by tutorial name, chapter, and page number). It provides consistent "Previous" and "Next" buttons at the bottom, options for exiting, and a table of contents. This type of navigation can also facilitate a user's ability to choose paths through information. This flexibility can encourage novices while not boring advanced learners. This allows the learner to customize the instruction, thus maintaining the learner's interest, an intrinsic motivational factor. This tutorial keeps text at a minimum, but also includes options for users who want more information. Throughout the tutorial, the life-saver icon

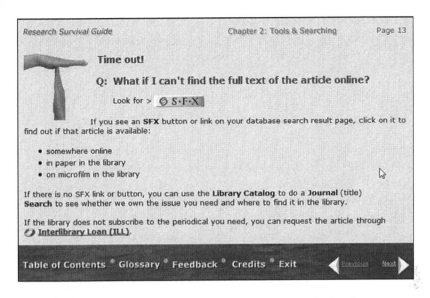

Figure 6.6 Internal examples of consistency in design from California State Library

Source: http://www.calstatela.edu/library/tutorial/toc.htm

is used to indicate that more information is available in a pop-up if the term is clicked. See the example in Figure 6.6 of the clickable term "Interlibrary Loan (ILL)" at the bottom on the left. Figure 6.7 shows

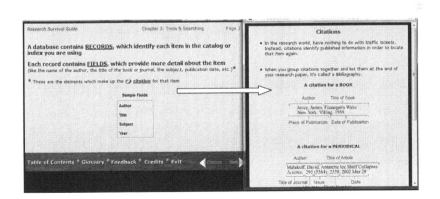

Figure 6.7 Example of consistent navigation and pop-ups for additional information from California State Library

Source: California State Library Research Survival Guide http://www.calstatela.edu/library/tutorial/toc.htm

another example of a life-saver with the clickable term "citation." When the term is clicked, another window pops up with additional information. These options allow the designer to keep the page concise, while providing additional information when a student requests it.

Consistency across tutorials in a series

Once the goals and objectives for instructional learning objects have been decided (regardless of the type of learning object: web page or screencast tutorial, podcast, video, PowerPoint, animation, etc.) think about elements that can be used throughout all associated objects. Such consistency across objects will help students feel more familiar with them. Betty (2008) described efforts to standardize several tutorials in order to make them intuitive to users. She concluded that using consistent features, such as standardized language and color schemes, may help minimize confusion among end-users, especially in sections that prompted user interaction. The tutorials also used common introductions and endings and short 10–15-second video clip introductions featuring members of the library faculty. Close captioning of audio and slide notes were also used in order to increase accessibility. Some common elements that could be used include:

- title of the series;
- the same introductory screen;
- a common logo, image, or graphic;
- the same color scheme and fonts;
- the same navigation elements and positioning of the index or table of contents; and
- the same closing screen.

Figures 6.8 and 6.9 show screenshots of the beginning and end of a tutorial that is part of a series from the University of Illinois. Each tutorial begins with the same ERIC title screen (with the title of the Part being viewed) and ends with the same Ask a Librarian screen to help direct students to additional help, if needed.

Figure 6.8 Example of a consistent introductory screen, University of Illinois

Figure 6.9 Example of a consistent closing screen, University of Illinois

Designing for different ability levels

Earlier in the chapter, the importance of assessing the audience prior to the creation of a tutorial to determine skills and previous knowledge was discussed. It is not possible to create one tutorial that will address all of the variations in ability and knowledge levels. However, the design of tutorials can include multiple options for students so that they can determine the material that is relevant to them. Some of the ways to accommodate different ability levels will now be examined.

Evaluate the prior knowledge of students

Somoza-Fernández and Abadal (2009) in their study of 180 tutorials found that most tutorials did not include systems for evaluating the prior knowledge of the students. Only 10 (6 percent) contained a test or pre-test to determine students' prior knowledge and skills. The option usually chosen was a pre-test in the form of a questionnaire. Because students come with different knowledge, experience, and learning styles, it is important to include some form of evaluation of students' prior knowledge in order to indicate the part of the tutorial that they should follow. The design of tutorials can include pre-tests embedded in them or can include periodic questions throughout to test knowledge. Once the results are shown, students should be given a choice of paths to take (e.g., to skip a section if they correctly answered the question or to go through a module for review).

Accommodate different levels

One way to accommodate different levels is to provide basic and advanced levels of the same subject so students can choose the appropriate content and paths based on their needs. Somoza-Fernández and Abadal (ibid.) found that only three percent of their sample provided this option. One size does not fit all when it comes to multimedia tutorials. Multimedia learning strategies that work well for learners with low existing knowledge may actually hinder learning for those with a higher level of pre-existing knowledge (Kalyuga, 2005).

Since it is difficult to create a single tutorial that works for all learners, ideally different versions of a tutorial would be available for different kinds of learners. If that is not possible, consider having pre-test questions that could analyze students' knowledge and recommend which sections they should take, or consider having links to "remedial" sections that beginning learners can follow but advanced learners could choose to bypass. In general, an index or table of contents with links to the topics in the tutorial can be a useful aid to beginners or advanced learners, as students can jump to their desired sections. Allowing control over pacing, the ability to skip some content, and control over features such as audio or text display is particularly important in screencasts for learners with different levels of knowledge.

Novices and beginners

Beginners learn more effectively when provided with structure and guidance, fairly detailed explanations, and opportunities to practice (Nguyen and Clark, 2005). For novice students, provide an outline of the content at the beginning of the tutorial or screencast (Clark and Lyons, 2010). An outline helps students create a conceptual framework for their learning, and lets them know what to expect so that they can absorb information better as they progress.

For beginners, provide:

- a clear structure, including an outline at the beginning
- detailed explanations
- practice opportunities
- an explanation of basic concepts
- worked examples
- multiple varied examples
- scaffolding (including explanations and links to underlying concepts).

Advanced learners

More advanced students learn better when they are provided with less structure and more control, such as the ability to skip sections, or to choose their own non-linear path through the tutorial content (Clark and Mayer, 2003; Nguyen and Clark, 2005). Therefore, for more knowledgeable learners provide less structure within the tutorial. For example, provide questions and problems for them to solve on their own at the end of the tutorial instead of worked examples throughout. To allow flexibility in navigating through the content, possibilities include providing a table of contents that allows students to choose which sections they wish to view, or breaking up a longer tutorial into small, focused sections and creating a series instead.

For learners with some background knowledge, provide:

- minimal explanations
- less detail
- less redundancy (e.g., words or graphics, not both)
- less structure, more control over content (e.g., branching, ability to skip sections)
- problems to solve.

Figure 6.10 shows an example of a tutorial from the University of Arizona that includes brief text information and then a video to show how to map concepts. This allows both the novice and the expert to access the information they need. The navigation on the left allows the user to pick and choose segments of interest.

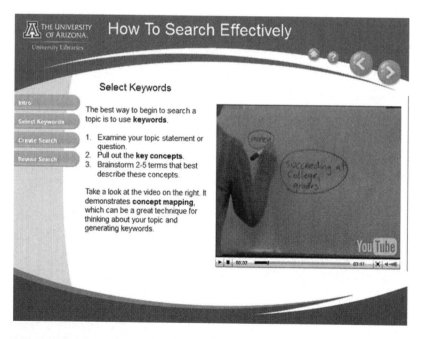

Figure 6.10 Options for the novice and the expert from the University of Arizona

Source: http://www.library.arizona.edu/tutorials/how_to_search_effectively/

Feedback

It is important to provide feedback as students go through the tutorial. Feedback can reinforce positive behavior and also correct students when they go wrong.

- *Type of feedback.* Effective feedback includes not only an indication of whether the response was correct or not, but also indicates the correct choice and the reasons why it is correct.
- *Checkpoints* (formative assessments). These can be interspersed to aid, as well as to measure, student comprehension and to assist in measuring the effectiveness of the tool and instruction.
- *Early success.* This is part of the feedback process. Assuming that the tutorial is interactive, an early question, task, or activity that results in success can be motivating to the student and can instill confidence and enthusiasm for continuing.

Feedback is an important aspect of interactivity and student engagement (Reece, 2007). Because many students are used to web- and e-learning situations where they get immediate feedback from their actions, they often expect feedback (Carliner, 2002). In addition, when they are new to a topic, learners need feedback to let them know how they are doing. Unless practice activities are accompanied by feedback, students may not know if they understand the topic properly, and may not be able to apply what they have learned effectively (Halpern and Hakel, 2003). This kind of feedback helps to build learners' confidence and increase their motivation (Stolovitch and Keeps, 2002).

Feedback can be built into screencasts or streaming media tutorials in a number of ways. For example, learners can see the consequences of their actions if search results are displayed after they type in a simulated search. Scenarios can allow learners to choose what to do, then show them what happens when they choose each action. Alternatively, quiz questions can be included to check understanding and display feedback immediately. Ideally, feedback should include explanations that show students why an answer or choice is right or wrong so that they can improve their understanding of the concepts involved.

Figure 6.11 is an example of feedback that goes beyond simply indicating if a response is correct or incorrect; it provides additional information that could further explain the process. The feedback to an incorrect response would also include the information provided in the feedback to a correct response.

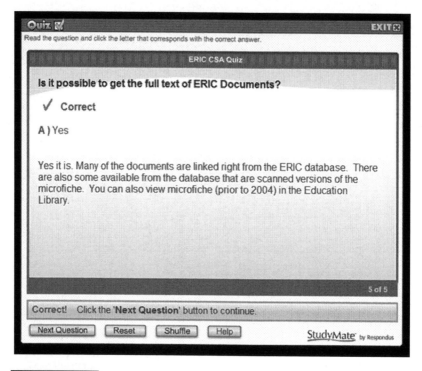

Figure 6.11 Feedback for an ERIC quiz from the University of Illinois

Source: http://www.library.illinois.edu/diglit/tutorial/eric/ericcsaquiz.htm

Other technical considerations

In screen capturing software there may be difficulty in rendering images and actions. Websites using large amounts of JavaScript to execute navigation and user interaction can be difficult to capture completely. For example, capturing drop-down or roll-over menus can be problematic, with the recorded images often not synchronized with the associated mouse event in the captured recording. However, nearly all screencasting software allows for the editing of slides, content, and audio after recording, and many of the quirks encountered during recording can be corrected during post-production.

Other considerations for design include screen resolution and usability. A general principle in web design is to provide content that is rendered in full at any screen resolution. Thus, it is more practical to record screencasts at a lower screen resolution (i.e., 800 × 600) than to try to compress images and text after capture. Doing so will also help limit the overall file size of the published project and increase its usability. Screencasts recorded at lower resolutions are also more likely to remain legible if the project is converted and uploaded to a video hosting site such as YouTube or blip.tv.

Plug-ins

Screencasting software requires plug-ins like Adobe Flash Player in order to render the end product. It is important to think about the resolution being used in production. Even if computers typically have the latest version of Adobe Flash Player, higher resolution results in larger SWF (ShockWave Flash) file size. This could still be problematic for people with a dial-up connection.

Accessibility

Making learning objects accessible includes providing alternate formats for accessing the object. With screencasting software it is possible to upload the script and synchronize it with the tutorial to provide captioning. While many of the commercial software products offer accessibility features like closed captioning and slide notes rendered by adaptive software, it is still a good idea to provide the tutorial content in alternate formats. Supplying a text-based version of the tutorial is a sound idea, and illustrates the library's awareness of the diverse learning styles and needs of patrons. At the University of Illinois, some faculty specifically asked for a web-based tutorial with text and screenshots because their distance learners could access that version more easily. Faculty have asked that PDFs of scripts are made available on the websites as well. It is important to consider how screen readers process the information, so checking with the institution's office for accessibility will be helpful.

Converting to multiple formats

Once the initial script and screencast is complete, consider providing alternate formats for better accessibility:

- Convert files to MP3 or MP4 formats. Most screencasting software provides options to convert to MP3, MP4 (very useful for uploading to ITunes U and mobile devices), a QuickTime format, as well as the Flash version.

- Upload to a streaming server or, if one is not available, create a channel in places like YouTube (which will compress and stream content).

- Provide a PDF of the script that is linked on the web page.

- Create a web page with screenshots of the tutorial for students who prefer scanning quickly to find information rather than trawling through the complete tutorial.

- Include links on the web page to other multimedia explanations, such as "Click here to see a demonstration," which will then open up a brief video tutorial on the subject – another good reason to create very short clips on concepts.

Assessment of the learning object

Another fundamental element of the tutorial is the implementation of some form of evaluation of a learning object. Somoza-Fernández and Abadal (2009), in their evaluation of 180 tutorials, looked at whether users were able to give their opinion on the usefulness of the tutorial, the learning process, and the formal aspects of the tutorial. Only 21 percent of the tutorials provided this mechanism. The instrument used most was the survey, followed by an online form and email. Directly soliciting user comments gives students an opportunity to voice opinions and suggestions on issues critical to them. Chapter 10 provides strategies for assessing learning objects.

Iterative testing is important in any learning object, from the initial concept to the script, from the first draft to the end product. Although early testing can be done with a few individuals, it is important to continue the testing throughout the development of the learning object and then periodically afterwards. Testing not only assists in understanding if the aims of the learning object are being addressed, but also whether the design, navigation, content, language, options, and interactivity are clear, self-explanatory, and facilitate progress. Chapter 11 provides strategies for the usability testing of learning objects.

Conclusion

Good design is critical to the success of a learning object. It is important to know and follow standards and conventions. Throughout the design process, from the brainstorming of ideas to the launching of the product, there needs to be iterative assessment to determine if the users are approaching, using, and understanding the object as intended. One of the key elements of good design is to be consistent (in language, organization, navigation, and actions). The design should be clean, with minimal "noise," and multimedia used only when it is appropriate, in order to help reduce the cognitive load on users. Cognitive load can also be reduced by making actions and options visible so that users immediately recognize what is possible.

Rather than creating a text-heavy object, alternate ways of presenting the information should be investigated, such as by using visuals, video clips, and examples, thus allowing the users to choose the mode that is best suited to their needs. Regardless of format, there should be help and documentation available (and easy to locate). Rather than including all of the information as text, additional tips or strategies can be made available through extra links or pop-ups for those who are interested in learning more. By creating flexibility within the object it can be used effectively by novices and experts, who can choose which options or features to explore. In addition, multiple formats of a learning object (such as web based, or produced as a screencast, PDF, MP3, MP4, etc.) will provide users with options to participate in the style that best fits their learning preferences.

The next two chapters further explore the importance of design. Chapter 7 provides suggestions for incorporating sound pedagogy in learning objects and Chapter 8 discusses options for incorporating interactivity.

References

Betty, P. (2008) Creation, management, and assessment of library screencasts: the Regis libraries animated tutorials project. *Journal of Library Administration*, 48(3–4): 295–315.

Bowles-Terry, M., Hensley, M.K. and Hinchliffe, L.J. (2010) Best practices for online video tutorials in academic libraries: a study of student preferences and understanding. *Communications in Information Literacy*, 4(1): 17–28.

Carliner, S. (2002) *Designing E-learning*. Alexandria, VA: ASTD Press.

Clark, R.C. and Lyons, C. (2010) *Graphics for Learning: Proven Guidelines for Planning, Designing, and Evaluating Visuals in Training Materials*. Hobeken, NJ: John Wiley & Sons.

Clark, R.C. and Mayer, R.E. (2003) *E-Learning and the Science of Instruction*. New York: Pfeiffer.

Cox, S. and Housewright, E. (2001) Teaching from the web: constructing a library learning environment where connections can be made. *Library Trends*, 50(1): 28–46.

Dewald, N.H. (1999) Transporting good library instruction practices into the web environment: an analysis of online tutorials. *Journal of Academic Librarianship*, 25(1): 26–31.

Dick, W., Carey, L. and Carey, J.O. (2000) *The Systematic Design of Instruction* (5th edn.). New York: HarperCollins.

Halpern, D F. and Hakel, M.D. (2003) Applying the science of learning to the university and beyond: teaching for long-term retention and transfer. *Change*, 35(4): 36–41.

Kahtz, A.W. and Kling, G.J. (1999) Field-dependent and field-independent conceptualisations of various instructional methods with an emphasis on CAI: a qualitative analysis. *Educational Psychology*, 19(4): 413–27.

Kalyuga, S. (2005) Prior knowledge principle in multimedia learning. In R.E. Mayer (ed.) *The Cambridge Handbook of Multimedia Learning* (pp. 325–37). Cambridge: Cambridge University Press.

Krug, S. (2005) *Don't Make Me Think: A Common Sense Approach To Web Usability*. Boston, MA: New Riders Press.

Mayer, R.E. (2006) Ten research-based principles of multimedia learning. In H.F. O'Neil and R.S. Perez (eds.) *Web-based Learning: Theory, Research, and Practice* (pp. 371–90). Mahwah, NJ: Lawrence Erlbaum Associates.

Mestre, L.S. (2010) Matching up learning styles with learning objects: what's effective? *Journal of Library Administration*, 50(7–8): 808–29.

Nguyen, F. and Clark, R.C. (2005) Efficiency in e-learning: proven instructional methods for faster, better online learning. *Learning Solutions*. Available at: *www.clarktraining.com/articles.php*.

Oehrli, J.A., Piacentine, J., Peters, A. and Nanamaker, B. (2011) Do screencasts really work? Assessing student learning through instructional screencasts. *ACRL National Conference A Declaration of Interdependence* (pp. 127–44). Philadelphia, March 30–April 2. Available at: *https://www.ala.org/ala/mgrps/divs/acrl/events/national/2011/papers/do_screencasts_work.pdf*.

Reece, G. (2004) American University library's information literacy tutorial. Available at: *http://www.library.american.edu/tutorial/index.html* (retrieved July 26, 2012).

Reece, G.J. (2007) Critical thinking and cognitive transfer: implications for the development of online information literacy tutorials. *Research Strategies*, 20(4): 482–93.

Rosson, M.B. and Carroll, J.M. (2002) *Usability Engineering: Scenario-based Development of Human-Computer Interaction*. San Francisco, CA: Morgan Kaufmann Publishers.

Somoza-Fernández, M. and Abadal, E. (2009) Analysis of web-based tutorials created by academic libraries. *Journal of Academic Librarianship*, 35(2): 126–31.

Stolovitch, H.D. and Keeps, E.J. (2002) *Telling Ain't Training*. Alexandria, VA: ASTD Press.

Su, S.-F. and Kuo, J. (2010) Design and development of web-based information literacy tutorials. *The Journal of Academic Librarianship*, 36(4): 320–8. DOI:10.1016/j.acalib.2010.05.006.

Pedagogical considerations for tutorials

Abstract: Creating meaningful content and incorporating sound online pedagogy is essential for effective multimedia instruction. Designing tutorials and web pages in a pedagogically sound way can provide opportunities for student exploration, creativity, and application of new understanding of difficult concepts to their own assignments. Effective pedagogy needs to include various approaches to learner motivation, module organization, and level of interactivity. Traditional instructional pedagogy has guided much of the simple skills instruction on the web, but librarians are also developing new ways of teaching in this medium. This chapter outlines some pedagogical considerations for generating meaningful content for both the novice and the advanced learner, and presents examples of instructional cognitive theories and how elements of the theories can be integrated into tutorials and learning objects.

Key words: pedagogy, online learning, tutorials, instructional design, multimedia instruction, cognitive theories.

Introduction

Instructional designers have devoted decades of research and development to creating models and processes to assist with the design and creation of instruction. For citations to some of the literature about these models see: Dewald, 1999a; Smith and Ragan, 2000; Mayer, 2001, 2006; Dempsey and Van Eck, 2002; Dick et al., 2005; Armstrong and Georgas, 2006; Hollis and Madill 2006; Smart and Cappel, 2006; Upton, 2006; Moreno and Mayer, 2007; Reece, 2007; Anderson et al., 2008; Palmer and Holt, 2009; Somoza-Fernández and Abadal, 2009. Good design only provides the shell of a learning object. Creating meaningful content and incorporating sound online pedagogy is essential for effective multimedia instruction. This chapter will provide some pedagogical considerations for generating meaningful content for both the novice and the advanced learner, and will present examples of instructional cognitive theories and how elements of these theories can be integrated into tutorials.

Meaningful content

Effective design is critical to the success of a learning object. However, if the content and message are not appropriate or relevant, the goals and objectives may not be accomplished. This section discusses suggestions for creating meaningful content and for providing it in short "chunks" to facilitate learning.

Appropriate content

Content should be focused around the goals of the learning object and presented so that it is easy to understand the main points. It is important first of all to decide on the scope of the learning object. Some library tutorials are created with a comprehensive scope equivalent to that of a credit-based class or of a face-to-face session. Others are specifically focused on conveying one concept or procedure, such as: the difference between a scholarly journal or popular magazine; how to search a particular database; or how to cite other works correctly.

Content should be as easy for learners to remember as possible by presenting it in ways that are effortless to process and understand. Kosslyn (2007) outlines a series of principles for effective PowerPoint presentations, which can also apply to screencasts and online multimedia. He recommends:

- giving an outline of what will happen right at the beginning to prepare students for what they will encounter;
- clearly indicating when each part is beginning and ending;
- stating each point explicitly and clearly;
- ending with a summary to help reinforce concepts in the student's memory.

Build connections/make it relevant

Since people understand and remember more easily if they can connect new information with something familiar to them, building connections with what learners already know is a key strategy for effective learning. When teaching how to search a database, for example, students may relate better if there are comparisons or analogies to other search tools that students already know, like Google or iTunes.

One way to make connections is to choose controversial, real-life topics to make relevance clear, to aid transfer, and to encourage the disposition of critical thinking. For example, in the American University Library's Information Literacy Tutorial (*http://www.library.american. edu/tutorial/index.html*), there are several topics that the students are asked to address or are used as examples. Throughout the tutorial the student is engaged in developing a research process to address the controversy of whether libraries should censor Internet use. This is something that is relevant to students and may engage them as they work through the tutorial. When developing content it can be useful to gather suggestions from faculty of current controversies that they use in teaching. Incorporating such controversies in tutorials may provide a connection for students, both in terms of other knowledge they have gained and also its relevance outside of a particular assignment.

Concept training

Tutorial instruction should not only be task based, such as training students in the mechanics of searching for information, but should also be concept based so that students recognize that the process discussed or used in that tutorial is transferrable and can be applied to other contexts. Dewald (1999a) also established that one of the fundamental indicators for a tutorial to be effective and to help students develop higher-order thinking skills is that it should teach concepts, not just the mechanics of searching. This is especially relevant in order for students to be able to transfer information to other applications. Library instructors typically emphasize concept training so that students can begin to understand that there are certain elements, features, or strategies of one database that they can apply to others. Various studies have evaluated tutorials and have concluded that the most successful tutorials (in terms of results) included concept training for both lower-order and higher-order information literacy instruction (Kaplowitz and Contini, 1998; Dewald, 1999a; Fourie, 2001; Tancheva et al., 2005).

Many library instruction tutorials include information about how to use certain tools appropriately to help students with library research or learning a library system, including search strategies, scholarly databases, citation styles, library online catalogs, quality Internet resources, journal articles, call numbers, reference resources, electronic mails, classification schemes, and citation management tools. Search strategy is one of the most popular topics, followed by selection and databases. It is possible to take any of these concepts and create a tutorial that illustrates how various aspects can be transferred to any number of other applications. It is unlikely that a library has the time or resources to develop a tutorial to demonstrate how to search every database. Plus, a student most likely would not want to go through every database.

Alternatively, one tutorial can be selected from a suite of tutorials to be representative of all those tutorials. Designers will need to determine the similar elements from those databases and then make it clear that although the tutorial is showing how to search using "X" database, these concepts apply to any of the tutorials in the suite.

Concept training can facilitate cognitive transfer. By creating the abstract conceptual framework in which the information is initially conveyed, the student may be able to distill the essence of the skill from the particular context in which it is taught. Students can also benefit from examples presented in multiple contexts. The exercises used should give students opportunities to apply the skill in new and different situations and should provide substantive corrective feedback. The multimedia learning environment should approximate as closely as possible the situation in which the skill or concept is to be applied, and then provide the opportunity for the learner to practice as many potential variations as much and as often as possible.

Modular design

Modules that provide information in small blocks, breaking it up into parts and sub-parts with summaries and reviews, help learners to organize the material in their own minds. Splitting longer or more complex content into small segments and arranging content in logical sequences also helps reduce content-related memory load in multimedia tutorials.

Breaking down instruction tutorials into manageable sections (modules), while remaining linear and allowing for the step-by-step acquisition of skills, prevents the user from becoming overwhelmed with information. Studies have shown that making short segments instead of longer videos or tutorials helps students to learn better and reduces the effort it takes for them to process information (Collins and Takacs, 1993; Vishwanatham et al., 1997; Dewald, 1999a and b; Nguyen and Clark, 2005; Lusk et al., 2008). Modules can facilitate self-directed learning by providing users with the option of either approaching the tutorial one section at a time or jumping between sections. This degree of choice is empowering to the user, but also serves to accommodate students with varying levels of knowledge and comprehension. Additionally, shorter tutorials are more likely to be viewed in their entirety, and thus more likely to fulfill their aim.

Uses for short tutorials

A common practice used in web-based library instruction is to create short modules to teach specific library skills and concepts. The overall result might mirror what a librarian would present in a face-to-face session. The design frequently follows a step-by-step progression of skills the librarian (or faculty member) believes students need in order to accomplish particular objectives (such as how to search a certain database, use a citation manager, or determine if an article is popular or scholarly). There may be periodic questions that the student needs to answer as they progress from one module to the next, and perhaps a final quiz.

This approach assumes that all learners have the same ability level and learning objectives. Rather than attempting to replicate a face-to-face session, tutorial designers can take advantage of the many options for inserting active learning, alternate pathways, and the strategic insertion of multimedia, and elevate the tutorial beyond a linear approach that does not serve all students' learning styles or abilities and, instead, aim for a cognitive model of instruction.

In addition to strategically placing tutorials on a library website, in course management systems or other platforms, librarians can index web-based tutorials and link to them from several high-profile portions of the website so that librarians, faculty, and students can quickly access either the whole tutorial or segments of tutorials as they are needed. For instance, during a reference consultation (either in person or through chat) the librarian could point to (or copy and paste) the web address of a specific chunk of a tutorial that may further answer a question. It may be that a student does not need the whole tutorial on how to find a database and search through it. S/he may only need the section that specifically describes how to narrow a search by using more appropriate subject headings. A tutorial that breaks down the concepts into smaller chunks offers a wider range of use.

Chunking by concepts

A good rule of thumb is to break down larger tutorials, covering multiple topics, services or features, into separate, smaller tutorials. For example, a single tutorial covering an article database could be divided into separate tutorials covering basic search options, advanced search options, use of the thesaurus, and so on. Shorter tutorials equate to smaller file sizes, which benefits both the end-user (faster downloads) and the university (which pays for the bandwidth). Each chunk or segment should focus on one major objective or section of the content. This helps learners to process information more easily, since they only need to concentrate on one point at a time.

Arranging instructional content in logical sequences also helps learners to process information better and pick and choose the sections they want to view or review. A good approach is to start with easier material and progress to more difficult material, and, similarly, to start with simple concepts and progress to more complex concepts or content. This technique also allows for frequent practice questions and feedback.

Basic and advanced levels – novice/expert

Another aspect that needs to be considered when designing online learning is that students come with different ability levels. Some may be novices, whereas others may be experts in one area or another. One common model that can be used is to incorporate a constructivist view on learning: learners construct new learning and new learning is filtered by their current knowledge state. In this way, students may choose content based on their own learning conditions and information needs.

Constructivist learning

Web-based education provides an opportunity to tailor approaches to create more learner-centered and constructivist learning options (Herrington and Standen, 2000; Dalgarno, 2001). Constructivism argues that humans generate knowledge and meaning from an interaction between their experiences and their ideas (Piaget, 1967, 1970; Von Glasersfeld, 1995). Constructivists believe that the world is constructed in the mind and personal constructions define personal realities (Jonassen et al., 1995; Savery and Duffy, 1995; Jonassen et al., 1999; Swan et al., 2009). Constructivist-based instruction firmly places educational priorities on students' learning. This view of learning is not listening and then mirroring, but rather participating and interacting with the environment in order to create personal meaning. Passive tutorials, such as many existing screencast video tutorials, do not engage learners in a way that helps them to build on their knowledge. Tutorials that incorporate different levels of activities, challenges, and options are more conducive to this approach.

Constructivist environments involve learners in knowledge construction through collaboration that allows for learning through interaction and reflection upon what has been learned through the process. The design of this process can occur prior to the design of tutorials and learning objects and again through the assessment phase. Tutorials can be created that allow for multiple paths based on students' choices and responses. In that way they can continue to construct their knowledge based on their existing knowledge and needs.

Some of the questions that can help guide the design of learning activities embedded within learning objects include whether the exercise:

1. focuses on addressing diverse perspectives;
2. requires higher-order thinking skills;
3. represents real-world examples;
4. provides scaffolding to assist students to move beyond what is known;
5. affords opportunities for self-reflection;
6. presents multiple representations of ideas;
7. allows for social negotiation; and
8. assesses the achievement of learning outcomes.

The above are questions that librarians and educators need to consider as they design and redesign their tutorials and learning objects to assess how well they align with student-centered learning.

An example of a tutorial that incorporates constructivism is *Søk & Skriv* (Search and Write) (*http://www.sokogskriv.no* and *http://sokogskriv. no/english*). This tutorial seeks to promote student learning by doing and reflecting. Students acquire new knowledge by reflecting upon their actions and the consequences of those actions. The newly achieved knowledge is integrated in the individual's knowledge framework and forms a new platform for reconsidering the problem at hand or solving new problems. When considering the pedagogy and design for this tutorial, Skagen et al. (2008) noted work by Tønseth (2004) that "emphasizes that it is of great importance for distance education students to relate their studies to their previous experience, and to be able to apply their new knowledge to their work context." The pedagogy underlying tutorial design should make the students responsible for contextualizing the research process in their own discipline and academic task. This then can assist in developing students' "learning-how-to-learn" abilities (Andretta, 2005), which can be applied in their professional life.

Personalization/scenario/cases

One way in which students can be active participants in choosing which learning object to use is for the tutorial to provide multiple paths that a student can take. One way to achieve this is to create a table of contents that is available at all times (either stationary or upon mouse movement) with chapters and sections outlined so that a student can pick and choose what will help them, rather than having to go through the whole sequence whether or not they need the information. Another way is to code the tutorial so that a student is directed to different parts of the tutorial, depending upon a response to a question or their selection.

Personalized characters

Some students appreciate connecting with a specific character or situation when working through a tutorial. Some tutorials ask students to choose a character and follow the character throughout the task. The goal is to connect the content of the learning object to a specific case (a fictitious student) with which users can identify. Examples include:

- *Søk & Skriv Advanced* (Search and Write) (*http://www.sokogskriv.no* and *http://sokogskriv.no/english* and *http://sokogskriv.no/english/index.php?action=static&id=4*). (See Figure 7.1.)
- *You Quote It, You Note It* (*http://library.acadiau.ca/tutorials/plagiarism/*). (See Figure 7.2.)

Meet Oda, Christian and Sofie

Search and Write present three students to you. Oda is a student of midwifery, Christian a student of economics and Sofie is studying the Middle-East.

You meet them while they are writing their assignments. The assignments are specific to their disciplines, but the work processes have many similiarities.

By reading their stories you gain insight in how the writing process within different field can pan out, what kind of challenges they meet and how they manage their ups and downs.

All three students use dialogue with others such as supervisors, peers or librarians when making their own decisions and to ensure work progress.

Oda
Midwifery studies

Christian
Economics

Sofie
Middle-east studies

Figure 7.1   Character choice from *Søk & Skriv* (Search and Write)

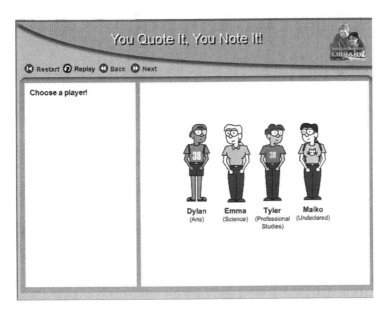

Figure 7.2   Character choice from *You Quote It, You Note It*, Vaughan Memorial Library

Source: http://library.acadiau.ca/tutorials/plagiarism

The University of Arizona Libraries created a tutorial that also asks students to choose a character. However, instead of using fictitious characters, the pictures are of real students. As the student rolls the mouse over the picture more information appears (see Figure 7.3).

The facility to choose a character with whom they may identify can provide a connection for the student between the real world and the content of the tutorial. In the study carried out for this book, the students generally liked the idea of "helping" someone through the process. When asked how they decided on a character one student said she chose the girl with the cat on her shirt because she liked cats. A few tried to find one who shared their major or who was of the same gender. When students rolled their mouse over a character the left frame of the screen filled with more information about the character. Students did not spend time reading the information. A few students did not understand how this process would help them to learn anything and simply chose the first character so they could keep moving through the tutorial. Other students

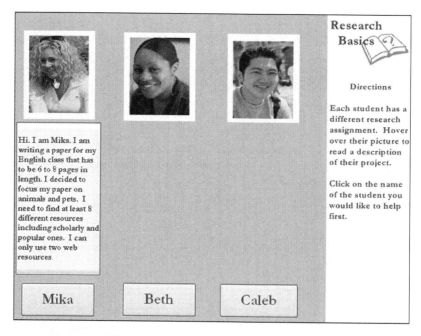

Figure 7.3 Character choice from Research Basics, University of Arizona

Source: http://www.library.arizona.edu/tutorials/research_basics/

did not find a student they could relate to so they just chose randomly. Some students also wondered if they would have a different (or better) experience if they chose a different character or scenario. Providing characters can be a way to personalize content, but some students might find it difficult to choose a relevant character and designers may need to consider carefully how to develop engaging characters.

Scenarios/concept-based topics

Concept-based instruction, which was presented earlier in this chapter, can help develop higher-order thinking skills. Using this approach through scenarios and controversial topics is a good way to personalize the tutorial experience for students. The choice of topics should relate to students' lives so that the relevance is clear, can aid transfer, and can encourage the disposition of critical thinking. Scenarios provide opportunities for students to reflect on a situation, apply their knowledge to the situation, and to engage in problem-solving activities. They can allow students to apply skills in an authentic and challenging environment. Scenarios could include a similar character that proceeds through different actions. The following list includes some tips for incorporating scenarios modified from a presentation by Blakiston and Mery (2010):

- Make the scenario as authentic as possible (through situations and images).
- Create real-world tasks that create problems the students need to solve.
- Make problems complex.
- Include a trigger-event where students need to make a decision.
- Include characters (and use them throughout the process).
- Allow students to choose characters (provide options for different interests and skill levels).
- Include a story element to add drama.
- Include guidance, feedback, and reflection.
- Prototype or storyboard first.
- Test the tutorial with potential users and modify it before making it live.

In the Research Basics tutorial by the University of Arizona Libraries, participants need to help a student find appropriate resources for a paper. After the participants have chosen a character they are given various questions and situations and need to respond. Figure 7.4 shows a screenshot that illustrates how the designers have incorporated many of the above bulleted suggestions. The paper requirement is very true to life for students and includes various options. They need to choose from several options, while understanding the complexities of the paper requirements. In this screenshot, choice two was selected to show the type of feedback that appears.

The tutorial continues with the chosen student dialoging with the tutorial participant. This helps to make the process more collaborative and more likely that students will relate to the experience. Notice also, in Figure 7.5, how this tutorial continues to provide the sections of the tutorial (although all but the current section is grayed out).

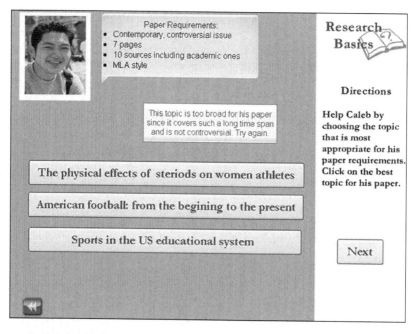

Figure 7.4 Narrowing a topic scenario from Research Basics, University of Arizona

Source: http://www.library.arizona.edu/tutorials/research_basics/

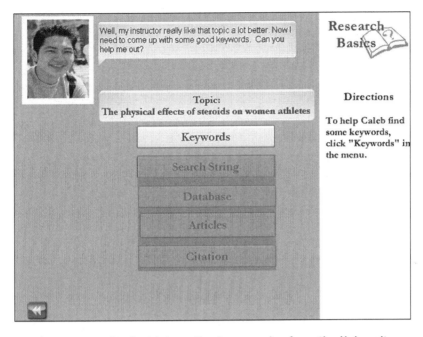

Figure 7.5 Student interaction in scenarios from the University of Arizona

Source: http://www.library.arizona.edu/tutorials/research_basics/

Cognitive science applied to instruction design

Sound pedagogy needs to be interwoven with good instructional design. It is important for the instructional designer to understand the principles of cognitive science and how they apply to effective instructional design for online learning. Concepts, such as working memory, cognitive load, production system theories of knowledge and learning, self-explaining behaviors, and transfer, all become important considerations for the instructional designer who must learn to use technology effectively and with intelligence, rather than simply because it is available and seems flashy or exciting.

Many designers experiment with adding flashy game-like components and strategies to their tutorials to hold students' attention. Clark and Mayer (2003) caution that if these are not designed well using empirically-tested strategies for multimedia instruction they could cause memory and cognitive overload, rather than facilitating knowledge construction.

What is cognitive load?

Cognitive psychologists have carried out research into the effective use of multimedia in learning. Much of this research looks into how people process information effectively, and is based on cognitive load theory (Sweller, 2011). According to cognitive load theory, short-term or working memory has a limited capacity and can only handle so much information effectively at one time. If a person's working memory is overloaded, that person may not be able to process anything well, thus leading to poor understanding, retention, and learning (Sweller, 1988, 1994, 1999, 2011; Chandler and Sweller, 1991, 1992, 1996; Mayer and Moreno, 2003; Nguyen and Clark, 2005; van Merriënboer and Sweller, 2005). There are three kinds of cognitive load to be aware of: intrinsic (related to the instructional content); germane (related to the activities that the students do); and extraneous (everything else) (Nguyen and Clark, 2005). For a summary of working memory and cognitive load theory see Sorden (2005). The load on working memory needs to be minimized in each of these areas so that people can process information more effectively and learn better.

This suggests that for instruction to be effective, care must be taken to design instruction in such a way as to not overload the mind's capacity for processing information. Rather than adding unnecessary "bells and whistles" to multimedia instruction, it is important to incorporate elements that contribute to instruction, but don't overload limited working memory. Multimedia, screencasts, and other types of animated media put high demands on short-term memory, since a lot of information (text, graphics, audio, motion) needs to be processed simultaneously (Betrancourt, 2005). The result may be that learners have difficulty in effectively processing the information. Activities should remain focused on the concepts to be learned, rather than trying too much to entertain. This is especially true if the entertainment is time-consuming to construct and is complicated for the learner to master. Working memory can be overloaded by the entertainment or activity even before the learner gets to the concept or skill to be learned.

Studies have shown that instruction using static graphics and visuals, like labeled screenshots, can be as effective or more effective for learning since it places fewer demands on our short-term memory (Clark and Lyons, 2004; Mayer, 2006; Mestre, 2010), leading to better understanding and retention. The words and graphics are processed simultaneously but use different parts of our working memory, and the effect is that each reinforces the other. However, words and graphics should be located near to each other so it is clear that they are connected; otherwise, it is more difficult for learners to process them together, increasing memory load (Mayer, 2006).

Minimizing extraneous memory load is especially critical for a successful screencast or streaming multimedia tutorial. Extraneous memory load is created by those elements of the screencast that do not contribute to the content or activities, and which therefore are not important to learning success. This is the kind of memory load which should be the easiest to reduce. When reduced, it is less likely that students' attention will be distracted from the content, and more likely that they will understand and learn successfully. Mayer (2003) suggests that since the visual and aural channels are separate, extraneous memory load is not created if different material is presented within the two channels. However, in the Mestre (2010) study, one of the main concerns of students in the screencast tutorials was that the narrator did not stop speaking when a call-out bubble appeared. Some students had difficulty with the bubbles for two reasons: first, they appeared over the existing screen and the student had to try to process what was in the bubble while still remembering what was on the screen; and, second, the student was still trying to listen to and process what the narrator was saying while looking at the new content in the bubble. Because the call-out bubble appeared on top of the existing screen, students did pay attention to it (as was intended). However, to reduce competing processes it could have been placed where there was no text and the narration could have ceased while the bubble was present. Figure 7.6 shows a call-out bubble appearing over part of a screen; this occurs at the same time as narration, typing in the boxes, scrolling of the closed captioning text, and the appearance of a blue arrow.

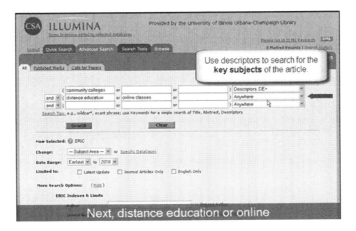

Figure 7.6   Too many simultaneous elements in a tutorial

Steps for reducing cognitive load

To reduce extraneous load the designer should take care to simplify and remove as much as possible that is not absolutely necessary to the content or activities. As part of his evidence-seeking efforts for the science of e-learning, Mayer (2001, 2003) presents nine major effects which emerged out of dozens of studies. These replicated effects are: modality effect; contiguity effect; multimedia effect; personalization effect; coherence effect; redundancy effect; pre-training effect; signaling effect; and the pacing effect. These are explained as nine effects, referred to here as principles in Moreno and Mayer (2000, 2007). In general, the following considerations should improve transfer and reduce cognitive overload in the design of instructional modules:

- Combine animation/pictures and narration as opposed to animation/pictures and on-screen text, i.e., students learn better in multimedia messages when words are presented as spoken language rather than printed text.

- Make narrations as conversational in style as possible and avoid using stiff third-person narration. This follows the personalization principle which states that better transfer occurs when narration is conducted in a conversational first- or second-person style.

- Present corresponding narration and animation simultaneously, both temporally and spatially. Temporal contiguity means that corresponding words and pictures should be presented at the same time, while spatial contiguity means that corresponding words and pictures should be presented near to rather than far from each other on a page or screen. In other words, don't place an important visual image on one page or frame, and then discuss it on a preceding or following page or frame without continuing to show the visual image.

  - Use words and graphics together (include the text within the graphic). Richard Mayer's research in multimedia learning has found that using words along with graphics produces more effective learning than using either one alone. The words and graphics are processed simultaneously but use different parts of working memory, and the effect is that each reinforces the other.

- When both words and pictures are presented, learners have the chance to construct verbal and visual cognitive representations and integrate them.

- Exclude extraneous material such as irrelevant video, animation, pictures, narration, and sounds.
  - Remove any unnecessary graphics, text, and audio since graphics and words that do not directly contribute to the main points can distract the learner's attention away from the main instructional messages (Mayer, 2006).
  - Avoid graphics or visuals which are merely decorative, or which generate associations that are interesting but not related to the main point (Clark and Lyons, 2004).
  - Make the remaining graphics as simple as possible, and consistent in style and format throughout the screencast in order to reduce the effort needed to interpret them (ibid.).

- Avoid combining animation and narration with the printed text when both are saying the same thing. When pictures and words are both presented visually and are conveying the same information, it can overload visual working memory capacity and actually reduces learning (Mayer, 2006). Only present words through one channel (either visual or aural, but not both at the same time).

- Do pre-training before presenting a narrated animation. It is better to do pre-training on each component so that the learners already possesses schemas for them before presenting material that requires the learner to integrate each component into larger schemas. This connects to the concept of chunking and building schemas.

- Use signal narrations to provide cues to the learner about how to organize material.

- Direct students' attention to the most important points (this reduces extraneous memory load and improves learning).
  - Show processes and tasks in context, such as where the search strategy help button is in a database search, as it is being discussed, rather than just talking about it. If students do not have context, they may not learn enough to apply what they are supposed to be learning (Clark and Lyons, 2004).
  - Highlight the most important part of the larger screen with visual or verbal cues so that students know where to direct their attention.

In screencasting software these visual cues might include using an arrow, circle, zoom feature, call-out button, highlighting of text, or grayed-out background to show the important area on the screen. Another strategy is to insert a title screen between sections to indicate a change in topic (see Figure 7.7). Verbal cues include putting captions on the screen, repeating or summarizing points, using tone and emphasis to indicate important points, or saying explicitly that a particular point is important. Figure 7.8 (on the left) illustrates the use of arrows to highlight the parts of a citation. The rest of the record has been grayed out. Figure 7.9 (on the right) is a screen capture as the narration continues to show further highlighting of this section.

- Create the opportunity for the learner to pace the presentation. Learners vary in the time needed to engage in the cognitive processes of selecting, organizing, and integrating incoming information, so they must have the ability to work at their own pace to slow or pause the presentation if necessary.

Figure 7.7   Example of a title page between sections to cue a change in topic, University of Illinois

Source: http://www.library.illinois.edu/diglit/tutorials/plagiarism/Plagiarism.html

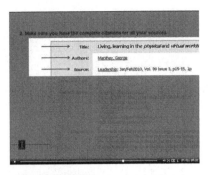

Figure 7.8 Example of grayed-out area to help focus attention on the main topic

Figure 7.9 More highlighting of specific features

Minimizing extraneous memory load is especially critical for a successful screencast or streaming multimedia tutorial. Extraneous load is created by elements of the screencast that do not contribute to the content or activities, and which therefore are not important to learning success. This is the kind of memory load which should be easiest to reduce. When reduced, it is less likely that students' attention will be distracted from the content, and more likely that they will understand and learn successfully. Above, reference was made to the tutorial that began with a snoring student. Yet students could not work out the relevance of that image. There was no reference to the image. The inclusion of the snoring character was probably to catch the students' attention, but it was confusing for students since they could not integrate it with the tutorial. Because they were focused on the image and the sound they did not read the text at the side but began clicking on the image, and were therefore distracted from the purpose of the tutorial (see Figure 7.10).

One of the most important questions to ask when designing screencasts or streaming video tutorials is whether the multimedia is needed at all, or whether the instruction could be delivered just as effectively some other way. Rather than having a "talking head," or some animation lecturing, or narration throughout a tutorial or video, is there some other way or combination of ways that might allow for active and relevant learning?

Figure 7.10 Snoring character introduction, Vaughan Memorial Library

Source: http://library.acadiau.ca/tutorials/plagiarism/

Models for integrating good pedagogy into tutorials

In the virtual environment, web and tutorial designers typically use multimedia that is intended to add excitement to the lesson, hold the learner's attention, and provide some active learning exercises. However, visual and auditory components that are intended to stimulate rather than educate do not always make for good instructional design in multimedia delivery, and can quickly become counter-productive to learning. When designing for online learning it is imperative to use good pedagogical principles. The American Distance Education Consortium (2003) lists the following principles (taken from *http://www.adec.edu/ admin/papers/distance-teaching_principles.html*):

- The learning experience must have a clear purpose with tightly focused outcomes and objectives.

- Web-based learning designs must consider the nature of content, specific context, desired learning outcomes, and characteristics of the learner. Learner-centered strategies include modular, stand-alone units that are compatible with short bursts of learning. Learning modules may also be open, flexible, and self-directing.

- The learner should be actively engaged. Active, hands-on, concrete experiences are highly effective. Learning by doing, analogy, and assimilation are increasingly important pedagogical forms. Where possible, learning outcomes should relate to real-life experiences through simulation and application.

- The learning environment should make appropriate use of a variety of media. Various learning styles are best engaged by using a variety of media to achieve learning outcomes. Selection of media may also depend on nature of content, learning goals, access to technology, and the local learning environment.

- Learning environments must include problem-based as well as knowledge-based learning. Problem-based learning involves higher-order thinking skills such as analysis, synthesis, and evaluation, while knowledge-based learning involves recall, comprehension, and application.

- Learning experiences should support interaction and the development of communities of interest. Learning is social and sensitive to context. Learning experiences based on interaction and collaboration support learning communities while building a support network to enhance learning outcomes. Multiple interactions, group collaboration, and cooperative learning may provide increased levels of interaction and simulation.

- The practice of distance learning contributes to the larger social mission of education and training in a democratic society. Changing mental models and constructing new knowledge empowers learners and encourages critical thinking. "Knowledge becomes a function of how the individual creates meaning from his or her experiences; it is not a function of what someone else says is true" (Jonassen et al., 1995).

Another model that is applicable to the development of tutorials and learning objects is that of Dick et al. (2005). This model reflects a systematic approach to instructional design based on nine components: identification of instructional goal(s); instructional analysis; analysis of learners and context; articulation of performance objectives; development of assessment instruments; development of instructional strategies; development and selection of instructional materials; design and implementation of formative evaluation of instruction; and the revision of instruction based on evaluation results.

Promote critical thinking

The goal of most instruction is to help learners think critically so that they can adapt their learning to new situations (i.e., transfer their learning). Teaching successfully with critical thinking in mind involves linking concrete skills and actions to a more conceptual framework. This connection between concrete actions and abstract principles creates better learning and retention, and helps students to apply what they learn in real-life situations more effectively (Commission on Behavioral and Social Sciences, 1999). Therefore, teaching for critical thinking involves students in more than just a series of steps and practice activities. Students need to see the steps put into a broader framework, and think about how the steps relate to a larger process so they understand why each is important. This can be done easily at a basic level by, for example, outlining the steps in the search process at the beginning of a screencast, and then clearly identifying each step as it is demonstrated.

Links to a conceptual framework can be established at a higher level by creating scenarios that place tasks in a wider context, for example by showing how to solve a commonly encountered problem. Figure 7.11 is a screenshot of the web page of the University of Maryland University

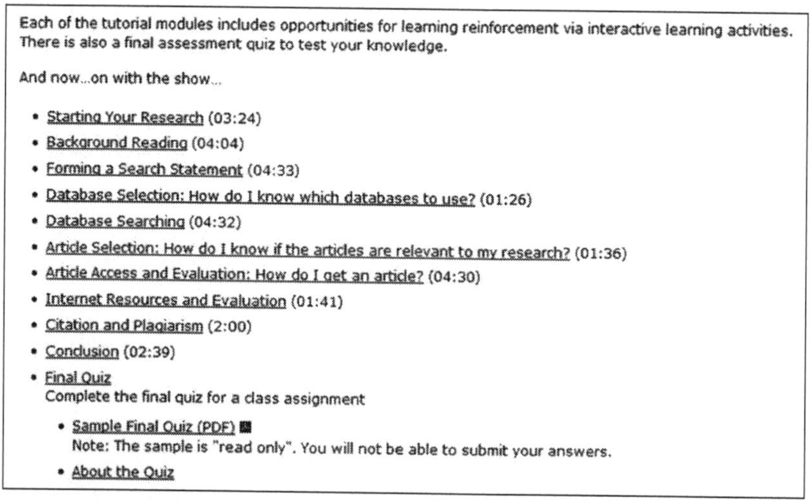

Each of the tutorial modules includes opportunities for learning reinforcement via interactive learning activities. There is also a final assessment quiz to test your knowledge.

And now...on with the show...

- Starting Your Research (03:24)
- Background Reading (04:04)
- Forming a Search Statement (04:33)
- Database Selection: How do I know which databases to use? (01:26)
- Database Searching (04:32)
- Article Selection: How do I know if the articles are relevant to my research? (01:36)
- Article Access and Evaluation: How do I get an article? (04:30)
- Internet Resources and Evaluation (01:41)
- Citation and Plagiarism (2:00)
- Conclusion (02:39)
- Final Quiz
  Complete the final quiz for a class assignment
    - Sample Final Quiz (PDF)
      Note: The sample is "read only". You will not be able to submit your answers.
    - About the Quiz

Figure 7.11   **Conceptual framework for tutorials from the University of Maryland**

Source: http://www.umuc.edu/library/libhow/research_tutorial.cfm. Secrets of My Research Success used with permission from the Information and Library Services, University of Maryland University College

College that includes the various segments of Captivate tutorials. These interactive Flash tutorials feature Quentin and his experiences in the research process. Each tutorial is embedded on a web page that includes the whole transcript beneath it.

An instructional design model that places a strong emphasis on knowledge transfer and critical thinking skills is that developed by Wiggins and McTighe (2005). This model is based on the backwards design and proposes "an approach to designing a unit that begins with the end in mind and designs toward the end." Consisting of three stages – desired results; accepted evidence of learning; and planning instruction and learning experiences – the goal of the model is to build deep, long-term understanding that helps students to connect facts, as well as to transfer acquired knowledge and skills to new contexts. A "student understands when he/she can explain, interpret, apply, have perspective, empathize, and demonstrate self-knowledge" (ibid., p. 338). This model requires students to be actively engaged with the material being presented (rather than passively watching) by prompting them to apply the information or to work with the information in some new way. Consequently, this model challenges instructors to address the following questions as they develop tutorials and learning objects: Does the learning object allow for active learning and critical thinking activities? Does the student need to apply the knowledge immediately?

Thompson and Yonekura (2005), from the University of Central Florida, simplify these steps in their model consisting of useful and reusable digital objects that include the following components: statement of a learning objective; presentation of content; an opportunity for practice; and assessment based on the achievement of the objective. According to their model, all four elements must be present for a component to be considered a learning object.

Strategies that allow students to think critically about tasks also include providing them with multiple, slightly different examples, or comparing good and bad examples. These strategies encourage students to evaluate the examples more closely and to apply what they learn to slightly different situations more effectively.

Bloom's Taxonomy (1956, 1972, 1984) provides a way to think about how instruction integrates critical thinking. The revised version of Bloom's Taxonomy presents different kinds of learning goals, organized on a continuum from simple and concrete to complex and abstract (Krathwohl, 2002):

- remembering
- understanding
- applying
- analyzing
- evaluating
- creating.

To promote critical thinking, it is also useful to concentrate on the more abstract and conceptual levels of learning (analyzing, evaluating, creating) in some screencast tutorials, rather than using only the lower three levels (remembering, understanding, applying). Education researchers Dunlap et al. (2007) developed a list of strategies that can help achieve different levels of Bloom's revised Taxonomy. To achieve the lower three levels of learning (remembering, understanding, applying), they recommend creating interactive activities for students that demonstrate concepts, provide opportunities to practice skills, or involve students in organizing or mapping what they know through concept or mind maps. To achieve the higher levels (analyzing, evaluating, creating), they recommend encouraging students to follow their own paths through the content, to access extra "enrichment" content, and to create interactive activities for students that help them assess and evaluate solutions, connect ideas, and create their own solutions to problems.

The American Distance Education Consortium also suggests the following as characteristics of quality web-based teaching and learning (available at: *http://www.adec.edu/admin/papers/distance-teaching_principles.html*):

1. fosters meaning-making, discourse;
2. moves from knowledge transmission to learner-controlled systems;
3. provides for reciprocal teaching;
4. is learner-centered;
5. encourages active participation, knowledge construction;
6. is based on higher-level thinking skills – analysis, synthesis, and evaluation;
7. promotes active learning;
8. allows group collaboration and cooperative learning;
9. provides multiple levels of interaction; and
10. focuses on real-world, problem solving.

Getting help with integrating effective pedagogy in multimedia

Most campuses have a teaching center that offers support for faculty (and librarians) in learning how to be effective teachers, both face-to-face and online. They can also provide support for best practices for integrating technology in online learning. Teaching faculty may take more advantage of this resource than librarians. In a study carried out by members of the Association of College and Research Libraries Education and Behavioral Sciences section (Mestre et al., 2011), the results of a survey that was answered by 97 librarians, mostly academic, showed that only one-fifth of the respondents had any training in teaching methods (either for face-to-face or online teaching). Most of them had only attended a conference program or workshop in the area of online teaching. Campus Centers for Teaching not only offer advice, workshops, training, and best practices, but may also offer incentives and support for modifying online courses to incorporate more active and collaborative learning. Additionally, there are ample opportunities to learn about effective instructional pedagogy by attending (in person or online) conference workshops, webinars, and presentations, many of which are free or offered at a low cost.

Conclusion

This chapter has focused on pedagogical considerations that librarians should consider when creating tutorials. Effective pedagogy needs to include various approaches to learner motivation, module organization, and level of interactivity. Traditional instructional pedagogy has guided much of the simple skills instruction on the web, but librarians are also developing new ways of teaching in this medium.

Designing tutorials and web pages in a pedagogically sound way can provide opportunities for student exploration, creativity, and the application of new understanding of difficult concepts to their own assignments. One approach to promoting students' learning is to help them develop their own understanding of concepts and skills, and apply learning in realistic settings. The unique capabilities of the web allow librarians to move beyond traditional pedagogical techniques to active, creative learning.

If learning objects and tutorials are well designed they can help students to decide what kinds of strategies they might want to use and what course of action to take in each phase. Students can focus on the particular piece of information that is most useful to them in relation to their academic work. Learning objects can be designed to help students in their individual research needs, whether these are to elicit brainstorming activities; to develop an outline; to learn of their information needs; or to learn of resources and strategies that will help them meet those needs. All of these approaches are beneficial to students, regardless of their learning style.

There are the best practices for developing effective pedagogies based on cognitive science and other library science research. These best practices should be kept in mind when designing online materials for library instruction. Bad design will distract students from learning the material. One of the goals of library instruction is to facilitate the transfer of learning, so it is important to facilitate that process through effective, pedagogically sound design and activities. The next chapter provides examples of ways in which to incorporate active learning and interactivity into learning objects.

References

American Distance Education Consortium (2003) *ADEC Guiding Principles for Distance Teaching and Learning.* Available at: *http://www.adec.edu/admin/papers/distance-teaching_principles.html.*

Anderson, R.P., Wilson, S.P., Livingston, M.B. and LoCicero, A.D. (2008) Characteristics and content of medical library tutorials: a review. *Journal of the Medical Library Association,* 96(1): 61–3.

Andretta, S. (2005) Information literacy: empowering the learner "against all odds." Paper presented at the LILAC Conference, April 4, 2005, Imperial College, London. Available at: *http://personalpages.manchester.ac.uk/staff/Drew.Whitworth/tangentium/andretta.doc* (retrieved July 25, 2012).

Armstrong, A. and Georgas, H. (2006) Using interactive technology to teach information literacy concepts to undergraduate students. *Reference Services Review,* 34(4): 491–7.

Betrancourt, M. (2005) The animation and interactivity principles in multimedia learning. In R.E. Mayer (ed.) *Cambridge Handbook of Multimedia Learning* (pp. 287–96). Cambridge: Cambridge University Press.

Blakiston, R. and Mery, Y. (2010) Scenario based e-learning: putting the student in the driver's seat. *26th Annual Conference on Distance Teaching & Learning.* Madison, WI. Available at: *http://www.uwex.edu/disted/conference/Resource_library/handouts/28769_10H.pdf.*

Bloom, B.S. (ed.) (1956, 1972, 1984) *Taxonomy of Educational Objectives.* New York: Longman.

Chandler, P. and Sweller, J. (1991) Cognitive load theory and the format of instruction. *Cognition and Instruction*, 8: 293–332.

Chandler, P. and Sweller, J. (1992) The split-attention effect as a factor in the design of instruction. *British Journal of Educational Psychology*, 62: 233–46.

Chandler, P. and Sweller, J. (1996) Cognitive load while learning to use a computer program. *Applied Cognitive Psychology*, 10: 1–20.

Clark, R.C. and Lyons, C. (2004) *Graphics for Learning: Proven Guidelines for Planning, Designing and Evaluating Visuals in Training Materials*. San Francisco, CA: Pfeiffer/Wiley.

Clark, R.C. and Mayer, R.E. (2003) *E-learning and the Science of Instruction*. San Francisco, CA: Jossey-Bass.

Collins, K.L.K. and Takacs, S.N. (1993) Information technology and the teaching role of the college librarian. *Reference Librarian*, 39: 41–51.

Commission on Behavioral and Social Sciences (1999) Learning and transfer. In J.D. Bransford et al. (eds.) *How People Learn: Brain, Mind, Experience and School* (pp. 39–66). Washington, DC: National Academies Press.

Dalgarno, B. (2001) Interpretations of constructivism and consequences for computer assisted learning. *British Journal of Educational Technology*, 32(2): 183–94.

Dempsey, J.V. and Van Eck, R.N.V. (2002) Instructional design on-line: evolving expectations. In R.A. Reiser and J.V. Dempsey (eds.) *Trends and Issues in Instructional Design and Technology* (pp. 281–94). Upper Saddle River, NJ: Pearson Education.

Dewald, N.H. (1999a) Transporting good library instruction practices into the web environment: an analysis of online tutorials. *Journal of Academic Librarianship*, 25(1): 26–32.

Dewald, N.H. (1999b) Web-based library instruction: what is good pedagogy? *Information Technology and Libraries*, 18(1): 26–31.

Dick, W., Carey, L. and Carey, J.O. (2005) *The Systematic Design of Instruction* (6th edn.). New York: Allyn and Bacon.

Dunlap, J.C., Sobel, D. and Sands, D.I. (2007) Supporting students' cognitive processing in online courses: designing for deep and meaningful student-to-content interactions. *TechTrends*, 51(4): 20–31.

Fourie, I. (2001) The use of CAI for distance teaching in the formulation of search strategies. *Library Trends*, 50(1): 110–29.

Herrington, J. and Standen, P. (2000) Moving from an instructivist to a constructivist multimedia learning environment. *Journal of Educational Multimedia and Hypermedia*, 9(3): 195–205.

Hollis, V. and Madill, H. (2006) Online learning: the potential for occupational therapy education. *Occupational Therapy International*, 13: 61–78.

Jonassen, D.H., Davidson, M., Collins, M., Campbell, J. and Bannan Haag, B. (1995) Constructivism and computer-mediated communication in distance education. *American Journal of Distance Education*, 9(2): 7–26.

Jonassen, D.H., Peck, K.L. and Wilson, B.G. (1999) *Learning with Technology: A Constructivist Perspective*. Upper Saddle River, NJ: Prentice Hall.

Kaplowitz, J. and Contini, J. (1998) Computer-assisted instruction: is it an option for bibliographic instruction in large undergraduate survey classes? *College & Research Libraries*, 59: 19–27.

Kosslyn, S.M. (2007) Clear and to the point: 8 psychological principles for compelling PowerPoint presentations. New York: Oxford University Press.

Krathwohl, D.R. (2002) A revision of Bloom's taxonomy: an overview. *Theory into Practice*, 41(4): 212–18.

Lusk, D., Evans, A.D., Jeffrey, T.R., Palmer, K.R. and Wikstrom, C.S. et al. (2008) Multimedia learning and individual differences: mediating the effects of working memory capacity with segmentation. *British Journal of Educational Technology*, 40(4): 636–51. DOI:10.1111/j.1467-8535.2008.00848.x.

Mayer, R.E. (2001) *Multimedia Learning*. New York: Cambridge University Press.

Mayer, R.E. (2003) Elements of a science of ELearning. *Journal of Educational Computing Research*, 29(3): 297–313.

Mayer, R.E. (2006) Ten research-based principles of multimedia learning. In H. O'Neil and R. Perez (eds.) *Web-based Learning: Theory, Research, and Practice* (pp. 371–90). Mahwah, NJ: Lawrence Erlbaum.

Mayer, R.E. and Moreno, R. (2003) Nine ways to reduce cognitive load in multimedia learning. *Educational Psychologist*, 38: 43–52.

Mestre, L.S. (2010) Matching up learning styles with learning objects: what's effective? *Journal of Library Administration*, 50(7–8): 808–29.

Mestre, L.S. et al. (2011) Creating learning objects for information literacy: a survey of librarian usage. *College & Research Libraries*, 72(3): 236–52.

Moreno, R. and Mayer, R.E. (2000) A coherence effect in multimedia learning: the case for minimizing irrelevant sounds in the design of multimedia instructional messages. *Journal of Educational Psychology*, 92: 117–25.

Moreno, R. and Mayer, R. (2007) Interactive multimodal learning environments: Special issue on interactive learning environments: contemporary issues and trends. *Educational Psychology Review*, 19(3): 309–26. DOI:10.1007/s10648-007-9047-2.

Nguyen, F. and Clark, R.C. (2005) Efficiency in e-learning: proven instructional methods for faster, better online learning. *Learning Solutions*. Available at: *http://www.clarktraining.com/content/articles/Guild_E-Learning.pdf*.

Palmer, S.R. and. Holt, D.M. (2009) Examining student satisfaction with wholly online learning. *Journal of Computer Assisted Learning*, 25: 101–13.

Piaget, J. (1967) *Biologie et Connaissance (Biology and Knowledge)*. Paris: Gallimard.

Piaget, J. (1970) *Logic and Psychology* (trans. W. Mays). New York: Basic Books.

Reece, G.J. (2007) Critical thinking and cognitive transfer: implications for the development of online information literacy tutorials. *Research Strategies*, 20(4): 482–93.

Savery, J. and Duffy, T. (1995) Problem based learning: an instructional model and its constructivist framework. In B.G. Wilson (ed.) *Designing Constructivist Learning Environments* (pp. 135–48). Englewood Cliffs, NJ: Educational Technology Publications.

Skagen, T., Torras, M., Kavli, S., Mikki, S., Hafstad, S. et al. (2008) Pedagogical considerations in developing an online tutorial in information literacy. *Communications in Information Literacy*, 2(2): 84–98. Available at: *http://www.comminfolit.org/index.php?journal=cil&page=article&op=viewFile&path[]=Fall2008AR2&path[]=74*.

Smart K. and Cappel J.J. (2006) Students' perceptions of online learning: a comparative study. *Journal of Information Technology Education*, 5: 201–19.

Smith, P.L. and Ragan, T.J. (2000) *Instructional Design*. New York: John Wiley & Sons, Inc.

Somoza-Fernández, M. and Abadal, E. (2009) Analysis of web-based tutorials created by academic libraries. *Journal of Academic Librarianship*, 35(2): 126–31.

Sorden, S. (2005) A cognitive approach to instructional design for multimedia learning. *Informing Science Journal*, 8: 263–79.

Swan, K., Garrison, D.R. and Richardson, J. (2009) A constructivist approach to online learning: the community of inquiry framework. In C.R. Payne (ed.) *Information Technology and Constructivism in Higher Education: Progressive Learning Frameworks* (pp. 43–57). Hershey, PA: IGI Global.

Sweller, J. (1988) Cognitive load during problem solving: effects on learning. *Cognitive Science*, 12: 257–85.

Sweller, J. (1994) Cognitive load theory, learning difficulty, and instructional design. *Learning and Instruction*, 4: 295–312.

Sweller, J. (1999) *Instructional Design in Technical Areas*. Camberwell, Australia: ACER Press.

Sweller, J. (2011) Cognitive load theory. In J.P. Mestre and B.H. Ross (eds.) *The Psychology of Learning and Motivation: Cognition in Education, Volume 55* (pp. 37–76). San Diego, CA: Academic Press.

Tancheva, K., Cosgrave, T. and Cole, V. (2005) *Cornell University Library (CUL) Instruction Services Survey: A User Assessment* [CUL Technical Reports and Papers]. Available at: *http://techreports.library.cornell.edu:8081/Dienst/UI/1.0/Display/cul.lib/2005-4*.

Thompson, K. and Yonekura, F. (2005) Practical guidelines for learning object granularity from one higher education setting. *Interdisciplinary Journal of Knowledge and Learning Objects*, 1: 163–79. Available at: *http://ijklo.org/Volume1/v1p163-179Thompson.pdf*.

Tønseth, C. (2004) IKT og læring – for hvem? In A.M. Støkken and J. Wilhelmsen (eds.) *Jeg har en motor inni meg som driver meg sjøl ... Livet som voksen fleksibel student* (pp. 101–20). Norgesuniversitetets skriftserie 2/2004. Tromsø, Norway: Norgesuniversitetet.

Upton, D. (2006) Online learning in speech and language therapy: student performance and attitudes. *Education for Health*, 19: 22–31.

Van Merriënboer, J.J.G. and Sweller, J. (2005) Cognitive load theory and complex learning: recent developments and future directions. *Educational Psychology Review*, 17(2): 147–77. DOI:10.1007/s10648-005-3951-0.

Vishwanatham, R., Wilkins, W. and Jevec, T. (1997) The internet as a medium for online instruction. *College and Research Libraries*, 58(5): 433–44.

Von Glasersfeld, E. (1995) A constructivist approach to teaching. In L. Steffe and J. Gale (eds.) *Constructivism in Education* (pp. 3–16). Hillsdale, NJ: Lawrence Erlbaum.

Wiggins, G.P. and McTighe, J. (2005) *Understanding by Design* (2nd edn.). Upper Saddle River, NJ: Prentice Hall.

8

Interactivity options for tutorials

Abstract: Good online information tutorials should effectively incorporate multiple instructional media into the web presence. They can be designed to incorporate many of the expectations that students have for design and interaction. Integrating a clear structure, outlines, multiple examples, exercises, self-assessment tests, and options that learners can pick and choose will offer the broadest flexibility for students. Online tutorials can offer students interactive exercises, realistic simulations of research problems, and immediate feedback to enable them to gauge their progress and refer to relevant parts of the tutorial for review, which can foster critical thinking. This chapter discusses the value of providing interactivity and active learning in tutorials as well as providing examples of exercises and interactivity. Also included are some strategies for incorporating instructional multimedia within tutorials to accommodate different learning styles and abilities, and checklists for the consideration of multimedia inclusion.

Key words: active learning, tutorials, online learning, learner controlled instruction, educational technology, learning activities.

Introduction

Multimedia applications can help with the learning process by providing examples and the ability to practice and work through a concept in ways that might appeal to a broad range of learning styles. This chapter provides a general discussion of the value of providing interactivity and active learning in tutorials as well as examples of exercises and interactivity.

The type of interactivity and exercises used in learning objects varies depending upon the type of software or web applications being used. Many screencasting tutorials serve as demonstrations of a concept, such as how to check out a book, how to use a self-check machine, how to narrow a search, etc. They are particularly useful if they are short. These types of guided demonstrations may serve as quick clips to offer on web pages or within other learning objects if users want to "see and hear" rather than just read how to do something. However, when tutorials are created to supplement or replace face-to-face instruction value is added when there is interactivity. Somoza-Fernández and Abadal's (2009) study found that the teaching methodology used in most tutorials (102 tutorials or 57 percent) was to present the content and consolidate it through exercises. Guided demonstration, such as how to search for information in catalogues or databases, was the second most used methodology (12 percent). They found only two tutorials (1 percent) which used problem-solving methodologies, which they attributed to the difficulty in developing them for online consumption.

Su and Kuo (2010) evaluated 37 tutorials and categorized them according to whether they used the following teaching strategies: active learning, situation simulation, and question-oriented. They found that situation simulation (similar to "guided demonstration" as used by Somoza-Fernández and Abadal above) was the most popular strategy (25 of the 37 tutorials, or 68 percent). Active learning (typically incorporating online exercises or quizzes to encourage interactions between the user and the tutorial, or chat with reference librarians) came in second (20 tutorials, or 54 percent). Question-oriented strategy (which helps students develop information literacy skills through solving an actual problem) amounted to 15 tutorials (41 percent). Although the Somoza-Fernández and Abadal and the Su and Kuo studies may differ in the way they define different teaching strategies found in tutorials, they both reveal that instructional designers are using various active learning and interactive techniques to foster active learning in the tutorials. Learning is an active, interactive process in which learners make meaning from new experiences.

Online tutorials can offer students interactive exercises, realistic simulations of research problems, and immediate feedback to enable them to gauge their progress and refer to relevant parts of the tutorial for review, which can foster critical thinking.

What qualifies as being interactive?

Many library websites that feature screencasting tutorials may describe themselves as being interactive, yet there is nothing really expected of the user, other than clicking on the start button. Some of the students in the usability study carried out for this book described the screencasting tutorial as interactive because they saw the narrator type in terms and work through a search. However, students are passive viewers of the information. Interactive, in this case, may mean that the learner has control over the pace and sequencing of materials (if there is a clickable index). This level of interaction is similar to an electronic textbook, where students can turn pages or jump to various sections. Interactions should be demonstrative, requiring the learner to show they understand a given point before proceeding to new material. There are differences in learning outcomes and in the subjective experiences offered between passive online tutorials (e.g., simply clicking "next" or "continue") and more interactive ones (e.g., students typing searches, answering questions, etc.).

Interactivity, as Hall (1997, p. 4) states, is what "distinguishes an information source from a learning experience." Interactivity contributes to learner motivation, aids learning by providing opportunities for students to practice skills, and allows for the assessment of student understanding at the completion of the learning module. Effective interactivity involves more than simply clicking on buttons or links. Learners expect interactivity to include control of and active engagement in activities (Sims, 2003), and feedback on progress also plays an important role (Reece, 2007).

According to Kolb's theory of how the learning process works, real learning cannot occur without participation in actual experience (MacKeracher, 2004). Therefore, providing students with some concrete, interactive activities to help them practice is important for meaningful learning. The Association of College and Research Libraries (ACRL) Characteristics of Programs of Information Literacy that Illustrate Best Practices (ACRL, 2003) and library researchers outlining best practices in online library instruction (Dewald, 1999b; Tempelman-Kluit, 2006; Reece, 2007) all recommend active learning or interactivity. Several studies have also shown that students expect and prefer interactivity, especially in multimedia learning (Sims, 2003; Markey et al., 2005; Armstrong and Georgas, 2006).

Johnson and Rubin (2011) evaluated 911 peer-reviewed journal articles about interactive computer-based training between 1995 and 2007. They categorized the type of interactivity in the training programs as either (a) machine paced or (b) student paced. Machine-paced interactivity only provided opportunities for the learner to pause or select sections. Student-paced interactivity required the learner to indicate when to advance (e.g., by clicking a "next" button). In their analysis of the results of the 79 articles that they chose to compare, the training that involved interactivity resulted in improved performance. Some of the suggestions they offer for best practices in interactivity include: using scripted instructional sequences; providing a high number of practice items; using auditory delivery; and integrating visuals and graphics in the training.

Incorporating the use of active learning increases intrinsic motivation by engaging the user in the learning process, and makes the tutorial more interesting and engaging (Allen, 1995; Dabbour, 1997; Dewald, 1999a and b; Weston et al., 1999; Dewald et al., 2000). Interactivity is also consistent with constructivist epistemology, which says that students construct their own learning and cannot absorb it passively from someone or something else; so the more active they are the more knowledge they construct (Jonassen et al., 1995; Driscoll, 2000; Vrasidas, 2000).

Interactivity and active learning

Interactivity is the online key to active learning. Students can respond to questions online with radio buttons, image maps, and forms, and they can receive immediate feedback through the use of CGI scripts. Frames allow the introduction of a second activity without leaving the instructional module, such as opening an online catalog in a separate frame for a practice session or a test of the student's newly learned skills. An engaging feature is to include activities to permit the movement of screen objects to clarify ideas and also to allow students to manipulate objects to show their understanding of concepts. Questions that promote evaluation, reflection, and creativity in students can be posed with forms for student writing, and the resulting essays can be reformatted by the computer and printed out for use by students and faculty. These elements allow educators to go beyond the simple presentation of information, allowing them to create web-based instruction that allows students to explore as they prefer, develop their own understanding of concepts and skills, and apply learning in realistic settings.

Chapter 7 discussed the importance of developing meaningful content in learning objects. In addition to content, interactivity, multimedia, and game-like qualities are identified as essential components in an effective online tutorial. An understanding of the importance of these features originated from researchers in the fields of psychology, cognitive science, and STEM (science, technology, education, and math). Library science researchers have benefitted from their work and have begun applying the suggestions to library instruction. For example, the ACRL Instructional Technologies Committee (2007) stated that web tutorials should include interactive exercises such as simulations or quizzes. This same view is shared by many other authors. For instance, as Anderson et al. (2008, p. 61) wrote: "These activities encourage active learning and allow students to respond to what is taught, while self-assessing their own learning." Tutorials should also provide a way to contact a librarian with any questions and provide feedback opportunities to comment on the tutorial's design or usefulness.

Undergraduate students, who may be the target audience for many of the learning objects being developed at higher education institutions, respond positively to the interactivity and the game-like nature possible in tutorials (Armstrong and Georgas, 2006). These digitally-savvy students are familiar with this type of learning environment, and may even expect it. Students are used to multimedia environments and to figuring things out online for themselves (Lippincott, 2005). They tend to value the convenience provided by technology, and expect to be engaged by their environments (Oblinger, 2008).

Active learning encourages students in the learning process to create their own understanding of the subject matter. Learners ideally should be able to choose their own, perhaps guided, paths through new information based on their own ability levels and objectives, and then apply the information to new situations, especially to their own situations. When students are able to see practical application of the knowledge, they are more motivated, and they can more easily merge the new information with their previous experiences. Multimedia is potentially useful in many situations, such as when showing processes in action or in adding opportunities for student interaction with the material in a realistic setting (Betrancourt, 2005).

Some initial considerations

In order to apply effective multimedia interactivity it is important to consider the desired type of student learning and then choose activities and interactions based on that. In multimedia instructional design, this suggests that a task analysis (pre-test) should be carried out to break down the skills and information that are needed in order to learn or perform the educational objective. The multimedia lesson should try to ensure that the learner has sufficient key core knowledge before trying to tackle an overall task that may be beyond the learner's current ability range, causing unnecessary frustration and possibly even causing the student to drop out of the activity. Some of the success for this will depend upon the software being used.

Activities for the student to complete during the screencast or streaming multimedia tutorial can also hinder learning by contributing to working memory overload. To minimize activity-related memory load, all activities should be within the capabilities of the students and the content and activities should be appropriate for the students' level of knowledge. If possible, different levels of activities should be offered so that the learner could choose by ability level or progress through activities sequentially.

There should be no technical difficulties to overcome. The technologies used should make everything easy to understand and to perform without assistance: from the initial click to start a screencast through any other tasks the student needs to complete, including any interactive exercises or quizzes. The interface and navigation should be clear and simple.

Planning for interactivity

When planning a screencast or multimedia instruction project, activities and interactions should be chosen that are based on the desired type of student learning; they should also integrate the steps and activities into a broader conceptual framework for students and show how they fit into larger processes. This can be useful to global learners. Activities should be chosen that help develop both higher levels of learning (evaluation and analysis) as well as lower levels of learning (understanding and applying).

A number of ways in which to accomplish interactivity were discussed in Chapter 6. Techniques such as using frames, buttons, forms, CGI-scripting, or screencasting software can be used to bring in a second activity without leaving the instructional module, such as opening an online catalog or a particular database in a separate frame for a practice session or a test of the student's newly learned skills. Other techniques such as drop-down menus, drag and drop objects, and games and puzzles can also be used to engage the learner. Some of these allow the learner to move screen objects to clarify ideas or to answer questions; this allows students to manipulate objects to show their understanding of concepts, which is helpful for the learner who likes to learn by doing.

Interactive activities

Learning transfer, or the ability of learners to apply what they have learned to actual situations, is a basic goal of teaching and learning (Commission on Behavioral and Social Sciences, 1999), but effective transfer of learning is difficult to achieve (see Mestre 2003, 2005 and references therein). Learning enough to apply new knowledge usually requires active engagement or practice in a realistic and authentic context (Halpern and Hakel, 2003; Nguyen and Clark, 2005; Clark et al., 2006; Dunlap et al., 2007). People are more motivated to learn when instruction is seen as relevant, and motivation increases learning success (Stolovitch and Keeps, 2002). Ideally, multimedia tutorials should include interactive activities that help students practice the skills and concepts being taught.

Tutorial content and activities should be appropriate for the students' level of knowledge. For example, one effective way to present information to beginners is through worked examples, which present a problem and then show the steps required to solve that problem (Renkl, 2005). At that point, a question can be posed to evaluate if the student understood the concept and can apply it. Research in cognitive science has shown that worked examples reduce memory load, hence allowing students to focus on what they need to understand (Sweller and Cooper, 1985; Paas and Van Merrienboer, 1994).

Interactivity should also allow the student to have some control. Control over the pace of the multimedia or screencast is one way to accommodate different ability levels and learning styles. There are three options for learner control over multimedia: control over content, control over help, and control over pace (Clark and Mayer, 2003). Control over the sequencing of content involves letting students have some choice over what path to take and what to do next. Control over access to help or learning support involves the ability to click on links for additional explanations or "bonus" material for remedial help, or the ability to find information about how to ask questions. The pacing principle (Moreno and Mayer, 2000) states that learners should be able to control the speed of, and pauses in, the multimedia lesson. This can be accomplished to a certain extent by including a control bar (generally generated in screencasting software). The control bar allows the learner to pause, rewind, and fast-forward the video. Students are then able to repeat sections or skip around, while engaging with the information on their own terms and at their point of need. This process can help them to become effective and independent learners. Researchers have found that learners prefer to have control over the pace of multimedia tutorials and that instruction is more effective when the learner has control (Kaplowitz and Contini, 1998; Dewald, 1999b; Holman, 2000; Fourie, 2001; Betrancourt, 2005; Veronikas and Maushak, 2005; Mayer, 2006). A table of contents with section markers should be available at all times to allow students to select their information.

For the novice learner

Novice learners are not always good at creating their own explanations for why or how processes work (Renkl, 2005). Examples should help learners make connections with the underlying concepts and principles rather than focusing just on the mechanics. This connection between the concrete and the abstract also helps students develop their critical thinking. Many tutorials simply demonstrate how to do something step by step (e.g., create a successful search strategy) but omit the principles that could apply to other situations.

Strategies to aid novice learners through examples include:

- Give an overview of a search process, then a demonstration of how a search works step by step, then give a summary of what happened and why.

- Give more than one example of a search, each with slightly different contexts (e.g., two different databases), so that students can see the principles that different searches have in common. Using multiple examples helps students create a better conceptual model of how the search process works, and therefore helps them to better apply what they learn to different situations (Commission on Behavioral and Social Sciences, 1999).

For the advanced learner

Advanced learners may not need or appreciate the repetitiveness of the above process. If possible, provide different paths for learners so that they can choose how much information they receive. Another strategy is to include a link to a video, another web page, or a pop-up window with more information for learners who do need extra help.

Branching and different learning styles

Successful tutorials include fundamental design elements that provide for students' varying learning styles. One way to accomplish this is with a "branching" design that allows students to choose both the order in which they wish to proceed and the level of difficulty (Dewald, 1999a; Fourie, 2001). This enables students who require more practice to receive it, while those students who have grasped a particular concept can confirm the fact and move on. Some tutorials also provide a guided tour in which a logical sequence is suggested (Cox and Housewright, 2001) or use a decision tree-based structure that mimics the research process (Kaplowitz and Contini, 1998). These options allow for multiple pathways through the tutorial, ensuring the flexibility that accommodates users of many levels.

Branching examples

The University of Arizona provides branching within its tutorials. When the student answers the question shown in Figure 8.1 they are taken to a page that helps them at their knowledge level (one page if they know the name of the resource and another if they do not).

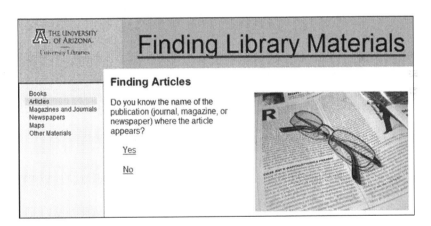

Figure 8.1 Example of branching from the University of Arizona University Libraries

Source: http://www.library.arizona.edu/help/tutorials/index.html

This type of branching activity is an effective strategy for the novice or the advanced learner. It builds on their previous knowledge and allows them to continue more quickly to their goal.

The option to navigate their own pathway through a tutorial and to access it from a distance also increases students' ability to receive instruction at their point and time of need. This both aids in the assimilation of knowledge (Dewald, 1999b) and allows the learning experience to be self-directed. Several scholars, including librarian scholars, have emphasized the importance of self-directed learning in teaching critical thinking skills to adult learners (Knowles, 1980, 1990; Gailbraith, 1991; Currie, 2000).

Activities that simulate a real context

Good activities should be meaningful to the learner and simulate a real context. As part of the interactive exercises, realistic simulations of research problems were discovered to be essential to the efficacy of tutorial instruction aimed at fostering critical thinking (Kaplowitz and Contini, 1998; Fourie, 2001; Salpeter, 2003). Scenario-based e-learning is considered to be useful with regard to enhancing student learning (Siddiqui et al., 2008). This can comprise short stories about people and their activities. They are often illustrative, focusing on particular novel or desirable features of a service or product, or the situation of someone who needs to solve a problem, or they can be used to compare and contrast extremes (with consequences). Scenarios can also encourage reflection. They can be scripted in narrative form or as conversations between two or more people, and they can include activities and choices for the student to make along the way.

When creating scenarios or simulations it is best to include situations, exercises, databases, dilemmas, and questions that students will actually encounter and that will help them complete tasks or solve problems they will actually need to solve. Simulations can provide valuable experience in applying new knowledge, either to contribute to the learning process or as an assessment of the learner's understanding. Programs such as Macromedia's Authorware or basic Flash allow designers to create exercises that allow students to move and manipulate objects on the screen. The use of graphics and motion can demonstrate activities that supplement explanations or allow users to engage in an activity that exhibits their understanding. Flash-based simulations such as drag and drop actions can be created to illustrate concepts (e.g., the movement of Venn diagrams to illustrate combining terms with Boolean connectors; placing books in appropriate subject boxes; or putting citations in the correct sequence). Figure 8.2 shows an example of a drag and drop activity that helps students to format a citation correctly. This tutorial does not include a pause feature or audio, however.

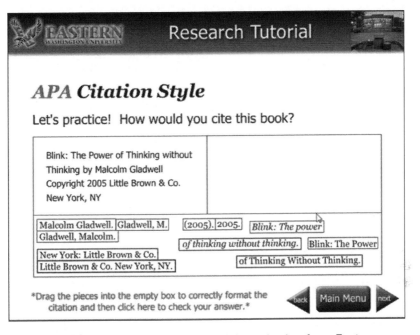

Figure 8.2 Example of a drag and drop citation from Eastern Washington University

Note: this version is out of date and reflects previous versions of APA and MLA. Regardless, the drag and drop interactivity is the feature of note here

Source: http://support.library.ewu.edu/reference/tutorial/flash/citation.html. Credits: Jonathan Grubb, who did all the work in Flash, and Ielleen R. Miller, Coordinator of Instruction.

The successful learning of even more complex knowledge requires the student to engage in the production of new knowledge, self-evaluation, reflection, and application of that knowledge. Tutorials should include questions and guidance to foster evaluation and reflection in the learner. Here are a few suggestions for ways in which to help students engage with more information if desired:

- Create simulations that engage students in exploratory-type activities.

- Provide a link to a search engine or website that enables students to try out a concept that was just presented in the tutorial.

- Provide links that go into more detail, with a pop-up asking "Want to know more? Click here."

- Provide a guided path, such as a framed table of contents, to allow free movement at any time.

Problem-based learning

Problem recognition tasks and problem-based learning can be used to foster recognition and identification skills. Creating these types of activities will focus on the student's ability to identify a problem and develop a solution to solve it. "Bloom's taxonomy hypothesizes that using problem-based learning will increase both the relevance and long-term retention of information learned" (Gilbert et al., 2006, p. 162). Scenarios and problem-based exercises should challenge students to think about an issue, respond to a question, and get immediate feedback.

Developing effective questions

Questions offer a way for students to process and reflect on the information that has been presented. They can also be used to evaluate knowledge and can promote creativity (especially if students are required to write responses). With questions and prompts, students are guided through complex thought processes to apply what they learn to their own situations. The questions, whether included throughout each module or at the end of the tutorial, should lead the student through a process, such as focusing a research topic, or developing or choosing terms to search in online databases, etc.

Johnson and Rubin (2011) evaluated 911 peer-reviewed journal articles published between 1995 and 2007 about interactive computer-based training. Based on their analysis they suggested some best practices for developing interactivity, including the following which pertain to questions and feedback:

- use a high number of practice items;
- keep responses at the overt level, as opposed to the covert level;
- provide options for learners to respond in the form of composing a response (fill-in-the-blank) rather than formats that merely ask the learner to select a response (multiple choice);
- provide feedback for all possible answers, both correct and incorrect;
- make incentives contingent upon specific performance during learning, not just simply for completing the program. This may foster improved performance.

Many tutorials use multiple-choice exercises, perhaps due to the limitations of the software. Even so, the construction of the questions, the choices, and the responses can be controlled by the designer, as well as the number of practice items and incentives throughout.

Corrective responses provided in exercises

Exercises should provide scaffolding not only in the original presentation of the information, but also in the corrective answers. Feedback should include corrective responses for all responses, rather than simply indicating if something was correct or incorrect. Students are thus provided with additional details and instruction when reading what the "correct" response was and why. With a multiple-choice option, instead of each response simply stating what the correct answer is, i.e., a, or b, or c, each response should also explain why. If a student selects an incorrect choice, there must have been something that led them to believe it might be correct, so addressing that (briefly) in the response may help them in the future. In some of the screencasting software there is a limit to the number of words that can be included in the responses. This means that the designer will need to think creatively about how to include helpful responses. Figures 8.3 and 8.4 give some examples of corrective responses.

In Figures 8.3 and 8.4, the feedback indicates whether the answer was correct and then reiterates why or provides additional instructional

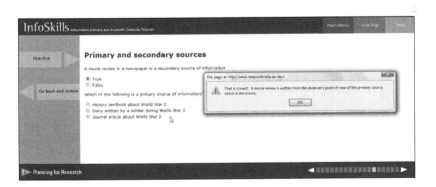

Figure 8.3 Example of feedback from the University of Newcastle

Source: http://www.newcastle.edu.au/Resources/Divisions/Academic/Library/information-skills/infoskills/index.html

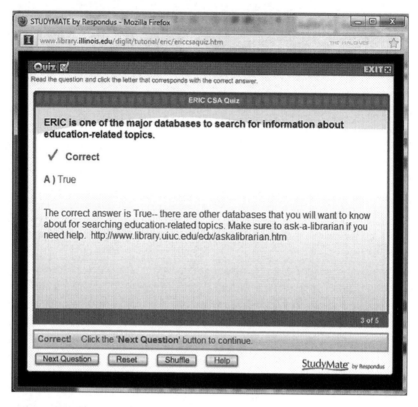

Figure 8.4 Correct response to a quiz from the University of Illinois

Source: http://www.library.illinois.edu/diglit/tutorial/eric/ericcsaquiz.htm

information. Figure 8.5 does the same thing using the quiz features in StudyMate. In addition to indicating that the response was incorrect, it also indicates what the correct answer is and why.

If feasible, it is useful to provide a link to explain or review the topic further. Depending upon the software, the student can be directed automatically to the point in the tutorial where that topic was covered. If not, it may be possible to include a hot spot or jump link to the chapter marking within the tutorial index so that students can review the information.

Exercises should also give students opportunities to apply skills in novel situations. By providing examples in which the skill is used in

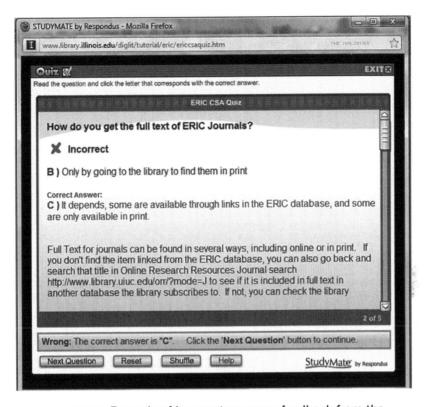

Figure 8.5 Example of incorrect response feedback from the University of Illinois

Source: http://www.library.illinois.edu/diglit/tutorial/eric/ericcsaquiz.htm

multiple contexts and by giving the student access to expert thought processes, a model for transfer is provided.

Using form boxes

With form boxes, students can be asked to type a response, write short essays, or address questions they wish to explore. Some programs have the ability to compile the individual's answers and present them on a new page to be printed out by the student and, presumably, to be used for research and shared with the course instructor. In some tutorials which use web pages, forms are frequently used for this purpose and responses can be emailed to both the student and the instructor.

Options that include typing

In addition to creating pop-up windows that link to a live website so that students can follow the tutorial and click or type information, other options also exist. The University of Texas at Austin created a web-based tutorial with form boxes for students to use. It allows students to type in phrases, and then provides scaffolding to take them through the process using their information (see Figure 8.6).

This is a very individualized approach to learning. The learner needs to reflect during each part of the process and then type responses. There are options for viewing examples on each screen to guide the student further. Students in the Mestre (2010) study were better able to recreate a search when they had followed the tutorial and entered their own terms in the database search, rather than when simply watching the narrator do a search. Figure 8.7 shows an example of a tutorial that requires the student to type in responses. Those responses are then used to generate the next task.

During each stage of the tutorial the student sees the previous information s/he typed. The student is then guided through each stage by building on that previous information. Eventually, the program combines the results into a search string that is then fed into the library catalog. The process scaffolds the student each step of the way, from topic development through to actually searching the library catalog. The program also allows students to email results (see Figure 8.8).

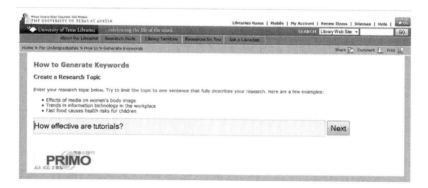

Figure 8.6 Ability to type in a phrase from the University of Texas Libraries

Source: http://lib.utexas.edu/keywords/

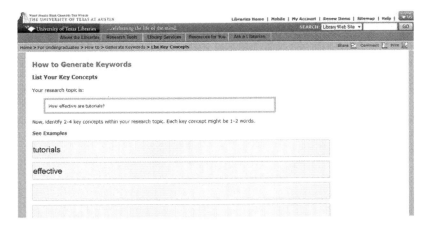

Figure 8.7 Forms that require students to type from the University of Texas Libraries

Source: *http://lib.utexas.edu/keywords/*

Figure 8.8 Email option form, the University of Texas Libraries

Source: *http://lib.utexas.edu/keywords/*

Seeking help

Of great value is the provision of live help while working through online instruction. This can be done by providing links to allow students to seek librarians' help through chat or instant messaging reference services.

Help within a tutorial

A tutorial can also include multiple "extra help" points for students. Figure 8.9 gives examples of icons that could be used when an additional point of information is available, such as a video clip, example, or more thorough explanation. These "extras" allow for students to choose whether or not to seek out more in-depth guidance.

Figure 8.9   Icons to indicate extra information available on a topic

Multimedia suggestions

Most commercial programs, like Adobe's Captivate and TechSmith's Camtasia, can create various types of interactivity, such as clicking on the screen and making something happen, entering text for a search, or inserting quiz questions. Adding interactivity in a screencast or streaming video tutorial can be a challenge, depending upon the software. However, there may be other ways to engage learners. For example, interactivity could be introduced by suggesting practice exercises at the end of a tutorial for students to try on their own, or by posing questions part way through the tutorial for students to think about.

Choice of audio

All tutorials with sound need to be captioned, or a script needs to be provided. Most screencasting tutorial software provides an option for users to turn on or turn off the closed captioning (cc). However, it is not as common to find tutorials that give the option to turn off the audio. Rutger's University Library tutorials include an option for students to choose whether or not they want to hear the audio; in either case the user is able to click through at their own speed (see Figure 8.10).

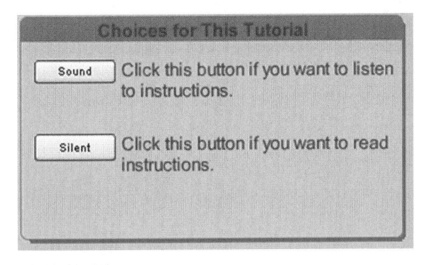

Figure 8.10   Rutger's University Library tutorial choices

Source: http://www.rci.rutgers.edu/~estec/tutorials/scholarly.htm

Animations and games

Flash elements can be incorporated into tutorials to allow for clickable regions. These provide a level of interactivity that can simulate games. Clickable regions (or hot spots) can be used for graphs, pictures, maps, or other objects. Some tutorials also take advantage of animations.

The tutorial shown in Figure 8.11 is an example of using clickable objects. In this case the student is asked to choose a player. When the student rolls the mouse over an individual more information appears about the character.

The game-like nature of some tutorials can be enticing. Encouraging interaction through games or simulations creates user involvement, which generates excitement. However, there is a balancing act needed in the creation of games and simulations. Both are unreal situations used to train for real situations. The engagement comes from a competitive aspect. There is a risk that the student will focus completely on the game and concentrate on beating the game rather than concentrating on the questions or statement being posed. To help with transferability, care should be taken to create game features that are engaging but not all-absorbing.

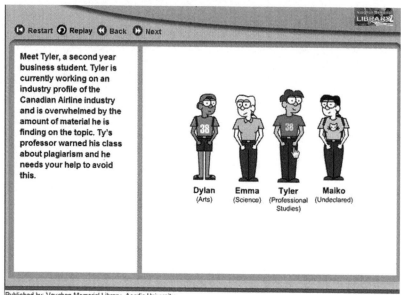

Published by: Vaughan Memorial Library, Acadia University

Figure 8.11 Use of clickable objects from a Vaughan Memorial Library tutorial

Source: http://library.acadiau.ca/tutorials/plagiarism

Pick and choose options

In the next example by Stony Brook University Libraries (see Figure 8.12), students are allowed to choose their path through the modules. This is no different from a table of contents but may appeal to students visually. They can see that all of the steps in the modules need to be completed in order to finish the research circle. As they roll over the name of the module more information about it is revealed. The tutorial provides multiple options for different learning preferences.

The screenshot in Figure 8.13 shows a typical screen that provides consistent navigation at the bottom, an option for a non-Flash version, an illustration, and underlined words that students can click on if they want a pop-up window to explain more. The screenshot shows the pop-up that appears if the word "indexes" is clicked. The tutorial was created using HTML, CSS, and a little bit of JavaScript.

In addition, the developers of the tutorial shown in Figure 8.13 used interactive screens (such as a Think Fast game, and Tiltometer) using

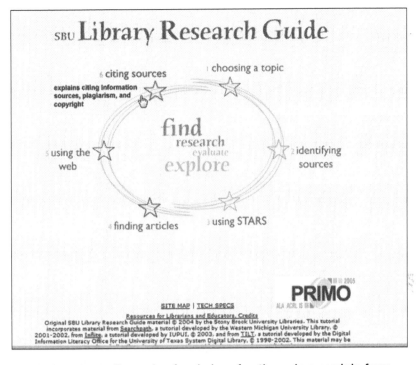

Figure 8.12 Example of a choice of pathway in a module from Stony Brook University

Source: http://www.library.stonybrook.edu/tutorial/index.html

Figure 8.13 Example of an extra-help pop-up from Stony Brook University

Source: http://www.library.stonybrook.edu/tutorial/mod1/06database.shtml#null

Flash that they got from another tutorial (TILT). Often, tutorial developers will give permission to download files and reuse them as is or to modify them.

An example of a clickable map is shown in Figure 8.14. Developed at the university library at Sonoma State University, it allows students to pick and choose a topic and then leads them through videos, pop-up windows with screenshots and information, or PDF documents with screenshots, step-by-step instructions, and links. After a quiz they can print out a certificate of completion. (Note that the institution has requested that it be noted that the quiz was a legacy from an earlier web page, that they are still developing an assessment for the tutorials, and that the quiz will be replaced.)

The UCI (University of California Irvine) Libraries have a series of tutorials (see Figure 8.15) which offer two ways of choosing information. In addition to selecting the module at the top of the page, they can also choose a more specific section in the left-hand column.

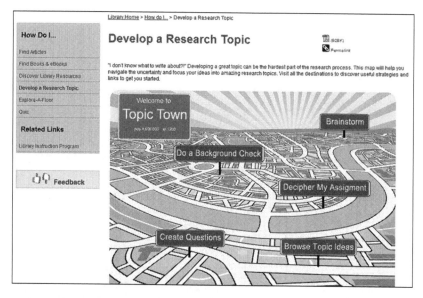

Figure 8.14 Clickable map example from the university library at Sonoma State University

Source: http://library.sonoma.edu/howdoi/researchtopic.php

Figure 8.15	Navigation options from the University of California Irvine

Source: http://www.lib.uci.edu/how/tutorials/LibraryWorkshop/begin.html

Credits: University of California Irvine Libraries Department of Education and Outreach

Pop-up exercises

In static web page tutorials, as well as in some screencast tutorials, it is possible to include a variety of multimedia options, including video clips and pop-up windows that allow students to work along with the tutorial. The example shown in Figure 8.16, from the University of Arizona, includes a variety of options for multiple learning styles. The tutorial provides a step-by-step approach (and table of contents), as well as video clips for the visual or auditory learner. These clips are interspersed throughout the tutorial to help students who want to learn more. Instead of the video clip opening in a new window it appears embedded in the same page. In addition, students can click on various segments and a new window opens to allow them to try a search.

The tutorial from the Carle Clinic Association shown in Figure 8.17 illustrates options such as a progress bar, an opportunity to get more information on the topic, and a feature that allows the user to write notes that can be printed out later. The "my notes" feature is very helpful for reflective learners.

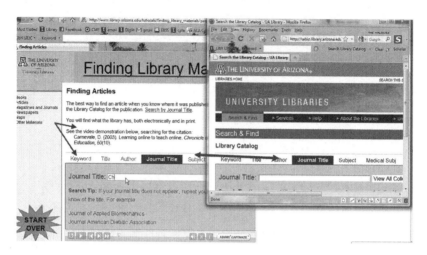

Figure 8.16 Example of pop-ups for exercises from the University of Arizona University Libraries

Source: http://www.library.arizona.edu/help/tutorials/index.html

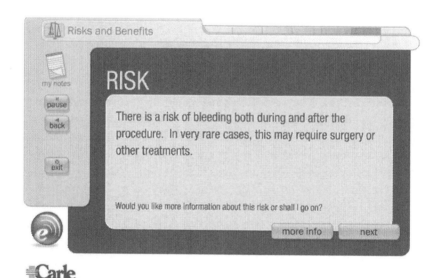

Figure 8.17 Carle Clinic tutorials

Source: http://www.carle.org/default.aspx

Concerns about adding multimedia

Overdoing it with animations

Flash elements provide excellent options for interactivity. However, if used badly they can create large, complicated animations that take a long time to download and don't add any value. It is better to have small, well-thought out examples of Flash animations that will add interest or functionality (and not get in the way). Some tutorials add a sound or something flashy when a certain response is chosen. During usability studies students should be asked if the animation is helpful and adds to the experience. Students will say if it is a waste of their time to watch or wait for it, or if it is a distraction.

Bandwith

Connectivity speed should still be a concern for designers. Multimedia applications take up tremendous resources in bandwidth (data rate). The amount, quality, and nature of digital media depend on the bandwidth of the delivery mechanism. Screencasting software provides options for rendering the product into multiple file sizes. It is still good practice to provide alternate formats for a tutorial (static web page with screenshots, link to a PDF file, link to a script).

Learning style considerations

The implementation of interactive online tutorials can provide flexible methods and options for students and can accommodate different learning styles. Depending on learning preference, students may approach exercises differently. Some learners prefer to have the learning material presented before the examples (reflective and sequential learners), whereas intuitive learners may prefer to have the examples before the learning material. Graf and Kinshuk (2006) studied students' behavior in online courses according to learning style preferences. The FSLSM was used in that study. The reflective learners spent more time on examples and dealt more intensively with outlines than active learners. Active learners performed better on questions dealing with facts. The sensing learners spent more time answering tests and revising them than intuitive learners. They also revisited learning material examples more often.

Sequential learners tended to start at the beginning of each chapter whereas global learners tended to skip learning objects and visit the course overview page more often.

Table 8.1 was developed by Graf (2007) to indicate various learner preferences using the FSLSM Index of Learning Styles (ILS) to show when outlines, exercises, examples, and content should be incorporated.

Table 8.1 *Adaptivity in Learning Management Systems Focusing on Learning Styles*, from Graf (2007)

Learning style by ILS	Features	Not recommended in VLE
Active	Many exercises Self-assessment tests Outlines once before content objects	Examples
Reflective	Outlines additionally between topics First the learning material in terms of content objects Afterwards examples A conclusion is presented immediately after all content objects	Exercises Self-assessment tests
Sensing	Many exercises Examples are presented before the abstract learning material Exercises and self-assessment tests only after the learning material	
Intuitive	Self-assessment tests and exercises are recommended to be presented before the learning material Examples are presented after the abstract content	Presentation of outlines between topics Examples and exercises
Sequential	Presenting first the learning material, then some examples, and afterwards a self-assessment test and some exercises Outlines are presented only before the content objects	
Global	Providing outlines additionally between the topics Presenting a conclusion straight after the content Providing a high number of examples after the learning material Examples, exercises, and self-assessment tests at the end	

The right-hand column indicates what was found not to be recommended in VLEs (virtual learning environments) for these preferences.

As indicated above, and as covered in previous chapters, learners differ in how they prefer information and exercises to be presented. This is summarized in Table 8.1 because of the added relevance that interactivity has for various learning styles. Global learners like to understand the big picture, and so prefer outlines. Because active learners like to learn by trying things out, they may benefit from multiple exercises, as well as a self-assessment test at the end of the tutorial. Reflective learners, who like to think things through, benefit from having content objects included before and after examples and tasks. Examples and exercises are important for sensing learners since they like learning data and facts. Intuitive learners may prefer the self-assessment tests and exercises up front since they like challenges. Depending on the results, they may then look for the content that explains the areas they answered incorrectly. Sequential learners like to learn in linear steps, and prefer to have examples first, then the self-assessment test and exercises (Graf, 2007).

Carmo et al. (2006) studied which type of activities can be used to support different learning styles in the learning environment. They discovered (through the use of the FSLSM and the ILS) that visual students had difficulties processing textual answers. The authors suggested also including visual activities in order to graphically create solutions. They found that visual/active learners were most likely to give answers graphically, and visual/reflective students did so using text. Carmo et al. suggest including problem-solving activities, recorded lectures, and discussions. In their study, sensory learners presented weak abstraction capacity so the authors suggest the inclusion of more examples and data. Overall, they conclude that the materials presented and used in activities should be a blend of concrete information and abstract concepts.

In addition, to help learners who prefer not to read large quantities of text – such as sequential, active, global, and visual learners – clear pathways and outlines are helpful. Interactive testing, exercises, diagrams, photographs, and other visuals can supplement the text.

When considering interactivity for tutorials and learning objects there are questions that should be asked to ascertain whether or not appropriate multimedia and exercises are being used. Appendix 6 provides a chart of strategies for incorporating instructional multimedia within tutorials to accommodate different learning styles and abilities. Those suggestions were derived from the various research studies covered in this book, and especially from student remarks and observations from the Mestre (2010) study. What follows now is an abbreviated checklist that may help when considering the inclusion of multimedia in tutorials.

A checklist for considering multimedia interaction

1. Are there a range of activities (especially remedial activities and extension activities) to meet the needs of learners with different abilities? What additional resources will learners have access to?
2. Are activities based on students' prior knowledge and skills?
3. Does the multimedia add meaning, value, or clarity to the situation?
4. Does the technology support the activities?
5. Are instructions clearly stated so that learners can progress through the activities effortlessly?
6. Do learners have choices about how they carry out a task?
7. How is support and feedback adapted to an individual learner's needs?
8. How will learners be assessed for each goal or outcome?

Conclusion

Today's students have been raised on the fast-paced edutainment in a media environment that specializes in short messages and multimedia, with news dispatched in sound bites and snippets of stories (Pressley, 2008). Good online information tutorials should effectively incorporate multiple instructional media into the web presence to convey the instruction in multi-stimulating ways (Zhang, 2006). They can be styled to incorporate many of the expectations that students have in terms of design and interaction. Integrating a clear structure and including outlines, multiple examples, exercises, self-assessment tests, and options from which learners can pick and choose will offer the broadest flexibility for learners. The use of interactivity can help students progress, providing a series of interactive exercises, such as clickable image maps, branching exercises, choices, and typing responses. This approach can help hold student attention and reinforce important skills by applying a hands-on approach.

Multimedia, screencasts, and other types of animated media put high demands on short-term memory, since a lot of information (text, graphics, audio, motion) needs to be processed simultaneously (Betrancourt, 2005). This means that it can be difficult for people to process information from multimedia effectively. Studies have shown that instruction using static graphics and visuals, like labeled screenshots, can be as effective or more effective for learning since it places fewer demands on our short-term memory (Clark and Lyons, 2004; Mestre 2010), leading to better understanding and retention. Since multimedia is inherently more difficult for learners to process, it should only be used as an instructional tool when it is helpful for learning. The first and most important question to ask when designing screencasts or streaming video tutorials is whether the multimedia is needed at all, or whether the instruction could be delivered just as effectively some other way. Multimedia is potentially useful in many situations, such as when showing processes in action, or adding opportunities for student interaction with the material in a realistic setting (Betrancourt, 2005). If it isn't necessary, however, avoid doing a multimedia tutorial or screencast.

To accommodate a broad range of learning styles, web and course designers need to move beyond text-based interactions and include visual or kinesthetic modalities, as well as intuition and thinking exercises. Reflective activities such as case studies, simulations, scenarios, concept mapping, mental imagery, or those that are problem based and require original responses (such as fill in the blanks), foster critical thinking. For the non-textual visual learner, one should add multiple sensory options such as animations, hands-on simulations, video clips, charts, pictures, graphic illustrations, and diagrams, as well as audio files for auditory learners. In addition to providing sequenced-learning strategies, the design of the site or tutorial should be flexible in order to allow students to choose the content, activities, and exercises, rather than being forced to proceed at the designer's pace. Thought should also be given to ways of including relevance and personalization for students and to allow students to choose a topic of personal interest. A self-directed, active learning approach (where learners are given the option of selecting life events and experiences as the basis of learning) should also be a goal, as should the ability of students to control their progress, and to get immediate feedback in a friendly, supportive manner.

References

ACRL Instructional Technologies Committee (2007) *Tips for Developing Effective Web-based Library Instruction.* Chicago, IL: Association of College & Research Libraries. Available at: *http://www.ala.org/ala/acrlbucket/is/iscommittees/webpages/teachingmethods/tips.htm.*

Allen, E.E. (1995) Active learning and teaching: improving postsecondary library instruction. *Reference Librarian,* 24(51–2): 89–103.

Anderson, R.P., Wilson, S.P., Livingston, M.B. and LoCicero, A.D. (2008) Characteristics and content of medical library tutorials: a review. *Journal of the American Medical Association,* 96(1): 61–3. DOI:10.3163/1536-5050.96.1.61.

Armstrong, A. and Georgas, H. (2006) Using interactive technology to teach information literacy concepts to undergraduate students. *Reference Services Review,* 34(4): 491–7.

Association of College and Research Libraries (2003) *Characteristics of Programs of Information Literacy that Illustrate Best Practices: A Guideline.* Available at: *http://www.ala.org/ ala/acrl/acrlstandards/characteristics.htm.*

Betrancourt, M. (2005) The animation and interactivity principles in multimedia learning. In R.E. Mayer (ed.) *Cambridge Handbook of Multimedia Learning* (pp. 287–96). Cambridge: Cambridge University Press.

Carmo, L., Gomez, A., Pereira, F. and Mendez A.J. (2006) Learning styles and problem solving strategies. *Proceedings of the 3rd E-learning Conference: Computer Science Education,* Coimbra, Portugal, September 2006.

Clark, R.C. and Lyons, C. (2004) *Graphics for Learning: Proven Guidelines for Planning, Designing and Evaluating Visuals in Training Materials.* San Francisco, CA: Pfeiffer/Wiley.

Clark, R.C. and Mayer, R.E. (2003) *E-learning and the Science of Instruction.* San Francisco, CA: Jossey-Bass.

Clark, R.E., Feldon, D.F. and Choi, S. (2006) Five critical issues for web-based instructional design research and practice. In H.F. O'Neil and R.S. Perez (eds.) *Web-based Learning: Theory, Research, and Practice* (pp. 343–70). Mahwah, NJ: Lawrence Erlbaum Associates.

Commission on Behavioral and Social Sciences (1999) Learning and transfer. In J.D. Bransford et al. (eds.) *How People Learn: Brain, Mind, Experience and School* (pp. 39–66). Washington, DC: National Academies Press.

Cox, S. and Housewright, E. (2001) Teaching from the web: constructing a library learning environment where connections can be made. *Library Trends,* 50(1): 28–46.

Currie, C.L. (2000) Facilitating adult learning: the role of the academic librarian. *Reference Librarian,* 33(69–70): 219–31.

Dabbour, K.S. (1997) Applying active learning methods to the design of library instruction for a freshman seminar. *College and Research Libraries,* 58(4): 299–308.

Dewald, N.H. (1999a) Transporting good library instruction practices into the web environment: an analysis of online tutorials. *Journal of Academic Librarianship,* 25(1): 26–31.

Dewald, N.H. (1999b) Web-based library instruction: what is good pedagogy? *Information Technology and Libraries*, 18(1): 26–31.

Dewald, N., Scholz-Crane, A., Booth, A. and Levine, C. (2000) Information literacy at a distance: instructional design issues. *Journal of Academic Librarianship*, 26(1): 33–44.

Driscoll, M.P. (2000) *Psychology of Learning for Instruction* (2nd edn.). Needham Heights, MA: Allyn and Bacon.

Dunlap, J.C., Sobel, D. and Sands, D.I. (2007) Supporting students' cognitive processing in online courses: designing for deep and meaningful student-to-content interactions. *TechTrends*, 51(4): 20–31.

Fourie, I. (2001) The use of CAI for distance teaching in the formulation of search strategies. *Library Trends*, 50(1): 110–29.

Gailbraith, M.W. (1991) *Facilitating Adult Learning: A Transitional Process.* Malabar, FL: Robert E. Krieger.

Gilbert, L., Mengxiong, L., Matoush, T. and Whitlatch, J. (2006) Assessing digital reference and online instructional services in an integrated public/ university library. *The Reference Librarian*, 46(95–6): 149–72.

Graf, S. (2007) *Adaptivity in Learning Management Systems Focusing on Learning Styles.* Ph.D. thesis. Vienna University of Technology.

Graf, S. and Kinshuk, S.G. (2006) Considering learning styles in learning management systems: investigating the behavior of students in an online course. In *Proceedings of the First IEEE International Workshop on Semantic Media Adaptation and Personalization (SMAP 2006)* (pp. 25–30). Athens, Greece: IEEE Press.

Hall, B. (1997) *Web-based Training Cookbook.* New York: John Wiley & Sons.

Halpern, D.F. and Hakel, M.D. (2003) Applying the science of learning to the university and beyond: teaching for long-term retention and transfer. *Change*, 35(4): 36–41.

Holman, L. (2000) A comparison of computer-assisted instruction and classroom bibliographic instruction. *Reference and User Services Quarterly*, 40(1): 53–60.

Johnson, D.A. and Rubin, S. (2011) Effectiveness of interactive computer-based instruction: a review of studies published between 1995 and 2007. *Journal of Organizational Behavior Management*, 31(1): 55–94. Available at: *http://dx. doi.org/10.1080/01608061.2010.541821.*

Jonassen, D.H., Davidson, M., Collins, M., Campbell, J. and Haag B.B. (1995) Constructivism and computer-mediated communication in distance education. *American Journal of Distance Education*, 9(2): 7–25.

Kaplowitz, J. and Contini, J. (1998) Computer-assisted instruction: is it an option for bibliographic instruction in large undergraduate survey classes? *College & Research Libraries*, 59(1): 19–27.

Knowles, M. (1980) *The Modern Practice of Adult Education: From Pedagogy to Andragogy.* New York: Cambridge.

Knowles, M. (1990) *The Adult Learner: A Neglected Species* (4th edn.). Houston, TX: Gulf Publishing.

Lippincott, J.K. (2005) Net generation students and libraries. *EDUCAUSE Review*, 40(2): 56–66.

MacKeracher, D. (2004) *Making Sense of Adult Learning* (2nd edn.). Toronto, ON: University of Toronto Press.

Markey, K., Armstrong, A., De Groote, S., Fosmire, M., Fuderer, L. et al. (2005) Testing the effectiveness of interactive multimedia for library-user education. *Portal: Libraries and the Academy*, 5(4): 527–44.

Mayer, R.E. (2006) Ten research-based principles of multimedia learning. In H. O'Neil and R. Perez (eds.) *Web-based Learning: Theory, Research, and Practice* (pp. 371–90). Mahwah, NJ: Lawrence Erlbaum.

Mestre, J. (2003) Transfer of learning: issues and research agenda. Report of a workshop held at the National Science Foundation. Available at: *http://www.nsf.gov/pubs/2003/nsf03212/nsf03212.pdf*.

Mestre, J. (ed.) (2005) *Transfer of Learning from a Modern Multidisciplinary Perspective*. Greenwich, CT: Information Age.

Mestre, L.S. (2010) Matching up learning styles with learning objects: what's effective? *Journal of Library Administration*, 50(7–8): 808–82.

Moreno, R. and Mayer, R.E. (2000) A coherence effect in multimedia learning: the case for minimizing irrelevant sounds in the design of multimedia instructional messages. *Journal of Educational Psychology*, 92: 117–25.

Nguyen, F and Clark, R.C. (2005) Efficiency in e-learning: proven instructional methods for faster, better online learning. *Learning Solutions*, November. Available at: *http://www.clarktraining.com/content/articles/Guild_E-Learning.pdf*.

Oblinger, D. (2008) Growing up with Google: what it means to education. *Emerging Technologies for Learning*, 3: 11–29. Available at: *http://partners.becta.org.uk/index.php?section¼rh&rid¼13768*.

Paas, F.G.W.C. and Van Merrienboer, J.J.G. (1994) Variability of worked examples and transfer of geometrical problem solving skills: a cognitive-load approach. *Journal of Educational Psychology*, 86: 122–33.

Pressley, L. (2008) Using videos to reach site visitors: a toolkit for today's student. *Computers in Libraries*, 28(6): 18–22.

Reece, G.J. (2007) Critical thinking and cognitive transfer: implications for the development of online information literacy tutorials. *Research Strategies*, 20(4): 482–93.

Renkl, A. (2005) The worked-out examples principle in multimedia learning. In R.E. Mayer (ed.) *Cambridge Handbook of Multimedia Learning* (pp. 229–45). Cambridge: Cambridge University Press.

Salpeter, J. (2003) Web literacy and critical thinking: a teacher's tool kit. *Technology and Learning*, 23(8): 22–34.

Siddiqui, A., Khan, M. and Akhtar, S. (2008) Supply chain simulator: a scenario-based educational tool to enhance student learning. *Computers and Education*, 51(1): 252–61.

Sims, R. (2003) Promises of interactivity: aligning learner perceptions and expectations with strategies for flexible and online learning. *Distance Education*, 24(1): 87–103.

Somoza-Fernández, M. and Abadal, E. (2009) Analysis of web-based tutorials created by academic libraries. *Journal of Academic Librarianship*, 35(2): 126–31.

Stolovitch, H.D. and Keeps, E.J. (2002) *Telling Ain't Training*. Alexandria, VA: ASTD Press.

Su, S.-F. and Kuo, J. (2010) Design and development of web-based information literacy tutorials. *The Journal of Academic Librarianship*, 36(4): 320–8. DOI: 10.1016/j.acalib.2010.05.006.

Sweller, J. and Cooper, G.A. (1985) The use of worked examples as a substitute for problem solving in learning algebra. *Cognition & Instruction*, 2: 59–89.

Tempelman-Kluit, N. (2006) Multimedia learning theories and online instruction. *College and Research Libraries*, 67(4): 364–9.

Veronikas, S.W. and Maushak, N. (2005) Effectiveness of audio on screen captures in software application instruction. *Journal of Educational Multimedia and Hypermedia*, 14(2): 199–205.

Vrasidas, C. (2000) Constructivism versus objectivism: implications for interaction, course design, and evaluation in distance education. *International Journal of Educational Telecommunications*, 6(4): 339–62.

Weston, C., Gandell, T., McAlpine, L. and Finkelstein, A. (1999) Designing instruction for the context of online learning. *Internet and Higher Education*, 2(1): 35–44.

Zhang, L. (2006) Effectively incorporating instructional media into web-based information literacy. *The Electronic Library*, 24(3): 294–306.

9

Assessment of learning objects

Abstract: The assessment of learning objects occurs in multiple stages, from the inception of a project through completion and then periodically thereafter. Assessment needs to be an ongoing process to ensure continued effectiveness, especially with learning objects. An outdated web-based tutorial, for example, could misinform, frustrate, and probably irritate participants. This chapter describes the role assessment plays in learning object design, and includes various assessment strategies that can be used to evaluate the effectiveness of learning objects. Topics include: Were the goals and outcomes accomplished? Is it intuitive (easy to use)? Is content appropriate? Is the multimedia appropriate? Are the exercises and learning experiences effective? Are there adequate feedback opportunities? What are the methods of assessment and the steps for assessment?

Key words: assessment, learning objects, tutorials, evaluation methods, online learning, user satisfaction.

Introduction

Throughout this book there has been frequent discussion of the need to assess learning objects in order to gauge whether they are meeting the established objectives and whether they are designed effectively for student engagement and learning. This chapter will provide an overview of various assessment strategies that can be used to evaluate the effectiveness of tutorials. Chapter 10 will discuss in more detail usability testing, which is a type of assessment that has been frequently used to evaluate tutorials.

How is success measured?

There are a number of measures that can be used to assess whether learning objects have been successful. Typically, assessment focuses on students' learning, as well as outcomes and opinions. Both quantitative and qualitative assessments can be useful for evaluating learning objects, such as tutorials, videos, and web pages. A general assessment focusing on quantitative methods might consist of measures such as surveys, questionnaires, internal checks, usage statistics, or analysis of pre- and post-test results. Qualitative methods such as usability testing, observations with screen capturing recordings and videos, interviews, focus groups, and user comments can provide more in-depth responses in terms of what students are experiencing.

Some of the questions one might ask during an assessment or evaluation of a learning object include the following: Were the goals and outcomes accomplished? Is it intuitive (easy to use)? Is content appropriate? Is the multimedia appropriate? Are the exercises and learning experiences effective? Are there adequate feedback opportunities? These are discussed further below.

Were the goals and outcomes accomplished?

During the design process of a learning object, goals and objectives should have been set. The goals should be specific, actionable, and realistic. The assessment of a learning object should include ways to measure if these goals and objectives have been met. The outcomes may differ, depending upon how closely participants attained these goals.

There are various ways to document evidence as to whether the goals of the learning object were accomplished.

- *Checkpoints*. A common practice is to include checkpoints throughout the tutorial or at the end. These might be in the form of a multiple-choice or fill-in-the-blank question to determine if the participant understands a process or concept. They might also direct a student to repeat a function (either within the tutorial or through an external link). For example, if one particular goal was that the user would be able to distinguish between an ED and EJ number in the ERIC database they could be given either a question or task that pertains to each.

- *Statistical tracking*. Most database vendors offer a way to view statistics of database usage. These, along with internal tracking, could be useful to determine increases or decreases in journal or database usage. Depending on the goal, one might want to determine if there was an increase or decrease in web or database activity after an assigned tutorial. For example, if a tutorial is assigned to a psychology class and the tutorial emphasizes that users should use the *PsycInfo* database, statistics could be gathered from some time before the assigning of the tutorial to a few weeks after the tutorial to gauge if there was a marked increase in the database usage. Another example would be to document changes in interlibrary loan (ILL) requests following an effort to push out a tutorial highlighting ILL/Document Delivery. For example, a continued high number of ILL requests for materials held by the library may suggest users lack the skills to locate the items from online databases. They may submit requests for items that are available through the library's online or print collection. If information is created in a learning object that is disseminated to students pertaining to a common resource that is hard to find, a measure of success could be a decrease in the number of ILL requests after some given time period. On the other hand, if the goal is to inform the user group of the availability of ILLs and how to request items, it would be important to track increases in usage after the creation of a learning object detailing the service, and track whether or not the requests were for items that could or could not have been found elsewhere in the system.

- *Log file analysis.* A log file analysis could be used to detail users' activity on the web. These files can be illustrative in seeing how students search. If the goal was to assess whether the instructions for using a multisearch feature on the website were clear, the logs of the searches could be analyzed to see how successful students were.

- *Web page analytics.* Analytics, such as Google Analytics, can be used to evaluate web activity or determine how long users spend on a given database/web page, or entry or exit points to databases. If one of the goals was to get students to access a database from a particular web page, the analytics could track entry points and patterns and assess if they have changed since an assigned tutorial on accessing information or databases. One of the objectives of the University of Mississippi Libraries home page usability study included determining whether 75 percent of the participants completed a task with the "most efficient number of clicks" (Stephan et al., 2006, p. 37). This study measured users' responses to questions by the number of clicks required to reach the resource, the time needed to complete the task, the completion of the task, and the satisfaction level of the participant. This type of measure helped them determine if their goal had been met and allowed them to focus on areas that needed improvement.

- *Tracking new accounts.* Another measure could include tracking new accounts. If a particular feature in a database was emphasized, such as exporting records to RefWorks (a citation management system), statistics for new accounts or the evaluation of entry points for students going into RefWorks during that time period could be tallied.

- *Evaluation of student work.* Following on from the above example of whether or not the students used the *PsycInfo* database, another measure could be to require students to email their database results to the librarian or faculty member, who could then assess the percentage of students who used the required database or searched according to the instructions in the tutorial. This could be extended to include the assessment of student papers at the end of the semester to determine the types of sources they used for their research. Although not immediate, it could provide evidence of how well the tutorial met its goals and objectives.

- *Pre- and post-tests.* The goal for the assessment carried out by Anderson and Wilson (2009) was to determine whether a passive or an interactive tutorial design better improves understanding of key concepts. They used pre- and post-test data to measure results. They also collected data regarding the participants' preference for taking an interactive versus a passive tutorial. Follow-up quizzes/feedback/activities/exercises on the related information from the tutorial are valuable ways to assess if goals and objectives have been met.

- *Student debriefing.* A valuable tool is to debrief with students after they finish working through a learning object. Questions can be asked to elicit whether or not the goals were met as well as to gain insight into adjustments that could be made.

- *Surveys.* Surveys can be used for multiple purposes, such as at the end of a semester on a course where students were asked to use a particular tutorial. Targeted questions could be asked to ascertain how well students retained information from the tutorial, whether they changed patterns or habits as a result of the tutorial, and other questions pertaining to the goals of the tutorial.

Is it intuitive (easy to use)?

Another question that is vital to assessing learning objects is whether the object is intuitive to use. Some of the key issues that designers hope to assess are difficulties in navigation and tutorial design, i.e., whether the tutorial is intuitive to users, and if the navigation and design enhance the experience. Evaluators may want to target specific elements such as the reliability of links and pop-up windows, the clarity of instructions, whether users notice a particular element (such as navigation, or the "Ask us" link), or the ease of use of the practice exercises and quizzes.

Is content appropriate?

Researchers may want to target how well content is presented. Is it too text-based, boring, or inappropriate for the target audience? Chapter 7 discussed suggestions for providing meaningful content and concept training. Student feedback in the form of a debriefing or through usability testing where students verbalize their thoughts as they progress through a tutorial can help to highlight how appropriate content is.

Is the multimedia appropriate?

As mentioned in previous chapters, tutorials can benefit from strategic multimedia applications to help accommodate various learning styles, interactivity, and engagement. However, multimedia should only be used if it improves, rather than distracts from, the learning experience. Does the inclusion of a Flash object increase student interactivity, engagement, or comprehension? During a usability study students will be able to voice their opinion of the value of any given multimedia application. It may also be possible to assess the value of applications by how well a student performs on an exercise or question. If there are opportunities for students to pick and choose or manipulate objects do they simply pick the first choice to keep things moving? Do they take the time to evaluate all of the possibilities, or could the task have been accomplished without the use of Flash elements?

Are the exercises and learning experiences effective?

If the goal is to create an interactive experience, then it is important to evaluate how students respond to the questions, exercises, and tasks they are asked to perform. Are there sufficient opportunities to practice? Are the tasks appropriate, self-explanatory, and educational? Do the exercises simulate real-world situations? Does corrective feedback accompany any response that students choose or give?

Are there adequate feedback opportunities?

Students' awareness of their actions and reflection on their own learning are essential. Accordingly, assessment should be process-oriented. It should give students feedback on their progress through the relevant requirements and objectives, and should be given in the course of the learning process. Feedback should support the learning and development process toward achieving the learning goals.

In addition to feedback pertaining to checkpoints throughout the tutorial, feedback pertaining to the design, content, and student experience is also important. This could be accomplished via a poll survey or question at the end of the tutorial that is directed back to the design team. It could also take the form of comments or attitudes expressed by students either as part of the tutorial or as part of the debriefing or usability study.

Debriefing can be very useful during a usability study. Follow-up questions after each task of a usability study can be designed to help capture qualitative data. The qualitative data revealed by participants' explanations of their choices can assist in measuring the level of learning achieved through viewing the screencasts.

Additionally, when the testing is finished, an overall debriefing of the pros and cons of the tutorial or web page, as well as students' thoughts on what they wish they had experienced or not experienced, can add additional information to future revisions.

Methods of assessment

Individual assessment looks at learning from the student's perspective and remains an important measurement component. Types of assessment tools include the following:

Pilot (beta) test

Once the beta design is ready, the designers or researchers should pilot it with a few individuals (or a couple of focus groups) to find out if the design and content are accomplishing the goals, as well as to find out how intuitive the design is for users. This component remains especially important since research suggests that individuals who utilize library tutorials are typically "self-directed and highly motivated" (Templeman-Kluit, 2006, p. 367) so this initial (and subsequent) assessment can help determine if users can proceed without additional guidance. The initial assessment would include evaluator observations as well as user comments to correct any inadequacies in the design and content.

Surveys/questionnaires

A common assessment practice discussed in the literature is surveys. Surveys measure issues such as student satisfaction and helpfulness of instruction, and can be used to determine the future direction of a course or program. Tutorial surveys may note the user's confidence in locating a specific database, or finding a copy of a particular magazine online. Moreover, these assessment techniques provide an opportunity for the student to rate the tutorial in terms of relevance, ease of use, and navigation.

Checklists

Checklists can be used to allow students to rate their interest in topics in a learning object and also to assess their skills and knowledge pertaining to a subject. These checklists can be used both in the design of a tutorial (based on student need for a tutorial) and also to evaluate how well the tutorial met the needs of the students. With faculty collaboration, these checklists could be distributed to students in a class prior to the creation of a tutorial so that the tutorial could be produced to suit student needs. Students could then be asked to complete a second checklist after finishing a tutorial. The responses would indicate how well the tutorial met the needs that students indicated prior to the tutorial design.

Pre- and post-tests

Pre- and post-tests are similar to checklists in that they may measure student needs before a tutorial and then evaluate how well the tutorial met those needs. However, unless the same student is asked to complete both, there is no way to measure change in a particular student's experience. Checklists can be useful in gathering information that may inform the design of a tutorial. If used after a participant completes a tutorial, they can provide information about the relevance of the tutorial or other attitudes and beliefs. Pre- and post-tests, however, are used with the same student to indicate whether that student was better able to complete a task, process, or function as a result of a tutorial.

Test/quiz results

Since most tutorials offer online quizzes or exercises the test results become great assets, providing a sketch of student competency on the issues presented, both during and after viewing the tutorial. If student performance is generally not as good as expected on a specific topic, the developer may need to revise that particular session.

Usability testing

Another assessment method mentioned in the literature is that of performing usability testing. This involves testing a target population to determine usability and asks students to provide feedback as they are observed performing tasks and exercises. Craven and Booth (2005, p. 190) suggested that these tests can illustrate users' opinion of a website, the usefulness of a service, the effectiveness of different search types and features, and "users' perception of the resource or service."

The usability study, by focusing on summative as well as performance assessment, appears especially suited for measuring users' learning through the tutorial. The participants' comments during the study also offer a source of data for individual assessment. Novotmy and Cahy (2006, p. 158) noted that they provided a "richer set of information for analysis than simply recording keystrokes." Chapter 10 is devoted to the topic of usability testing.

Comparison of groups

As more institutions develop online instruction and tutorials, there is a desire to assess whether the online product is as effective as in-person instruction. To compare the two types of instruction, studies often divide multiple sections of the same class, either student selected or instructor divided, into online only or in-person instruction. They usually include a pre- and post-test in order to compare the two groups. Other uses could be to test groups who used a tutorial and groups who didn't and compare the results.

Faculty inclusion in assessment

Faculty feedback sessions are also helpful in assessing the usefulness of a tutorial and the accuracy of representation of content and pedagogy for that discipline. They can provide both direct and indirect benefits. If there is a number of faculty reviewing the tutorial they can each focus on a specific aspect; for example, one might focus on grammar and typographical errors, another on navigation, another on exercises and responses. If faculty members come from different disciplines they can discuss together if the information is transferable across disciplines and if the content can be adjusted to be applicable to more than one discipline.

Within specific courses faculty can also involve students in the design and evaluation of tutorials. They can have students take a survey or pre-test as a way of helping librarians gather information on goals and objectives for a particular tutorial. Once designed, faculty can ask students to take the tutorial and then participate in a post-test evaluation of the tutorial. Results from tutorial exercises can also be sent to the faculty member. As previously mentioned, faculty can also provide an end-of-semester assessment by evaluating student papers or bibliographies to see if they improved. Some of this is subjective, but, generally, faculty will be able to judge if a bibliography or paper makes better use of scholarly resources as a result of a tutorial. With faculty involvement there can be both formative and summative assessment. Formative assessment occurs during the learning experience and includes feedback to both instructor and student. Summative assessment happens at the end of the course to ascertain the achievement of the learning objectives.

Usage statistics

Tracking usage statistics can be helpful in determining what individuals use and how they access those resources. Even though it may be difficult to attribute any changes in patterns over time to the fact that a tutorial is available to explain best practices, there may be indicators that could be used.

Analytics can track usage in a given time period, which may help document whether the tutorial had the desired action of directing students to a particular resource. Google Analytics is a free service that allows users to track usage statistics for their websites. It requires creating an account, setting up profiles for the website(s) you want to track, and then adding nine lines of HTML code generated by Google Analytics to each web page you want to track. The code generated by Google Analytics includes references to the remotely hosted JavaScript file (ga.js) used by Google to collect data, the account number, and a reference to the JavaScript function. Most screencast software programs publish tutorials for use on the web as a Shockwave Flash (.swf) file, with an accompanying HTML and JavaScript file used to render the tutorial in a web browser. Before placing the tutorial online, the published HTML file needs to be edited so that it includes the analytics code. As more accurate data are collected with the integration of the analytics code into the tutorial files, the library can better determine how much of each tutorial is viewed.

With the use of Google Analytics or the integration of JavaScript calls into .swf tutorial files, data can be collected that accurately record bounce rates and times of visits. These data can allow for better understanding of the use of each tutorial, including whether or not there is further interaction with a web page or whether the student leaves or goes to another page. They can help the designer understand student patterns and whether or not additional information or exercises need to be incorporated into a tutorial. They can also document how long a student spends on a tutorial. If the estimated norm should be five minutes, the usage statistics can reveal if students are leaving too early or whether or not they are engaging in particular sections or exercises for longer periods. By tracking the sections that are being jumped or those that are being used more heavily and for longer periods, the designers may be able to revise aspects to engage learners in more appropriate ways. During a post-test these analytics can track how students proceed to their required task.

Focus group interviews

Assessment can also be accomplished by interviewing students during their learning process. One method is to use focus group interviews. Effective focus groups typically consist of eight to ten participants. The facilitator (better to be someone not involved with the project so that there is no bias in questions asked) uses scripted broad questions (non-leading) that are asked of each group. One person can facilitate while another records the responses. A useful technique is to project the notes on to a large screen so participants can see the points and revisit them.

Often, results from questionnaires are used as topics for further exploration in focus group interviews. Students and faculty can be invited to participate in a series of focus groups pertaining to specific questions. Responses can be valuable in helping to decide content, design, or other variables for a tutorial. Where there is a prototype ready for viewing, a small group of students can be brought together to view and discuss the prototype (with scripted questions by the researchers). The results of this evaluation can expand the researchers' knowledge of the students' experience and their views on the design, content, usability, and purpose of the tutorial. The students' feedback can also lay the groundwork to improving and developing the learning environment and content in the tutorial or learning objects.

Individual interviews

Individual interviews are also instructive, although very time-consuming to conduct and transcribe. The number of participants involved will depend upon the variables that are being tested and the target audiences involved. Conducting interviews or usability study interviews with even a small number of individuals may help to point out patterns, reactions, attitudes, difficulties, or concerns that would not be captured with other methods. Participants are able to express reasons why they approach a task in a particular way more fully when allowed to verbalize a response. Chapter 10 provides some examples of usability study interviews.

Multiple assessment instruments

Designers have a variety of assessment tools and options available to them. Choices may be made based on budget, software capabilities, access to participants, and time. It is best to incorporate a variety of assessment strategies. Means and Haertel (2003) promoted the use of multiple forms of assessment to measure the impact of learning technologies. They argued that "No single study, genre of studies, or methodology is adequate to the task" (ibid., pp. 257–8). In addition to the types of methods described above, eye tracking and recordings can help provide triangulation to assessment studies.

Eye tracking

Eye tracking data can be used to confirm the data collected by video, audio, and the time and error logs during the think-aloud protocol (used in usability studies). Eye tracking recognizes the human pupil and records the movement and fixation of the eyes when viewing images or websites. The equipment can be calibrated to track which parts of a screen are being viewed. Some software can generate a "heat map" to show, through colors, where viewers focused their attention. With eye tracking it is possible to document eye patterns on a page and to learn what attracts students' attention. During the Mestre (2010) study, because eye tracking equipment was not used the researcher needed to observe how students looked at the page, or skimmed the page, and then made notes. It was also important that the students described what they were doing. Eye tracking equipment would make this much more precise and non-intrusive. One of the common uses of eye-tracking equipment in usability testing is to confirm data that is collected by other sources (Karn et al., 1999). The results can help with decisions about modifications to be made to pages in order to make sure the most relevant information is being viewed. (See Cooke (2005) for an article that describes the use of eye tracking for usability.)

Recordings

Recordings (i.e., time log, video, audio, and eye-tracking data) can be used for triangulation with the data collected by the usability staff during the observed think-aloud protocol. A full repertoire of collected data could consist of a list of usability problems, quantitative data from logs, and qualitative data from participants' verbal reports during each session, including any follow-up debriefing with the participants (to ensure they had a chance to describe their experience fully).

Steps for assessment

The following bullet list provides suggestions for assessment. These have been modified from Masemola and De Villiers' framework (2006) for the usability testing of interactive e-learning applications in cognitive domains.

- Work with campus experts on assessment design (decide which aspects are to be measured and their metrics, i.e., if the objectives in the screencast are clear; if navigation is clear, etc.). Determine if there will be a control group.

- Submit forms for the institution's IRB (Institutional Review Board) or equivalent unit that oversees research procedures and ethics. Even usability testing in designing web-based tutorials is considered research with human subjects, and has strict monitoring requirements. This is discussed further in Chapter 10.

- Formulate the documents required – these will include the initial test plan, task list, information document for participants, checklist for test administrator, and pre- and post-test questionnaire to measure learner satisfaction and changes required post-testing.

- Create a marketing plan with incentives. Create a plan as to how participants will be recruited and how incentives will be funded.

- Pilot with a few participants and refine the test plan, task list, and information document, based on the knowledge gained from the pilot.

- Conduct identical pre- and post-tests (regardless of target audience or if there is a control group).

- Conduct the main usability testing.

- Provide follow-up questions/debriefing.

- Analyze the results (coding responses).

- Write up results, draw conclusions, make recommendations, and revise.

Assessment and maintenance of tutorials

Throughout the scores of journal articles related to tutorial assessment, the following are some of the common areas that authors/researchers redesigned after carrying out assessments of tutorials or web pages.

Navigation

- Navigation was made more consistent and clearer in the areas which had caused confusion during testing.

- A context sensitive link (on the left-hand side) was added to allow users to pick and choose a section or module.

- The number of links was reduced by incorporating more tutorial content into the main pages and reducing external links.

Design elements

- More color was added through the use of colored fonts and bullets.
- More graphics were introduced in which the text was inside the graphic, rather than separate to the graphic.
- The quality was improved to give a more professional look (smoothness in video, audio quality, voice sound, consistency with images, font, colors, headings, etc.).

Content

- Tutorial content was shortened considerably by removing sections that students consistently identified as either too basic or as something already known.
- Sections were expanded based on student feedback as to where more information was needed (or links to additional information were provided).
- A virtual tour of the library, as requested by student testers, was also added.
- Help buttons ("Ask a librarian") were added.

Personalization elements

- Characters were introduced for students to choose from; this character would then guide the student through the tutorial.
- Different pathways were added so that a student could choose the type of examples or information they wanted (based on knowledge, interest, or need).
- Scenarios were incorporated which provided examples that students had previously mentioned were relevant to them.
- Questions and tasks were constructed which would be relevant to something current in, or of interest to, students' lives (e.g., by using a popular television show, actor, group, athlete, dilemma).

Readability/language

- Tutorials were made less text intensive, with more emphasis given to presenting information in small chunks of text or using bullet form, with bolding of key terms for easier reading.

- Tables were introduced extensively to improve ease of scanning.

- Wording was tightened up.

- Descriptions that were identified as confusing or jargon-intensive were simplified.

- Explanations were expanded (or reduced) in areas which had been identified as inadequate.

- Questions were reworded to enhance clarity and to reflect the revised tutorial content.

Interactive exercises

- More interactivity was added through the use of clickable image maps to facilitate a learning-by-doing process in the library catalog and journal article modules.

- The number of examples was reduced, or increased (depending upon assessment).

- Short (15–30-second) video clips were added as an option to "See how this is done" for those individuals who wanted a demonstration or more information.

- "Try it now" or "Now you try it" links were provided to allow the user to practice tasks when demonstrated.

- New questions were designed to increase the number of hands-on exercises geared to evaluating students' ability to apply core skills and concepts.

- Interactive practice exercises were introduced extensively at the point of relevance throughout the tutorial (such as: a search of the library's catalog and journal indexes; a visit to specified websites in order to answer questions; or an exercise to practice and reinforce what the student had just learned).

Quizzes

- Short assessments were incorporated within the web page/tutorial, which if answered correctly would allow the student to proceed; if not answered correctly, the student would be directed to additional information or help.

- Quizzes were added or reworked (with results sent to a faculty member and/or a librarian). Some quizzes were revised to emphasize the application of skill, rather than just to test facts and knowledge.

Conclusion

The assessment of learning objects occurs in multiple stages, from the inception of a project through completion and then periodically thereafter. It needs to be an ongoing process to ensure continued effectiveness, especially with tutorials. An outdated web-based tutorial could misinform, frustrate, and probably irritate participants. Ideally, the tutorial should be reviewed periodically by the design and development team, with reference to user feedback. Although there are many methods for evaluating learning objects, one of the best is to incorporate student feedback. User comments and attitudes are important in tutorial assessments. Participant responses can provide suggestions for areas such as those that Lindsay et al. (2006, p. 435) identified when assessing their information literacy tutorials: increased interactivity, practice opportunities, and "shorter with less writing and more pictures."

Bury and Oud (2005) also illustrated the role of user comments in affecting usability testing outcomes. They designed their assessment of the online information literacy tutorial to include task performance activities as well as student input on the navigation, design, and effectiveness of the tutorial. Participants also answered questions as they worked through the tutorial, which resulted in more detailed and specific responses.

In the Mestre (2010) study, the pre- and post-tests revealed such startling results that the very notion of providing screencasting tutorials was called into question. Students were not able to recreate a search after watching the screencasting tutorial. They were much more able to recreate a search after progressing through the web-based static tutorial with screenshots. The initial hypothesis had been that students would much prefer the screencast tutorial over the static web-based tutorial. However, based on results and student feedback, it was clear that students not only preferred the static web-based tutorial, but performed better after completing that tutorial. The responses from students redirected the design process from a path of phasing out the static web-based tutorials to one of augmenting them to include "clips" of the screencasting tutorials to enhance instruction. Without various assessments, this information would not have been gathered. The time, effort, and money invested in the tutorials would have been wasted if the result was that students did not benefit. However, after engaging in various assessment methods, the redesigned tutorials, based on students' perspectives, can now achieve what the designers had envisaged.

The following chapter explores usability testing further, including the issue of active student engagement in the evaluation process.

References

Anderson, R.P. and Wilson, S.P. (2009) Quantifying the effectiveness of interactive tutorials in medical library instruction. *Medical Reference Services Quarterly*, 28(1): 10–21.

Bury, S. and Oud, J. (2005) Usability testing of an online information literacy tutorial. *Reference Services Review*, 33(1): 54–65. DOI:10.1108/009073205 10581388.

Cooke, L. (2005) Eye tracking: how it works and how it relates to usability. *Technical Communication*, 52(4): 456–63.

Craven, J. and Booth, H. (2005) Putting awareness into practice: practical steps for conducting usability tests. *Library Review*, 55(3): 179–94.

Karn, K.S., Ellis, S. and Juliano, C. (1999) The hunt for usability: tracking eye movements. In *CHI 1999 Extended Abstracts on Human Factors in Computing Systems* (CHI EA 1999) (p. 173). New York: ACM. DOI:10.114 5/632716.632823. Available at: *http://doi.acm.org/10.1145/632716.632823*.

Lindsay, E.B., Cummings, L., Corey, M., Johnson, C.M. and Scales, J.B. (2006) If you build it, will they learn? Assessing online information literacy tutorials. *College & Research Libraries*, 67(5): 429–45.

Masemola, S.S. and De Villiers, M.R. (2006) Towards a framework for usability testing of interactive e-learning applications in cognitive domains, illustrated by a case study. *Proceedings of the 2006 Annual Research Conference of the South African Institute of Computer Scientists and Information Technologists on IT Research in Developing Countries* (pp. 187–97). October 9–11, 2006, Somerset West, South Africa. DOI:10.1145/1216262.1216283.

Means, B. and Haertel, G.D. (2003) Cross-cutting themes in research design for technology. In G.D. Haertel and B. Means (eds.) *Evaluating Educational Technology: Effective Research Designs for Improving Learning* (pp. 257–8). New York: Teachers College.

Mestre, L.S. (2010) Matching up learning styles with learning objects: what's effective? *Journal of Library Administration*, 50(7–8): 808–82.

Novotmy, E. and Cahy, E.S. (2006) If we teach, do they learn? The impact of instruction on online catalog search strategies. *Portal: Libraries and the Academy*, 6(6): 155–67.

Stephan, E., Cheng, D.T. and Young, L.M. (2006) A usability survey at the University of Mississippi Libraries for the improvement of the library home page. *The Journal of Academic Librarianship*, 32(1): 35–51.

Templeman-Kluit, N. (2006) Multimedia learning theories and online instruction. *College & Research Libraries*, 67(4): 364–9.

10

The value and process of usability studies

Abstract: One effective method used to evaluate web pages and tutorials is that of usability testing. Usability testing is multifaceted and can meet multiple goals. One of its values is that it can help define the nature of existing problems much more precisely than using only quantitative measures. By using various methods in a study, such as recording, video, eye tracking, log analysis, think-aloud protocols, and debriefing, a more extensive picture is revealed.

In addition to providing invaluable information on the effectiveness of a web page, learning object, or tutorial, usability testing allows researchers to gather information and identify problem areas not found through other assessment methods. This chapter discusses the purpose and methods of usability testing and provides some examples.

Key words: usability testing, learning objects, evaluation methods, online learning, program effectiveness, user satisfaction.

Introduction

To succeed in web-based instruction, students need an interface that has a high degree of usability. Usability testing measures the performance of end-users as they progress through a predefined set of tasks on the system or program being evaluated. The goal is to identify problems and areas that are unclear or difficult to navigate for the user and to identify how well the program, web page, or software meets specific usability criteria. The testing generally takes place in a private room or lab while evaluators observe and record the activities of the participants as they proceed through the tasks. The data are later analyzed to determine how easy the product was to learn, and how effective and enjoyable it was – from the user's perspective. This chapter will discuss the purpose and methods of usability testing and provide some examples, along with student perspectives.

Definitions of usability testing

The International Organization for Standardization, ISO 9241-11 (ISO, 1998; Bevan, 2006), defines usability as the extent to which a product can be used by specified users to achieve specified goals with effectiveness, efficiency, and satisfaction in a specified context of use. Using this standard, the usability of an application can be assessed through the three key quality criteria, namely: effectiveness – a measure of how well the user is able to use the application to achieve his/her goal; efficiency – a measure of the speed with which the user can complete tasks; and satisfaction – which is a subjective measure of how pleasant it is to use the system.

A simplified definition of site usability is the way in which the user *actually* navigates, finds information, and interacts with the site (Wood, 1998; Goto and Cotler, 2002). According to Dumas and Redish (1994, p. 4), "usability means that people who use the product can do so quickly and easily to accomplish their own tasks." Their definition rests on four assumptions concerning users:

1. usability means focusing on users;
2. people use products to be productive;
3. users are busy people trying to accomplish tasks; and
4. users decide when a product is easy to use.

Usability guru, Jakob Nielsen (1993), defines a usable interface as one which is:

- easy to learn (learnability)
- efficient to use (efficiency)
- easy to remember (memorability)
- causes few errors (error freeness)
- pleasant to use (satisfaction).

Purpose of usability testing

Usability testing is a process used to evaluate interactive applications before they are uploaded to be used by the general public. It is a way to capture users' interactions with a particular online application, such as a software program, a database, a tutorial, an online course, or a website. As mentioned above, through this process the evaluator observes users while they navigate a site to perform specific tasks. The evaluator (or the program itself) collects data on how users experience the visual, aural, and textual design of a site or program.

Usability testing provides designers with valuable clues regarding how a user understands and navigates through the layout of a site. It can also provide insight into a user's understanding of the terminology used to describe particular applications and access points. Typically, web usability testing is carried out with the goal of establishing where in a site users become frustrated and where the major trouble spots lie.

Regardless of the effort that goes into the creation of a tutorial or web page, the real test lies in how the user interacts with and responds to the final product. Although the designer may have followed all of the correct design elements and criteria, these will be irrelevant if the user doesn't approach the product in the way that the designer intended. The user can provide valuable insights into revisions that might be needed in terms of organization, layout, content, navigation, interactivity, use of terminology, amount of text, images, and use of multimedia. Users can also provide subjective responses as they work through the product, as well as express their satisfaction or dissatisfaction. In the end, though, the real test is whether or not the product accomplishes what it set out to do. After working through the tutorial, for example, was the user then independently able to complete the task illustrated or described in the tutorial? Librarians create tutorials and guides to help users navigate through the databases or other library services that are presented online. Yet, many are created and uploaded without having their usability tested. Good design includes an understanding of the users' needs, and the ability to create an interface that includes content, tasks, exercises, and feedback that allows the user to grasp its meaning and to interact successfully with it. Unless the design meets users' needs, the site may be misinterpreted, ineffective, or unusable.

Usability testing helps designers to understand how to improve a site. Testing can provide invaluable input so that the developer can make choices for the site. It is an opportunity to watch how people (novices, rather than the experts who designed the site) use a site or tutorial and where they run into trouble. These insights help the revision process. Through usability testing, a website, tutorial, or other learning object can be improved to allow students or users to interact with the interface to complete tasks in a manner that is natural and intuitive to them. The result is that users do not have to waste time trying to figure out the interface and can proceed through the tasks efficiently.

Methods

Librarians may use many methods to evaluate tutorials and web pages. Student evaluation, questionnaires, quiz results, staff testing, and observations are common first methods. There are various approaches to usability testing. Heuristic evaluation, naturalistic observation, and interviews are briefly described below as they include components that make up usability testing.

Heuristic evaluation

The heuristic method evaluates a product using a list of preferred attributes. Turner (2002) developed a heuristic checklist (Heuristic Evaluation by Proxy). The list was to be used as a method for quickly identifying any website design problem areas. The seven main categories (further subdivided into 55 subcategories) of the list are: navigation; page design; content; accessibility; media use; interactivity; and consistency. Although quick and inexpensive to conduct, Jeffries and Desurvire (1992) cautioned against carrying out a single heuristic evaluation to assess an interface, and instead advocated for usability testing in order to uncover more serious and consistent problems. Wichansky (2000) noted that there was no acceptable substitute for applying actual user data to the analysis of product usability. She concluded that one highly effective method was the quick study, where a small number of subjects are used to collect and analyze data to be used by designers to quickly make correct design decisions.

The use of a small number of subjects is also something that is prevalent in more user-based methods, such as interviews and usability studies. Heuristic evaluations can overlap with usability studies by incorporating some of the methods used in naturalistic observation.

Naturalistic observation

Naturalistic observation is a method that involves observing subjects in their natural environment. The goal is to look at behavior in a natural setting without intervention. This can be applied to tutorial or web-based evaluation if subjects are given a task and asked to go through the process without intervention from the researcher, in order to observe the "natural" way a subject would proceed. Researchers may take notes or tallies of various behaviors they observe. This could also include taking time samplings. For example, in the Mestre (2010) study, time marks were taken to document how long it took students to get to the requested database when they were on the "Online Research Resources Page," as well as their various unsuccessful attempts. Of value in these types of situations is to understand why students chose the paths they did. This type of observation can then be extended into more robust usability testing that includes debriefing and interviews.

Interviews (inquiry method)

Interviews are part of an inquiry method that is typically designed to gather information on users' experiences and preferences. Inquiry methods may include focus groups, interviews, debriefing, surveys, self-reporting logs, and journaled sessions.

Bury and Oud (2005) in their assessment of a library tutorial conducted an informal brief interview to give students the opportunity to make general comments or share impressions which might not have surfaced during the scripted questions. Students were given a standard list of questions as a handout, were asked to answer these questions while working their way through the tutorial, and were left on their own to do so. This process had similarities to the inquiry method of usability testing as the student did much of the recording using journals or self-reporting logs (Hom, 1998). Many of the questions asked were designed to determine students' impressions or levels of satisfaction with areas of the tutorial design, navigation, and content as opposed to determining their level of efficiency or success in carrying out specified tasks. The results obtained were, therefore, based largely on what students said rather than observations of what they did.

Usability testing

Usability testing combines the above methods into one process, although researchers may use various components based on what is being assessed.

Usability metrics

In general, the two forms of usability metrics are quantitative data (aimed at measuring user performance) and qualitative, subjective data (aimed at measuring users' perceptions about the application) (Nielsen, 1993; Barnum, 2002). Both of these can be used during a study by including observation and verbal student feedback.

The following list highlights some examples of performance measures that are used in website testing:

1. number of mouse clicks to get to a particular point;
2. number of errors users make in getting to the desired point;
3. number of repeated errors;
4. number of times the user asks for help or clarification;
5. time spent reading (determined from think-aloud protocol);
6. time taken to complete tasks;
7. number of incorrect or correct answers on a quiz.

Other measures can be used that require the participant to verbalize their thoughts as they go through the web page or tutorial. They can be instructed to comment on any (or all) of the issues indicated in the bullet list that appears below as they progress, and can be reminded to do so. These are especially useful when evaluating tutorials and can help to identify other potential tutorial problems which may not have been identified previously using other evaluation methods.

Bury and Oud (2005) looked at the following areas in focusing their usability questions to evaluate Laurier Library's information literacy tutorial. The assessment included quantitative as well as qualitative methods:

- *Navigation.* How easy is it to navigate within the tutorial (including moving backwards and forwards, links to external pages, etc.)?
- *Design.* Is the page design appealing and effective or are improvements needed?
- *Layout and presentation of information.* Does the right balance exist between textual and non-textual information? Is the layout of information on pages conducive to effective learning?
- *Interactivity.* Is interactivity effective? Is there an appropriate amount of interactivity or is more needed? If so, where would it be most useful?

- *Use of language.* Is language pitched at the right level? Is it clear or obtuse? Is the tone right?

- *Content.* Is tutorial content too commonsensical or too advanced? Is information felt to be relevant by students? Is there too much detail or length and if so where? Is there unnecessary repetition and if so where? What useful information did students learn, and what did they know already? Which were the best and worst modules?

- *Tests.* Were self-test exercises and quizzes clear, reasonable, and helpful?

During a debriefing of the study, additional questions could be asked of the participants, such as: What was missing? What would have helped? What problems did they encounter? Where were they confused?

Guidelines for usability testing

Usability testing can reveal the things that are or are not important to users. It can also highlight topics that were omitted that should not have been. Usability testing involves one person at a time being shown how, or asked, to work through something while being asked questions or asked to perform a task while being observed. Testing should be iterative and not done at the last minute before something is launched. It is inportant to test early in the design so that improvements can be made. Otherwise, lots of time, energy, and resources could be expended completing a project only to test and find out that a redesign is needed – requiring more time, energy, and resources. It is especially important to catch users before a site is in use and the users are comfortable with it. By engaging a few users during different stages of development and redesign the process can becomes more fluid and efficient.

Formal usability testing consists of observing and recording users carrying out specific requested tasks. Fundamental guidelines recommended by Dickstein and Mills (2000) relating to the preparation and execution of formal usability testing are as follows:

- decide what to test;

- design scenarios which will require the user to perform tasks you want to test;

- write a script for administering the test to ensure consistency;

- ask the testers to think aloud as they work through the tasks;
- have a moderator/facilitator who asks questions;
- have a recorder who transcribes what is observed (this can be done using software);
- identify individuals to act as testers who are representative of your target user population;
- offer some kind of incentive for testers;
- make sure there is a quiet (private) place to carry out the testing;
- record the test results as soon after the test as possible;
- analyze the test results and recommend redesigns to correct problems that are identified.

Process for performing usability studies

Although the following will vary depending upon the situation, the steps can be applied and modified as needed.

Process with participants

- introduce yourself and give a brief overview of what will happen in the session;
- sign any necessary forms;
- answer any questions;
- get background information from the participants (or at the end of testing);
- carry out a pre-test if applicable;
- start the usability testing, reminding participants to provide reactions and relate what they are thinking;
- carry out a post-test if applicable;
- perform a debrief with the participant at the end: overall reactions, suggestions for improvements, etc.;
- give participants any incentives that were offered as part of the study;
- review the results immediately.

Examples

Bowles-Terry et al. (2010) conducted a usability study of one–two-minute brief instructional videos to investigate whether watching a video tutorial enabled a student to complete the task described in the tutorial. The approach they used was similar to that recommended in Dickstein and Mills' (2000) guidelines above:

- develop real-life scenarios that require users to perform specific tasks;
- write a script for consistency between testers;
- provide compensation for the testers' time;
- choose volunteers from the general student population;
- set up a quiet place in which to conduct the testing;
- ask testers to think loud as they perform the tasks.

The investigator interviewed the students about their library experience and asked each student to complete an unfamiliar, library-related task (e.g., request an article photocopy through ILL or deposit an item in the institutional repository), an approach referred to by Krug (2006) as "key task testing." Students were instructed to think aloud about what they were doing and why as they attempted to complete the task. Screen movements and audio were recorded with Camtasia software. After attempting to complete the task, students viewed an online video tutorial about the task they had just attempted, and then offered general impressions and specific feedback about the instructional video. If students were at first unable to complete the task, they returned to the task after viewing the video to see if the tutorial had prepared them to complete the necessary action. All but one of the students were able to complete the task after viewing the video.

Mestre (2010) also used the above process in her usability study to determine if the screencast tutorials that were developed were effective for students from different cultural groups. In her study, though, instead of choosing volunteers from the general student population, volunteers from various ethnic groups were targeted (Latinos, African Americans, Native Americans, Asian Americans, Anglo Americans). Additionally, students were asked to take two learning style inventories prior to the study which would help in understanding approaches taken during the usability study and preferences for the design, interactivity, and multimedia applications used. Mestre's study (ibid.) included both a pre-test and a post-test (after viewing a tutorial) where students attempted to find articles on a specified topic. In the study, students were asked to go through the process with three tutorials (a static web page tutorial with screenshots, a screencast video tutorial, and a Flash-based interactive tutorial). At the end of each, students participated in a debriefing.

Additional tips that may help when working with students in a study are as follows:

- Give subjects clear instructions both written and verbally.
- Tell them how long it will take to complete the test tasks.
- Tell them what types of tasks they will perform.
- Ask them to state what they believe they will be doing and ask for any questions.
- Stay quiet and out of sight while conducting the test (unless it is really essential to intervene to get them back on track).
- Take a lot of notes during the test, even if it is being recorded.
- At the end of the study ask the subjects about their overall impressions.
- Ask the subjects for their suggestions for improvement.

Recording student interactions

In order to capture the testers' movements a screen recorder can be used. There are various programs that successfully accomplish this, e.g., Camtasia, Captivate, and Morae. These are described further in the chapter on resources in this book (Chapter 12). These products also record the participant's voice. This frees the focus of the researcher from note-taking while simultaneously recording the testers' thought processes, to be transcribed at a later date.

Think-aloud process

In addition to capturing the movements and observations of a student during the usability test, it can be helpful to include the student's narrative during the process in order to provide more information. The use of a think-aloud protocol specifically reveals users' difficulties in the comprehension or use of a website or tutorial since their spontaneous comments reveal both the location and nature of any difficulty. For example, one student comment from the Mestre (2010) study was, "I can't figure out if I'm supposed to click on this person or not."

The think-aloud process encourages participants to verbalize their thoughts, feelings, expectations, and decisions while interacting with the application (Dumas 2003). By "thinking aloud," or talking about what they are doing as they are doing it, each participant reveals their thoughts as they complete each task, giving the researcher insight into why each action is being performed (Ericsson and Simon, 1993). According to Nielsen (1993, p. 19), "this additional insight into the user's thought process can help to pinpoint concrete interface elements that cause misunderstanding so they can be redesigned." This can help evaluators to understand the reasons behind users' actions, as well as explain the misconceptions users might have about the system. Participants may feel uncomfortable talking through their actions so may need to be reminded periodically to "explain what you are doing; explain why you chose a selection," etc.

This narration also helps if a researcher is employing use-of-time patterns, such as recording the time spent in navigation and reading screen information, and the time spent on actual learning activities. It can give clues as to why it took a participant extra time to choose something or if there were any confusions based on language, organization, or design on that particular page. In the example of the Mestre (2010) study, the results indicated that students spent between 45 seconds and three minutes getting to a particular resource. Without the think-aloud process, the evaluators may never have known why or what students were thinking as they tried to figure out what to do next.

In this process, prior to the start of each testing session students are instructed to verbalize as they begin and end each task. For example, as they begin each task students will say, "I'm beginning Task 1," and as they complete each task they will say, "I'm finished with Task 1." They are instructed to move along to the next task after completing the previous task, and to identify which task they are working to complete. If students do not believe they can complete a specific task, they are instructed to verbalize their difficulty; that they are unable to complete the task, and are moving on to the next task. The students determine whether they have completed a task and when to move on to the next task. However, in some cases, the researcher may need to intervene if too much time is spent trying to figure out a task, and direct the student to the next task.

As previously mentioned, participants may need some prompting throughout the process to remember to verbalize their thoughts. Adebesin et al. (2009) used co-discovery (co-participant) testing where two users collaborate with each other while exploring the application being evaluated. During the process they verbalize their thoughts as they interact with each other and the application, using a single workstation. In this situation, the verbalizing is more natural because it involves a conversation between two people (Nielsen 1993; Wilson, 2004). Adebesin found that individual test participants struggled with think-aloud and remained mainly silent during testing sessions, making it difficult to make such distinctions. Various authors, including Nielson (ibid.) and Wilson (ibid.) have acknowledged this problem that occurs with individual participants.

The two observations of co-discovery testing revealed that co-participant testing has the potential to reduce the level of intervention by the test administrator, and is especially relevant for testing e-learning, where collaboration is currently promoted as a useful form of learning. If not using the co-discovery method, it becomes very important to have a researcher present who can prompt the participant to verbalize thoughts. Once the session is over, the data need to be collected and transcribed for later review by the researcher.

Eye tracking

Eye tracking can be combined with usability testing. This involves sophisticated monitoring and recording of eye movements on different screen regions to determine whether important information is attended to by participants (Pretorius et al., 2005). Eye tracking equipment is used to identify the specific areas of the website or tutorial that students look at and shows the amount of time students spend looking at each area.

Time log data

Data from each test session can also be captured through a written time log, video, audio recordings, and eye tracking equipment. A time log records the time automatically and can be used to record the users' activities as they attempt to complete each task. It records the time each user spends completing each task and the time between tasks. If one of the researchers is in a separate room, a keyboard input device can be connected to the time log recording equipment in that room to allow the researcher to make observation notes while testing is conducted, especially if using a two-way mirror process.

Using this method the researcher can enter notes about each participant's activities as they work through each task. Additional details about the participant's activities (e.g., whether or not each task was successfully completed; if the participant became frustrated with one task, stopped, and moved on to the next task; or was stopped by the researcher in the room due to time constraints) can be recorded in the time log. A printed time log can be produced for each test session. Then, at the end of the usability testing sessions, data from the time log can be entered into a spreadsheet for analysis.

Resources needed for usability testing

IRB (Institutional Review Board)

In university settings there is usually an IRB that requires various protocols to be followed when students are being evaluated as part of a research project. In the case of web or tutorial testing, it may be possible to work with the IRB to have an open-ended agreement for web testing that allows ongoing usability testing. Testers would need to have approved appropriate forms regarding the study which would later be given to participants to sign. The completion of this process may take several months so it should be planned well in advance. The process will ask for all information pertaining to the target population, each part of the study, questions asked of the participants, directions, forms, evaluations, resources, potential harm to participants, and incentives.

Goals of evaluation

It is assumed that comparable sites or tutorials have already been reviewed in pre-testing in order to determine elements of style, organization, design, or interactivity for the proposed site or tutorial. During this phase several participants or a focus group could help identify viable features for use. Once a mock-up is ready, several different participants or another focus group could be asked to give preliminary impressions of what does or does not work. When the final product is ready for testing, the researchers will need to identify the specific goals of the evaluation. These may be based on previous concerns during the evaluation of the mock-up or they may be a set of new goals.

Researchers

The number of researchers needed can vary depending on the type of usability testing being done. If recording software is being used, a moderator/facilitator may be all that is needed to guide the participant through the process. If there is no recording software, it may be helpful to have an additional person to record observations and comments. Also, if the researchers are not expert at performing data analysis they will want to recruit/employ someone who is able to do so.

Participants

If possible, the goal should be to recruit participants from different age groups, majors, backgrounds, and experiences. It is best to try to recruit students who might actually use and benefit from the tutorial (e.g., education students, first-year students) – in short, users who reflect the target audience of the tutorial or site. However, a variety of perspectives is useful, especially when testing if the design works for both novice and expert. Individuals who are not from the target audience may be able to discover areas that are unclear.

Number of participants to test

There is no hard and fast rule as to how many people to recruit. Meaningful and accurate results can be obtained from very few users. Nielsen (2000) asserts that it is only necessary to test five users, unless a site will be used by several user groups. Krug (2006) maintains that as few as three or four users will suffice, since the first few users are likely to encounter all of the most significant problems. Ultimately, "As you add more and more users, you learn less and less because you will keep seeing the same things again and again" (Nielsen, 2000, p. x). The goal would then be to test again, after revisions, with different users. With only three to five people to test it would be possible to make conclusions and begin revisions more quickly than when wading through so many notes that may be repetitive.

However, it may be important to determine if users from different populations approach the site or tutorial differently, which could lead to increasing the number of participants to add diversity – for example five freshmen, five seniors, five faculty members – especially during subsequent testings. In the case of the Mestre (2010) study it was important to recruit more participants in order to include students from different ethnic groups and with different learning styles.

Location

The preferred location is any room that offers privacy so that the individual can be without distractions and feel comfortable speaking aloud during the process. Often, the IRB will stipulate conditions such as a private room for testing.

In terms of more formal labs, some researchers use two connected rooms with a two-way mirror to observe and hear each session, along with audio equipment to record each session. In lieu of using a two-way mirror, a testing lab can be a separate room equipped with a computer, desk, office chair, telephone, and whiteboard.

Equipment

Digital equipment in the testing lab records video and audio, and creates a time log of participant navigation through the course site. Some labs have an unobtrusive ceiling-mounted bubble camera to record audio and video, whereas other labs use a free-standing video camera mounted on a tripod, or, if using a laptop, the tester can use the camcorder. Some set-ups allow for the video to transfer immediately to a usability lab that may have a large flat-screen monitor for immediate viewing by a researcher. For a basic usability study the typical equipment consists of a computer and preferably some screen capturing/recording software like Camtasia, Captivate, or Morae to record both the audio and mouse clicks of the user. Capturing the audio is important not only to catch the reasons why a user chooses to do or not to do something, but also to capture their tone of voice (indicating frustration, etc.). Some testers still use camcorders to record sessions, but the playback and pinpointing of sections is much more cumbersome than with screen capturing software. Depending on the equipment being used, the researcher may or may not opt to be in the room with the participant (to prompt, guide, instruct). When the researcher is not present in the room, participants will need to have a telephone or some other option to contact the researcher for assistance.

Eye tracking equipment in combination with cameras captures images of the student's computer screen, the keyboard, and the participant's face together with the participant's eye gaze position and duration. These can be viewed simultaneously, or the camera can be moved to project just one of these views (or to change the angle of the camera) for closer examination as the student proceeds through the tasks.

Script

A well-designed script that can be used for all participants is important. It provides the purpose and goals for the testing, any IRB information, pre- and post-tests, and questions and instructions to be given during the testing. Some references to resources for scripts are included in Chapter 12 and in Appendices 2 and 3. Some basic guidelines and questions to use in the development of scripts include:

- Briefly review the purpose of the study and what the participants will be asked to do.

- Ask participants to perform a preliminary evaluation of the site/ introduction to a tutorial. Do they understand the purpose of the site, the value, how it's organized etc?

- Ask participants to do something and watch how they do it, asking them to "talk aloud" as they are clicking to explain why they are doing what they are doing. Try to make the task relevant to them so they will be more invested in going through the process and can use their personal knowledge to guide them, e.g., "Find a database in your major area of study."

- After the task, ask a series of questions as part of a debriefing of the experience.

- Provide contact information and a copy of their signed consent form for them to take away.

Cost

It is usually advisable to offer some incentive to participants. Often it could be a small gift card to somewhere local, perhaps a coffee shop. At the university level, incentives are typically between US$10 and US$15 for an hour. Often, student workers are asked to participate in studies and if approved they could count this time as a work hour (rather than receiving an incentive). Businesses might pay considerably more per hour (US$50 and above).

Promotion

Advertisements and flyers should be simple and catchy so that people will notice them: "We need to have a few people look at our tutorial and give us some feedback. It's very easy and will take about 45 minutes. You'll be paid _____ for your time." Some visual element can also help grab attention.

Iterative testing and analysis

Iterative testing of a product is very important in order to make changes throughout the design of a learning object. The testing begins with brainstorming ideas for the project (perhaps with a small group) and continues through prototypes and the final product and then again after revisions are made. Figure 10.1 is an example of what a usability testing design might look like, beginning at the top.

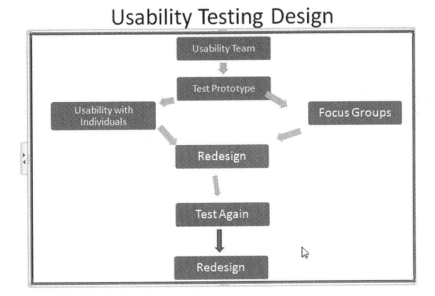

| **Figure 10.1** | Usability testing design flow chart |

Usability analysis

An analysis of the results of the study should be done as soon as possible after testing in order to generate additional questions for follow-up interviews. This may consist of both quantitative and qualitative analysis. The data that were collected via video and audio equipment can be recorded to DVD for later review by the researcher. Notes should also be recorded after each interview while still fresh in the memory, and then transcribed.

Quantitative

Statistics based on items that could be tracked with a definitive response can be compiled. Examples of quantitative data include questions that can be answered "Yes" or "No," such as "Did the participant progress from point A to point B as expected without difficulty?" These can be entered into statistical software packages for later analysis. Data such as tracking when pauses occurred, when participants had questions, and when participants exhibited confused body language can also be tallied, along with the time stamp or location in the product where the question, pause, or confusion was noted. Consistently low quiz scores for certain questions can also be noted as they may point out the need for better explanations of some concepts.

Qualitative

There are several qualitative methods in usability testing that can produce additional information to be analyzed. These include:

- the think-aloud protocol data as captured by the video and audio media;
- the time/error log as captured by the time recording equipment;
- eye tracking data;
- summary interview data (such as debriefing remarks).

There will be a number of qualitative responses: observations that can be analyzed throughout the transcript, body language, pre- and post-tests, and debriefing. The development of a good chart or form to record results will make it easier to categorize results to make sure that predetermined questions are being answered.

With a chart such as that shown in Table 10.1, recordings can be made of relevant occurrences that are observed (or mentioned by the participant during think-aloud).

Table 10.1	Example of common themes based on the Mestre study (2010)

	Uses ORR* before tutorial?	Focuses on images first?	Able to recreate search?	Favorite part of tutorial?	Least favorite part of tutorial?
Capture 1	No – uses easy search	Yes, then the text	Yes	Pictures	Text
Capture 2	No – clicks on articles (information only)		Yes		
Capture 4	No – uses easy search	Reads text first	Yes, but went through easy search	Step-by-step images	Opening up a new window
Capture 5	Goes to UGL website and finds articles	Yes	Yes, after going back to the tutorial	Pictures and highlights	All the writing
Capture 9	No – goes to article locater, then easy search	Yes	Not through ORR. Uses easy search and then finds ERIC		
Capture 10	Uses easy search	Both images and description	Easily – copies and pastes URL and types ERIC		
Capture 11	Yes goes there first, but types in keywords – no results – so goes back to easy search	Bold words first, then pictures	Yes, corrects herself a couple of times		

Note: * Online Research Resources, a web page which lists and links to all the online resources of the library

Some of these responses could be transferred into quantitative results by tallying how many times instances occur, such as:

- Accessed the ERIC database by going through ORR: (2 students).

- Accessed the ERIC database by going through easy search: (16 students).

- Clicked on the link in the tutorial to get to the ERIC database: (2 students).

- Could not get to the ERIC database: (1 student).

The use of a spreadsheet to tabulate and analyze the data is useful, as is the use of statistical software packages.

Themes

In order to analyze the student interviews, think-alouds, and debriefing remarks it helps to create categories of recurring themes. Examples may be categories such as:

- Navigation comments ("I wish there was some table of contents somewhere at all times so I could know where I am in the tutorial and even skip around").

- Language/terminology comments ("What does ILL mean?"; "I didn't understand all that about 'descriptor'").

- Clarity of instructions ("There should be an example"; "I didn't quite understand what they wanted me to do on this part"; "Too much information").

- Narration comments ("She went too fast narrating"; "That was pretty monotone"; "I like that it was a female").

- Interactivity comments ("Pop-up X didn't stay up long enough"; "I wanted to do something, not just watch them do it"; "It was helpful to see the steps"; "I would rather have a link so I could try it out"; "I wasn't sure if I was supposed to click on this image to have it do something or go to the next task").

- Image comments ("That image was a little blurry"; "Images could be larger"; "Text should be embedded in image"; "Not clear what that image is showing or explaining").

- Text comments ("Too text based"; "Too many instructions; just give me the bullets"; "I don't want to read so much").

- Content comments ("This is too repetitive"; "It would have been good to have an example on this part – too ambiguous"; "Too much information"; "I already knew this. Couldn't you have a 'skip this part if you know it' button or a 'jump ahead button' for people who know it?").

- Design elements ("That red color was hard to read"; "The font was way too small").

- Test comments ("Doing this is teaching me a lot about keywords").

It may be useful to create separate files/Word documents for each category. If the study provided hypotheses, the categories could be arranged around them to help analyze feedback that would either support or invalidate the hypotheses. Additionally, categories could be arranged under the goals of the study.

Correlation

When carrying out an analysis, various questions will emerge that may indicate a need to correlate how someone responded to a particular question/direction and how well they did on another aspect of the testing. Correlation is a statistical measurement of the relationship between two variables. The definition from the Blackwell Dictionary of Sociology (correlation, 2000) is:

> The correlation coefficient (also known as the Pearson product – moment correlation coefficient) is represented by r. Its numeric value ranges between –1.0 and +1.0, with the positive or negative sign indicating the direction of relationship and the number itself indicating the strength of the relationship. A value of 1.0 (positive or negative) indicates a perfect relationship, which means that knowing X allows us to predict Y without error. A value of 0.00 indicates no relationship, which means that in trying to predict values of Y we will make as many mistakes knowing X as we will not knowing X.

If an individual does not improve in a task (assuming s/he also did a pre- and post-test) it may help to go through the transcripts/observations of the testing to see if they correlate with any particular measure (such as if the participant scored highly as an aural, kinesthetic, or visual learner). Also, computing correlations between pairs of questions/items may help determine patterns.

Common problems

Common problems should be obvious if mentioned by multiple participants and these are the ones that the design team may want to address first, depending upon how easy they are to fix.

Fixes

- Evaluate what should be corrected. Be careful not to fix something just because users did not get it at first. Assess what it was that caused the difficulty and see if there is a way to make it clearer. It may not be better to add more text explanations. Perhaps something could be taken away or rearranged (to help make something clearer) instead of adding something on. Another option would be to include an additional link for "Tell me more."

- Evaluate new feature requests. Students may have many suggestions, but they may not be immediately feasible. These can be added to a "parking lot" for later discussion.

- Fix the obvious. These are the things that become clear as soon as participants come across them and experience difficulty (such as, "There is nothing to say to click on a person to begin. I just see images of characters in the middle of the page").

- Fix what is easy to fix. If making some text bolder or larger would help make it more obvious, that is an easy fix.

- Consider the impact on the rest of the design. When changing one aspect, what happens to the rest of the content on the page? Will the rest of the content still be emphasized appropriately?

Conclusion

Usability testing is multifaceted and can meet multiple goals. One of its values is that it can help define the nature of existing problems much more precisely than solely using quantitative measures. By using various methods such as recording, video, eye tracking, log analysis, think-aloud, and debriefing in a study a more extensive picture results.

In addition to providing invaluable information on the effectiveness of a web page or tutorial, usability testing allows researchers to gather information and identify problem areas not found through other assessment methods. For example, participants might identify content that they feel is missing from the tutorial that would help them understand a process better. They might suggest different terminology, examples, or the inclusion of a pop-up with a definition, a virtual map, or a video clip to demonstrate a concept or how to do something. Student feedback can inform the designer of areas or concepts that are already known, and, thus, are not critical for inclusion. In such an instance, designers might include branching to accommodate novice and expert users. Feedback can also alert designers to the areas or concepts that students feel are the most important, as well as to exercises that would help to complement the content. No matter what method is used, it should be part of a continual or iterative process of assessment and improvement (Head, 1999).

References

Adebesin, F., Villeirs, R. and Ssemugabi, S. (2009) Usability testing of e-learning: an approach incorporating codiscovery and think-aloud. In *Proceedings of the 2009 Annual Conference of the Southern African Computer Lecturers' Association* (pp. 6–15). Eastern Cape, South Africa: ACM.

Barnum, C.M. (2002) *Usability Testing and Research*. New York: Longman.

Bevan, N. (2006) *International Standards for HCI*. Available at: *http://nigelbevan.com/papers/International_standards_HCI.pdf*.

Bowles-Terry, M., Hensley, M.K. and Hinchliffe, L.J. (2010) Best practices for online video tutorials in academic libraries: a study of student preferences and understanding. *Communications in Information Literacy*, 4(1): 17–28.

Bury, S. and Oud, J. (2005) Usability testing of an online information literacy tutorial. *Reference Services Review*, 33(1): 54–65.

correlation (2000) In *The Blackwell Dictionary of Sociology*. Available at: *http://www.library.illinois.edu/proxy/go.php?url=http%3A%2F%2Fwww.credoreference.com/entry/bksoc/correlation*.

Dickstein, R. and Mills, V. (2000) Usability testing at the University of Arizona Library: how to let users in on the design. *Information Technology and Libraries*, 19(3): 144–51.

Dumas, J.S. (2003) User-based evaluations. In J.A. Jacko and A. Sears (eds.) *The Human-Computer Interaction Handbook*. Mahwah, NJ: Lawrence Erlbaum Associates.

Dumas, J.S. and Redish, J.C. (1994) *A Practical Guide to Usability Testing*. Norwood, NJ: Ablex Publishing Corporation.

Ericsson, K.A. and Simon, H.A. (1993) *Protocol Analysis: Verbal Reports as Data* (Rev. edn.). Cambridge, MA: MIT Press.

Goto, K. and Cotler, E. (2002) *Web Redesign: Workflow That Works*. Indianapolis, IN: New Riders.

Head, A. (1999) Web redemption and the promise of usability. *Online*, 23(6): 20–3.

Hom, J.T. (1998) The usability methods toolbox. Available at: *http://www.usability.jameshom.com/*.

ISO (International Standards Organization) (1998) ISO 9241-11:1998: Ergonomic requirements for office work with visual display terminals (VDTs) – Part 11: Guidance on usability. Available at: *http://www.iso.org/iso/search.htm?qt=iso+9241-11&sort_by=rel&type=simple&published=on&active_tab=standards*.

Jeffries, R. and Desurvire, H. (1992) Usability testing vs. heuristic evaluation: was there a contest? *ACM SIGCHI Bulletin*, 24(4): 39–41. DOI:10.1145/142167.142179.

Krug, S. (2006) *Don't Make Me Think: A Common-sense Approach to Web Usability*. Berkeley, CA: New Riders.

Mestre, L.S. (2010) Matching up learning styles with learning objects: what's effective? *Journal of Library Administration*, 50(7–8): 808–82.

Nielsen, J. (1993) *Usability Engineering*. Boston, MA: Academic Press, Inc.

Nielsen, J. (2000) *Designing Web Usability*. Indianapolis, IN: New Riders.

Pretorius, M.C., Calitz, A.P. and Van Greunen, D. (2005) The added value of eye tracking in the usability evaluation of a network management tool. *Proceedings of the 2005 Annual Research Conference of the South African Institute of Computer Scientists and Information Technologists (SAICSIT)* (pp. 1–10). Available at: *http://portal.acm.org/citation.cfm?id=1145675.1145676*.

Turner, S. (2002) The HEP test for grading website usability. *Computers in Libraries*, 22(10): 37–9.

Wichansky, A.M. (2000) Usability testing in 2000 and beyond. *Ergonomics*, 43(7): 998–1006.

Wilson, C. (2004) *Usability Techniques: Pros and Cons of Co-participation in Usability Studies*. Available at: *http://stcsig.org/usability/newsletter/9804-coparticipation.html*.

Wood, L.E. (1998) Introduction: bridging the design gap. In L.E. Wood (ed.) *User Interface Design: Bridging the Gap from User Requirements to Design* (pp. 1–14). Boca Raton, FL: CRC Press.

11

Marketing learning objects for broad visibility

Abstract: Academic libraries have the opportunity through their web pages to make their resources very visible to their university community. The role of branding and marketing library resources is critical to helping users understand that it may be worth their while to explore what is offered on the web page or in a tutorial or other learning object. This chapter includes strategies for publicizing and marketing websites and tutorials by working with faculty, using social networking tools, and creating online and print marketing. Included are sections on: the message; working with faculty to promote tutorials and websites; social network tools; making resources more visible; and some suggestions for promoting, linking, and embedding learning objects.

Key words: marketing, library services, learning objects, social networks, metatags.

Introduction

The best-designed websites and tutorials take considerable time and resources to develop. Even if they are available through various mediums and venues, they may still go unused if they are not marketed adequately. Students rate convenience over quality. They want to get information fast and be able to use the resources intuitively. Internet search engines, rather than libraries, are relied on by college students because of their speed, convenience, and ease of use (OCLC, 2010). These factors play a major role in the selection of Internet resources over library resources. The 2010 OCLC study results showed that not a single survey respondent (of the 2229 participants) began their information search on a library website, instead using search engines or resources like Wikipedia as their first stop. However, library websites were used by a third of the respondents, even if they were not the first place they would look for information. The top two reasons participants in the survey did not use the library website was that they didn't know it existed (39 percent) or they preferred to use it in person (28 percent). Other reasons for not using a library site were that other websites had better information or that they couldn't find the site. Of interest is that nearly half of the respondents indicated value in the self-help materials available at the library. Tutorials, videos, and other learning objects would fall into the self-help category. Academic libraries have the opportunity through their web pages to be very visible to their university community. The role of branding and marketing library resources is critical to helping users understand that it may be worth their while to explore what is offered on the web page or through a tutorial.

This chapter provides various strategies for publicizing and marketing websites and tutorials by working with faculty, using social networking tools, and creating online and print marketing. In order to be able to promote or embed tutorials, videos, and podcasts into multiple venues quickly, it is important to remember to produce them in, or convert them into, multiple formats, such as narrated PowerPoints, MP4, MP3, downloads that open with Windows players or QuickTime. These formats allow users to download the material to their device of choice. It is also important to create options for users to view the information on a static web page (with additional options to link out to extra material), and, along with captioning material, to include the script of any video tutorial (either through a PDF or Word document). For an example of the representation of various formats see:

- Lonestar: *http://www.lonestar.edu/library/15286.htm*. Shows the QuickTime video, a link to YouTube, and a link for the script.

- Dalhousie chart with different formats of tutorials (Flash, YouTube, podcast, PDF script): *http://www.library.dal.ca/How/LibCasts/*.

The message

The message (whether print or electronic) that is disseminated can be one to alert students, faculty, and staff to the presence of the tutorial, video, or web page, as well as to the benefits or objectives. Another short message should be prepared to accompany any publicity pertaining to the resources. Messages could also contain quotes from those who have used the resource that might entice others to try it. Whatever the medium or mode of publicity, the message should end with a "hook" to get the intended audience to actually click on the link (and remember to include the link) to get to the tutorials or web pages.

Working with faculty to promote tutorials and websites

One of the most effective ways to bring visibility to a library tutorial is to work with faculty in the design of the tutorial to see that it brings value to the objectives and goals of a particular course. Once developed, faculty can easily link to the tutorial or embed it within their course website or course management system. The following list highlights some ways in which a faculty member can assist in the marketing of a tutorial.

- *Embed objects in course management systems.* Faculty can either link to a tutorial or embed it within their course site. The tutorial will then be easily accessible to students at the point of need in the course. However, if the tutorial provides information that faculty expect the student to master, then students should be required to complete it. A study carried out by Harkins and Rodrigues (2011) found that unless a tutorial was required or sufficiently embedded in a course management system, few students would voluntarily choose to complete it. Out of 75 respondents, only 12 (16 percent) provided feedback on the tutorials. One reason for this, according to the authors, could have been a perceived low value of online tutorials, or because the tutorial wasn't required. With so many other requirements, students may say that they don't have the time to do something extra, unless they can see its value clearly.

- *Link the objects in bibliographies, guides, and web pages.* Instructors are usually very willing to add relevant library resources and tutorials to their bibliographies and guides. Periodically, librarians should send personal notes to faculty about a resource that they think will be helpful to students and specifically suggest that it be included (or linked) from web pages and bibliographies. Because students frequently consult their course pages there is a much better chance of students seeing and clicking on the links.

- *Include a notice of the objects in faculty and student listservs/ newsletters.* Each semester librarians can send an update of new resources to these listservs and newsletters. A particular heading that is used each time can help alert readers to something that may be useful. The heading could be something like: "New and noteworthy from the library"; "Librarian's corner"; "Tips from the librarian"; "Research strategies from the librarian." Information should be succinct and easy to scan. Librarians need to work with faculty to get an ongoing spot in their departmental newsletter.

- *Alert faculty to objects that would be useful for them to show in classes.* It is less common for faculty to spend class time pointing out a particular library resource. This is another opportunity for librarians to show faculty how a particular resource will help a student accomplish a required task. However, to do so, librarians would need to know the syllabus for a course in order to know when a resource would complement that course. Many subject librarians routinely ask faculty for their syllabi and class bibliographies so that they can add in suggested library resources for a particular theme or day. Faculty would then be able to spend a few moments in class either highlighting or showing the resource.

Social network tools

The OCLC report (2010) found that 92 percent of college students use social networking sites. Many libraries have a presence on social networking sites. These are excellent avenues for highlighting announcements for library tutorials and learning objects that can help students with research. Figure 11.1 is a screenshot of the undergraduate library web page at the University of Illinois which uses various social networking tools.

The screenshot shows multiple social networking tools being used:

- Google Map (upper right-hand corner) which allows students not only to see the location of the undergraduate library but also to interact with location information.

- Instant messaging ("Ask a librarian") so students can chat with a librarian.

- Twitter feed which announces various research tidbits and suggestions. Many libraries and faculty have Twitter feeds that provide research tips, help, tidbits, and interesting strategies for using various library tools. Often, these feeds occupy a standard spot on library home pages, visible to thousands of students each day. A periodic mention

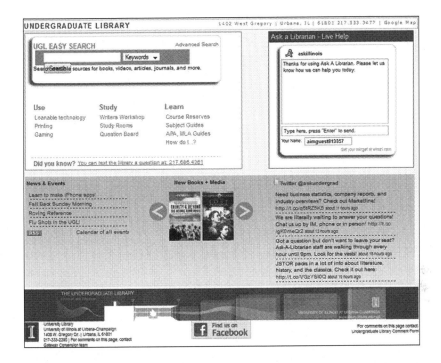

Figure 11.1   Example of social networking at the undergraduate library, University of Illinois

Source: http://www.library.illinois.edu/ugl/

of a specific tutorial or web page can be tweeted, in relation to how it can help a student. For example, the undergraduate library at the University of Illinois banks Twitter feeds that get displayed throughout the day. Examples include:

– When researching diseases, meds, or other med topics, try starting with Medline, easy to use, easy to understand: *http://t.co/8XSUAZFf.*

– Want to do academic research on movies? Sports? Fashion? Research these topics and more with Pop Culture Universe: *http://t.co/5mLvIyCm.*

– Need help figuring out how to use the ERIC database. View these tutorials at: *http://www.library.illinois.edu/diglit/blogs/eric.html.*

■ Blog (News and Events on the left-hand side) with announcements.

■ RSS feeds (web feed formats used to publish frequently updated works) are used in the New Books + Media rotating display. Students can subscribe to RSS feeds for Twitter as well.

- Facebook (bottom middle part of the page). Twitter feeds can also be directed to the library Facebook page. Frequently, new library videos or resources are embedded in the Facebook post to make it convenient for students to simply click on the resource.

- "Did you know?" Although this is not a social network tool, it is a rotating element on the page that attracts the attention of students.

In addition to pushing out announcements and resources using the library's social media and network tools, librarians should also explore the availability of these tools more broadly on campus and submit announcements and posts there as well.

Making resources more visible

The importance of metatags

In order for potential users to find tutorials or web pages it is critical that appropriate metatags, metadata, and subject headings be added wherever possible. In addition to using the title of a web page, a metatag is used by search engines to allow them to more accurately list a site in their indexes. Metatags need to be manually inserted in web page documents and online guides (like LibGuides). They can also be inserted during the processing stage of a tutorial, video, or other learning object, sometimes by clicking on author options. Figure 11.2 is an example of the page source for a web page that shows the metatags for name, description, keywords, author, and copyright.

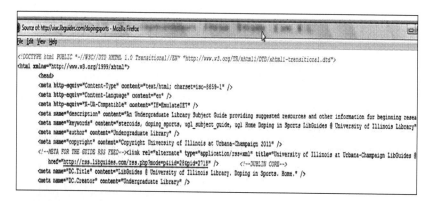

Figure 11.2 Example of page source showing metatags

Some web authors make the default metatags "all." Although this may seem like a good way to get all of the content indexed in search engines, some search engines only index a number of characters in the page, so some of the important characteristics may not be indexed. Also, even if the whole page is indexed, there may be terms that describe the page that are not included in the page. For example, a web page that describes how to use the ERIC database may not include phrases a student would use to find this resource such as, "finding information in ERIC" or "how to use ERIC."

A search of the tool using the library and university website search engine, Google, Bing, or any search engine will show how findable the product is. For example, a typical statement a student might type in a search engine to see how to use the ERIC database might be something like, "help with ERIC" or "how to search ERIC." Users may not think of adding the term "tutorial." Therefore, it is wise to use phrases similar to those used by the typical user. The goal is to have the ERIC tutorial that was developed appear close to the top of the results, or at least on the first page. If it doesn't, the links that do appear first should be examined to see what tags were used so that yours can be modified appropriately. Here are a few sources with suggestions on how to make a site more visible on the web:

- META builder. This page provides a form that generates HTML META tags for inclusion in HTML documents, including title, description, keywords, owner, author etc.: *http://vancouver-webpages. com/META/mk-metas.html*.

- Heng, Christopher (2008) How to improve your search engine ranking on Google. *Thesitewizard.com*. Available at: *http://www. thesitewizard.com/archive/google.shtml*.

- Heng, Christopher (2010) Why is my site not ranking in the search engines? Reasons for poor search engine ranking and how to make it rank better. *Thesitewizard.com*. Available at: *http://www.thesitewizard. com/sitepromotion/reasons-website-not-ranking-in-search-engines.shtml*.

The location of the learning object within web pages

A tutorial, video, or other learning object that is buried under several layers on the library website runs the risk of low use unless users know to search for it. Typically, users will not exert a lot of effort searching for an item, so it is best to make the pathway obvious. If there is some indication on the front page that tutorials are available a student may be more likely to make the effort to click on the link. Learning objects need to be easily findable, not just by students but by librarians who want to be able to direct a student to one as part of a reference question (face-to-face or virtual chat). The University of Illinois Library's video tutorials are currently two clicks away from the library homepage but had not been discovered by any participants in the Mestre (2010) study until they were directed to the videos during usability studies. One of the reasons for this may be due to terminology. The homepage has a link to LEARN to use the library. It also has a link to Subject Resource Guides. Either of these links seem like good options to students. However, when they click on either page there are so many categories and links that students may get overwhelmed. Due to recent usability testing, these terms and the locations on the pages are being changed to be more user friendly.

The multiple ways in which a student looks for information is another reason that links to tutorials and learning objects should be included in as many places as possible. Instead of just relying on including the tutorial in the main tutorial list, it should also be included in any relevant subject guides, on the database page (if it is a tutorial that pertains to a particular database), and on a help page. Tutorials should be placed on pages that are directly relevant to a student's point of need. In a study carried out by Bowles et al. (2010, p. 25), one student said, "It wouldn't occur to me to go to a page *just* for tutorials. But if I were on a page, say, about the main stacks, and a tutorial was linked to the bottom of that, it would be helpful."

Su and Kuo (2010) evaluated 37 tutorials from PRIMO (a database of online tutorials and other instructional resources, maintained by the ACRL). The presumption was that a tutorial posted on the top layers of the library website would have higher visibility. Most tutorials were two clicks from the library homepage (14, or 38 percent). An almost equal number of tutorials were three clicks way (13, or 35 percent). Only seven tutorials took one click to find (19 percent). One took as many as four clicks. Most contributors managed to situate tutorials one or two clicks away from the library homepage (57 percent). The results may suggest that librarians have become aware of the effect of website positioning. Tutorials buried in deeper layers, e.g., three or more clicks away, are less likely to be found.

Suggestions for promoting, linking, and embedding learning objects

The list below includes ideas for making learning objects more visible. Working with colleagues and faculty across campus is vital to finding relevant places to embed and link the learning objects.

- Determine the places that students look for information and situate tutorials there. Video tutorials have the potential to provide point-of-need instruction, but first librarians must find out what students need and the optimal places to post tutorials in terms of student access.

- Highlight an embedded video or tutorial on a web page and change it each month.

- Include tutorials on database pages. It seems obvious that pages which discuss databases should also include links to tutorials related to those databases. This is not common, unfortunately. For an example of how this is done on Brandon University's databases' pages see: *http://www2.brandonu.ca/library/databases/psychology.html*.

- Post a link to "Tutorial help" on the Help link (which is usually available on every library web page). For an example from Brandon University Libraries' help page see: *http://www2.brandonu.ca/library/infoservices.html*.

- Use selected pop-ups on web pages to highlight a new tutorial. Using pop-up messages can be annoying if overdone so these should be used selectively.

- Include new resources in newsletters, flyers, displays, bookmarks, and table tents. In addition to providing an announcement of a new learning object in online newsletters (both internal to the library and though other institutional channels) flyers can be made up to highlight a particular resource and placed on tables within the library, posted throughout departments, or even posted in bathroom stalls. The undergraduate library at the University of Illinois rotates bathroom stall flyers monthly. These flyers highlight services within the library or services by library partners (such as the careers center or the health center). Monthly rotating table tents (which are small flyers placed on tables) also provide tips and research strategies. These are great marketing tools because of the high number of students that see them (see Figure 11.3).

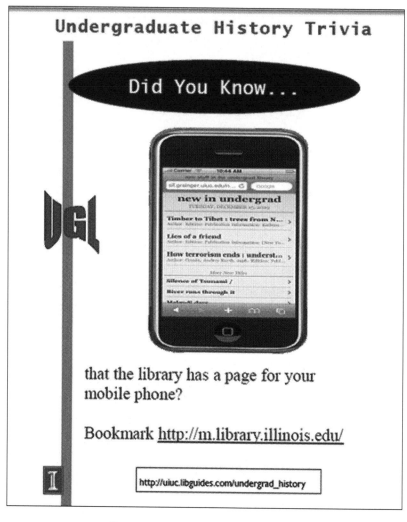

Figure 11.3 Example of table tent content highlighting mobile apps from the University of Illinois

Figure 11.4 is an example of a bathroom stall flyer that was converted to a smaller size to be also used as a table tent.

- Take advantage of displays. Displays are excellent ways in which to highlight new resources. Massey University Libraries maintains a marketing blog of examples. For an example of a display that was created to publicize their new "Discover database" which simulates a Google-style search see: *http://alisonwallbutton.wordpress.com/tag/displays/.*

| **Figure 11.4** | Example of a bathroom stall flyer from the University of Illinois |

The display also includes quotes from students. The complete marketing blog, "Marketing matters for librarians," is available at: *http://alisonwallbutton.wordpress.com/category/promotion/*.

- Incorporate videos into the institution's digital repository. This may also assist with findability and raise awareness of their availability.

- Include tutorials within subject guides. Many library subject guides may include links to tutorials. However, embedding the tutorial is much more effective. This can be done through web pages or in products like LibGuides. Subject librarians usually highlight relevant databases for specific topics. Figure 11.5 is an example of an embedded tutorial and illustrates how tutorials and videos can be embedded in an online subject guide. This guide highlights various learning objects and the page specifically discusses image tools. If a user is on this page it makes sense to include any tutorials related to the content of the page, such as the tutorial for Snag It (on the left-hand side).

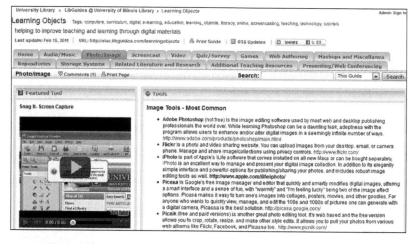

Figure 11.5 **Example of an embedded tutorial videoclip in a LibGuide from the University of Illinois**

Source: http://uiuc.libguides.com/content.php?pid=64638&sid=477614

- Download learning objects to commercial sites like YouTube, Google Video, ANTS, SlideShare, Screencast.com, MERLOT, and Vimeo. Most of these provide free accounts. These sites offer streaming capabilities that make embedding the learning objects into other pages and guides very easy. These resources are described in more detail in the next chapter.

- A video sharing site where users can easily upload and share videos not only provides a free way to stream videos and video tutorials, but is highly visible and popular with students. As YouTube is commonly acknowledged as an entertainment venue, it is questionable how many viewers would type in the right keywords to search for an information literacy video, or change gears and start watching if they actually bumped into one. Most YouTube videos are short and motion-picture based. While such a video requires a shorter attention span, it also makes squeezing in a content-rich information literacy video an almost impossible task, not to mention the issue of incorporating a large amount of text. Although the videos can be produced in modular format, they are not as easy to organize as web-based tutorials. Nevertheless, a YouTube or LibTube library video can be an excellent marketing tool with which to lead students back to web-based tutorials on a library homepage.

- Share with other libraries. By using multiple marketing venues other librarians may discover tutorials and learning objects that they could use. Librarians can opt to provide the code for their tutorial (especially if they use a Creative Commons license). Some of the repositories allow educators to download learning objects and modify them, although the originating library would then be credited in future iterations of the tutorial resulting from the code.

- Create a promotional video to highlight tutorials or resources. Student involvement with these videos is essential. They do not have to be produced professionally but should still be of high quality. Here are some examples:

  - "Academic Search Premiere: the library minute series" from Arizona State University: *http://www.youtube.com/watch?v=Yqtyxfdvai4&f eature=player_embedded*. This includes some humor, talking heads, and screen captures of the Academic Premier database.

  - "Who will help me?" from University of Alberta Libraries: *http://www.youtube.com/watch?v=uiLq2axJPew&feature=player_embedded*.

  - "UGL intro rap video" from the undergraduate library at the University of Illinois: *http://www.youtube.com/watch?v=rhY0gYKOT8c*.

  - "Introduction to the UGL" at the University of Illinois: the library has an ongoing PowerPoint digital display that changes weekly. It features various services, resources, and technology of interest to students. For an example using narrated PowerPoint that was converted into Camtasia to provide streaming see: *http://www.youtube.com/watch?v=NzIl5ichELA*.

Other resources

Library conferences and webcasts offer many opportunities to learn about marketing strategies. Many library sites (especially public libraries' sites) often include a section on events, exhibits, or programs. These are useful as they give examples of the ways in which the libraries market and publicize their efforts. The following list suggests some resources that might help in putting together a marketing plan:

- Library Marketing Plan Workbook: *http://www.nmstatelibrary.org/ docs/development/planning/Marketing_Plan_Workbook.pdf*. This includes sections on: Why marketing?; The basic steps of the marketing plan; Develop your marketing message; Determine your marketing medium(s); Set marketing goals; and Develop the marketing budget. The PDF includes templates available at: *http://www.stlib. state.nm.us/files/Marketing_Plan_Template.doc*.
- Ohio Library Council (2008) Marketing the library: *http://www.olc. org/marketing/*. Intended more for public libraries, but contains six self-paced modules that cover the steps of marketing. Includes categories (on the left-hand side) for overview, planning, products, promotion, Internet, and Ohio examples.
- Charlene McCormack and Doreen Harwood (2008). Marketing plan tutorial. University of Washington Bothell: *http://library.uwb.edu/ guides/tutorials/marketingtutorial/framedtutorial.html*.
- See also Appendix 5 for a sample communication plan.

Conclusion

Librarians and digital resources can play a critical role in today's students' life-long learning. Marketing is the key to pushing out the value of these resources. Preparing a marketing plan that involves all of the stakeholders will contribute to reaching users successfully. Marketing should be offered in multiple delivery modes to meet different user patterns, situations, and information needs. Librarians should take advantage of all of the publicity and marketing channels available to them, as well as be creative in generating others.

References

Bowles-Terry, M., Hensley, M.K. and Hinchliffe, L.J. (2010) Best practices for online video tutorials in academic libraries: a study of student preferences and understanding. *Communications in Information Literacy*, 4(1): 17–28.

Harkins, M.J. and Rodrigues, D.B. (2011) Where to start? Considerations for faculty and librarians in delivering information literacy instruction for graduate students. *Practical Academic Librarianship: The International Journal of the SLA Academic Division*, 1(1): 28–50.

Mestre, L.S. (2010) Matching up learning styles with learning objects: what's effective? *Journal of Library Administration*, 50(7–8): 808–82.

OCLC (2010) *Perceptions of Libraries, 2010: Context and Community*. Dublin, OH: OCLC. Available at: *http://www.oclc.org/reports/2010perceptions/2010perceptions_all_singlepage.pdf*.

Su, S.-F. and Kuo, J. (2010) Design and development of web-based information literacy tutorials. *The Journal of Academic Librarianship*, 36(4): 320–8. DOI: 10.1016/j.acalib.2010.05.006.

12

Resources

Abstract: Throughout this book, references have been made to various learning style questionnaires, tutorials, software, scripts, and other resources that can be used to create or locate learning objects. This chapter provides information pertaining to those and other resources that may be of use in the creation of learning objects. The resources below may require subscription fees, unless otherwise indicated. The Appendices contain additional specific examples. Many of these resource categories can also be found in an online version that will be frequently updated, see: *Learning Objects*, a LibGuide developed at the University of Illinois: *http://uiuc.libguides.com/learningobjects*.

Key words: learning styles, learning objects, multimedia, screencasting, multimedia tools, technology tools.

Resource categories are:

- Learning style inventories
- Repositories and sites for hosting learning objects and tutorials
- Organizations/websites devoted to online learning
- Storyboarding sites
- Free CGI scripts on the Internet
- Scripts for usability studies
- Screen capture tools
- Screencasting tools, including screencasting help, open source tools, and commercial software
- General software for creating learning objects
- PowerPoint/Flash conversion
- Images (image sites, image capturing and editing tools)
- Audio (recording, editing, music, sound effects)
- Video and software to integrate photos, videos, and audio (video editing and other software)

- Puzzles/games/activities

- Simulation/scenario/animation tools

- Mobile applications

- Test/assessment tools, and

- Eye tracking software and equipment.

Learning style inventories

Although there are many more, the following were discussed in this book:

- Barsch Learning Style Inventory (BSLI) provides a free inventory and score for each of three learning modalities – visual, auditory, and kinesthetic – at: *http://ww2.nscc.edu/gerth_d/AAA0000000/barsch_inventory.htm.*

- Dunn and Dunn Learning Style Questionnaire (LSQ). Variations available for purchase at: *http://www.learningstyles.net/en/our-assessments.*

- Entwistle Revised Approaches to Study Inventory (RASI) and Approaches and Study Skills Inventory for Students (ASSIST).

  - PDF available at: *http://www.nottingham.ac.uk/integrativelearning/images/File/Project%20Showcase/18-itemEntwistlesRASI.pdf.*

  - ASSIST scoring key: *http://www.etl.tla.ed.ac.uk/questionnaires/ASSIST.pdf.*

- Felder and Soloman Index of Learning Style Questionnaire (ILS) at: *http://www.engr.ncsu.edu/learningstyles/ilsweb.html.* This web page links to an online free learning style assessment based on the four dimensions of the Felder-Silverman model: active/reflective, sensing/intuitive, visual/verbal, and sequential/global. Additional links include validation studies, articles, and Dr. Felder's homepage.

- Flemming VARK Questionnaire ("How do I learn best?") at: *http://www.vark-learn.com/english/page.asp?p=questionnaire.*

- Gregorc Mind Styles Delineator available for purchase at: *http://gregorc.com/instrume.html.*

- Hermann Brain Dominance Instrument (HBDI) is a 120-question diagnostic survey that identifies your preferred approach to emotional, analytical, structural, and strategic thinking (right vs. left brain).

More information at: *http://www.hbdi.com/* and available for purchase at: *http://www.coco.co.uk/prodhbdi.html*.

- Honey and Mumford Learning Styles Questionnaire (LSQ). There are two versions of the LSQ: the 80-item original questionnaire and a 40-item questionnaire, both available at: *http://www.peterhoney.com/*.

- Kolb's Learning Style Inventory (LSI) available for purchase at: *http://learningfromexperience.com/tools/kolb-learning-style-inventory-lsi/*.

- Myers-Briggs Type Indicator available for purchase at: *https://www.cpp.com/products/mbti/index.aspx*. A variation of the test is available free online at: *http://www.humanmetrics.com/cgi-win/jtypes2.asp*.

- Rey, which assesses spatial and visual memory (Rey and Osterrieth, 1941, 1944, 1993). Available for purchase at: *http://psycnet.apa.org/index.cfm?fa=buy.optionToBuy&id=1992-25787-001*.

- VAK Visual, Auditory and Kinesthetic Survey available free at: *http://www.nwlink.com/~donclark/hrd/styles/vak.html*; *http://www.vaknlp.com/vak.htm*, and *http://www.brainboxx.co.uk/a3_aspects/pages/vak_quest.htm*, among other sites.

Repositories and sites for hosting learning objects and tutorials

There are many sites available that allow individuals to download learning objects. Some of these are very well-known and popular sites such as YouTube, Google Video, ANTS, Slideshare.net, Screencast, MERLOT, and Vimeo. Most of these provide free accounts. These sites offer streaming capabilities which allow the embedding of learning objects into web pages and guides very easily. The following list highlights some of the most common sites, which are either repositories for learning objects or they offer hosting solutions (free or by subscription).

Common repositories for locating learning objects (or contributing to the site)

- ANTS (Animated Tutorials Sharing Project). This is a collaborative project for sharing screencast tutorials for databases, catalogs, etc. Tutorials can be embedded in your own website or downloaded and used as a starting point for developing new tutorials. To view content and to contribute to tutorials visit the wiki at: *http://ants.wetpaint. com/*.

- Tutorial files on Screencast.com: *http://www.screencast.com/users/ ants*.

- Tutorial files on DSpace at the University of Calgary: *https://dspace. ucalgary.ca/handle/1880/43471*. Resources and examples related to the design of tutorials and learning objects, such as scripts used for usability studies, guidelines for designing tutorials, and descriptions and links to tutorials.

- *Blip.tv*. This allows free access to videos in a wide range of topics (usually part of a series). It also provides a dashboard for creating a series: *http://blip.tv/*.

- Google Video. In addition to its video search function, there is also a video uploader page (requires a free account): *http://www.google. com/videohp*.

- iTunesU from Apple: *http://www.apple.com/education/itunes-u/what- is.html*. This site provides educational podcasts, lectures, and learning objects, as well as the ability to upload podcasts. Examples from the University of Illinois Libraries are available at *https://itunes.illinois. edu/* in the Public Access area. You will need to download the free iTunes software: *http://www.apple.com/itunes/overview/*.

- Knoodle (an SK Telecom Americas portfolio company). This is primarily a tool for uploading PowerPoint and video to the web. It also includes a virtual classroom and some learning management features: *http://www.knoodle.com*.

- LibGuides from Springshare. These are web-based guides (with templates that allow the linking and embedding of videos and streamed learning objects). Examples are available at many library sites. See, for example: *http://uiuc.libguides.com/index.php*, and the learning objects guide at: *http://uiuc.libguides.com/learningobjects*. More information about LibGuides is available at: *http://www. springshare.com/libguides*.

- The Learning Edge EQUELLA LCMS (The Learning Edge International). This is a digital repository from Australia that incorporates learning objects, learning content management, and integrated content authoring. It is now owned by Pearson Education: *http://www.equella.com/*. For more information see: *http://www. thelearningedge.com.au/*.

- LION (Library Information Literacy Online Network). Participants in this project agree to make episodes openly available for others to link to, embed, share, download, or edit, provided the appropriate credit is assigned to the author (further information about all rights can be found by looking at the Creative Commons license associated with each episode). A variety of software is used to create these objects, see: *http://liontv.blip.tv/*.

- MERLOT (Multimedia Educational Resource for Learning and Online Teaching) offers a free, online repository for educational materials: *http://www.merlot.org*.

- PRIMO (Peer-Reviewed Instructional Materials Online). This database includes peer-reviewed instructional materials (in a variety of formats) created by librarians to teach people about discovering, accessing, and evaluating information in networked environments. Reviewed by members of the ALA ACRL Instruction Section: *http://www.ala.org/apps/primo/public/search.cfm*.

- Resource pages – screencasting and online tutorials. This is a wiki that lists tutorials created with a variety of software, including PowerPoint, Flash, Camtasia, and Wink. There are sections for school, public, and academic libraries: *http://lib20.pbworks.com/w/page/16753986/resources-screencasting*.

- *Screencast.com*, by TechSmith. In addition to free uploading and hosting of videos created with Jing and Camtasia (with a free account) there are options for sharing and embedding: *http://screencast.com/*.

- *Slideshare.net*. This site provides access to PowerPoint presentations and allows uploading (free account). Once PowerPoints have been uploaded they are streamed. It has editing tools to synchronize the audio and slides: *http://www.slideshare.net*. Examples include:

  - What is Library 2.0: *http://www.slideshare.net/sirexkat/what-is-library-20* (Kathryn Greenhill, Murdoch University).

  - Slidecasting 101: *http://www.slideshare.net/jboutelle/slidecasting-101*. Learn how to create a slidecast on *Slideshare.net*.

  - Slidecast on Slidecasting: *http://www.slideshare.net/pollyalida/slidecast-demo*. More details on creating a slidecast (by Polly Farington).

- TeacherTube. This site is a great free resource for instructional videos, documents, audio, and music files. With a free account learning objects can be uploaded: *http://teachertube.com/*.

- YouTube. In addition to finding learning objects, uploading is also available with a free account: *http://www.youtube.com/*.
- Vimeo. Vimeo provides free access for viewing files and offers options for uploading, including album options. Vimeo also offers Vimeo PRO and Vimeo Plus for more advanced options and features (for a fee). See, for example: *http://vimeo.com/dallibraries/albums*. For more information see: *http://www.vimeo.com/plus*.

Podcasting repositories

- *Digital podcast.com*. Includes a subject directory and sections for audiobooks, sound effects, podcast equipment, making a podcast, promoting your new podcasts: *http://www.digitalpodcast.com/*.
- iPodder. Hand-picked, peer-reviewed podcasts: *http://www.ipodder.org/*.
- iTunes. In addition to the enormous selection of audio files, you can also get access to iTunesU for university related podcasts: *http://www.apple.com/itunes/*.

In addition, there are a few general pages that may be of interest. They provide many more options than were listed above:

- For many categories, a PDF is available at: *http://www.trimeritus.com/vendors.pdf*.
- For many open source tools see: *http://sourceforge.net/*.
- Another site that is helpful for learning about options for uploading to websites is: *http://www.trimeritus.com/vendors.pdf* (Don McIntosh, December 2011, *Learning Management Vendors*, p. 100).

Organizations and websites devoted to online learning

- Educause. This is a nonprofit organization that provides programs, professional development activities, applied research, strategic policy advocacy, teaching and learning initiatives, and online information services. See their resources page (*http://www.educause.edu/resources*) for a repository for the use and management of information technology in higher education. For more information about Educause see: *http://www.educause.edu/*.

- Library Information Technology Association (LITA). This is a division of the American Library Association and is comprised of members interested in leading-edge technology and applications. It offers continuing education, guidelines, and a journal: *http://www.ala.org/lita/about*.

- The Sloan-C Consortium: Individuals, Institutions, and Organizations Committed to Quality Online. Education (Sloan-C). This organization provides workshops, conferences, webinars, publications, and reports, and is dedicated to integrating online education into the mainstream of higher education: *http://sloanconsortium.org/*.

- United States Distance Learning Association (USDLA). This association provides advocacy, networking, and information about online trends through web-based training, conferences, and publications: *http://www.usdla.org/*.

- WCET. This is a cooperative (WICHE Cooperative for Educational Technologies) that accelerates the adoption of effective practices and policies, advancing excellence in technology-enhanced teaching and learning in higher education. They offer resources, webcasts, and conferences related to online learning: *http://wcet.wiche.edu/*.

Storyboarding sites

- The eLearning Coach. These storyboard templates have been donated by the e-learning community for you to download and use for projects. There are a variety of types so you can pull features from one and add them to another. Available at: *http://theelearningcoach.com/resources/storyboard-depot/*.

- Illinois Online Network, Learning Styles and the Online Environment. University of Illinois. Available at: *http://www.ion.uillinois.edu/resources/tutorials/id/learningStyles.asp*.

- Resource Engineering Power Book Builder (Resource Engineering). A tool for developing PowerPoint storyboards and turning them into ToolBook courses. Other tools and the Esprit-LMS for ToolBook are offered at this site: *http://www.toolbookdeveloper.com*.

- xinsight. Storyboard templates: *http://xinsight.ca/tools/storyboard.html*.

Software

- Atomic Learning. StoryBoard Pro Software. This is freeware. *http://www.atomiclearning.com/storyboardpro*.

- Power Production Software. This is a site that offers a variety of software for storyboarding: *http://www.powerproduction.com/*.

- Other free storyboarding options:
  - *http://www.newfreedownloads.com/find/storyboard.html*
  - *http://www.freefilmsoftware.co.uk/*
  - *http://www.soft32.com/download_104137.html*
  - *http://www.bobsedulinks.com/software.htm*
  - *http://www.freedownloadmanager.org/download/storyboarding_software/*.

Free CGI scripts on the Internet

The following is a list of resources for librarians to access free CGI scripts on the Internet. It involves cutting and pasting CGI codes into header and body parts of HTML pages. In most cases, instructions for using them are simple and clear:

- CGIScripts.directory.com: *http://www.cgiscript-directory.com/*.
- CGI resource index: *http://cgi.resourceindex.com/*.
- Free CGI scripts: *http://www.free-cgi.com/freecgi/hosting/index.php*.
- FTLS.org – free CGI archives: *http://www.ftls.org/en/examples/cgi/*.
- HotScripts.com: *http://www.hotscripts.com/*.
- Krystyna's CGI Scripts for Educators: *http://www.tesol.net/scripts/scriptsdetails.html*.
- Matt's Script Archive: *http://www.scriptarchive.com/*.
- Scriptsearch.com: *http://www.scriptsearch.com*.

Scripts for usability studies

Ballard, J. (2010) *Website Usability: A Case Study of Student Perceptions of Educational Websites*. Unpublished dissertation, University of Minnesota. Appendices A and B include forms and scripts for usability studies. Available at: *http://conservancy.umn.edu/bitstream/91797/1/Ballard_umn_0130E_11150.pdf*.

Blummer, B. (2007) Assessing patron learning from an online library tutorial. *Community & Junior College Libraries*, 14(2): 121–38. Available at: *http://dx.doi.org/10.1300/02763910802139397*. Also includes in Appendix I: interest/knowledge/skills checklist; and in Appendix II: usability tests, questions, and problem-recognition tasks.

Bowles-Terry, M., Hensley, M.K., Janicke Hinchliffe, L. (2010) Best practices for online video tutorials in academic libraries: a study of student preferences and understanding. *Communications in Information Literacy*, 4(1): 17–28. Includes the process and questions asked during the study.

Bury, S. and Oud, J. (2005) Usability testing of an online information literacy tutorial. *Reference Services Review*, 33(1): 54–65. Includes questions asked about each module.

Mestre, L.S. (2010) Matching up learning styles with learning objects: what's effective? *Journal of Library Administration*, 50(7–8): 808–29. See Appendices 2 and 3 in this book for the actual scripts.

Oehrli, J.A., Peters, A. and Nanamaker, B. (2011) Do screencasts really work? Assessing student learning through instructional screencasts. *ACRL* (pp. 127–44), March 30–April 2, 2011. Philadelphia, Pennsylvania. Appendices A and B in the article have the assessment survey and the complete script using Qualtrics assessment software (pp. 136–44).

Rohmann, G., Tempelman-Kluit, N. and Pavelsek, M.J. (2002) Web usability testing: three cases from NYU libraries. *Connect*. Available at: *http://www.nyu.edu/its/pubs/connect/archives/spring02/libraries.html*. For their script see: *http://www.nyu.edu/library/resources/usability/testing2.htm*.

Song, L., Singleton, E., Hill, J. and Hwa Koh, M. (2004) Improving online learning: student perceptions of useful and challenging characteristics. *Internet and Higher Education*, 7: 59–70. Appendix A in the article includes the interview protocol.

Screen capture tools

The screen capture tools mentioned below allow for snapshots to be taken of screens. Some of the software has very basic editing tools and other software is more robust. Most of the following are free or can be purchased at very low cost from the company website. As an alternative, those on a budget may wish to try free screencasting software such as Jing or Wink. While limited in terms of the number of features they possess they do provide basic functionality, interaction, audio, and a simple intuitive interface to work with. Documentation and links to the software can be found at the project websites. See the following LibGuide for print screen and snapshot options for additional resources: *http://uiuc.libguides.com/content.php?pid=64638&sid=477614*.

- Aviary. Put "*http://aviary.com*" in the front of any web page URL. That web page then comes up inside an image editor, including graphics and effects editor. This is a free scaled down version of Photoshop: *http://aviary.com/*.

- Camstudio is a free version of Camtasia that allows for screen captures and screencasting. It does not have the robust editing features however: *http://camstudio.org*.

- Easy Capture is free and captures screenshots, including windows screen capture, scrolling windows screen capture, and selected-regions screen capture. It also allows you to edit the screen captures and add balloon stamps: *http://www.xydownload.com/easycapture/*.

- FireShot add-on is useful for free quick website screenshots. This is an add-on for browsers (Firefox, IE, Google Chrome) (built-in screen capture options to get the screen shots): *http://screenshot-program.com/fireshot/*.

- Gadwin offers a free or pro account to perform full- or window-screen captures, with some editing features: *http://www.gadwin.com/ printscreen/*.

- HardCopy is a free screen capture software that enables you to print or save the current window or screen – whether you are taking screenshots to produce documentation, printing off records, or anything else. Not as robust as Gadwin or Snagit but if you don't want to annotate, it is fine. You could import it into a graphics program to annotate: *http://www.gen.hardcopy.de/*.

- Jing is free for screen captures and screencasting: *http://www. techsmith.com/jing.html*.

- MWSnap is a free program for taking screen captures of a desktop, an active window, menu, or a specified part of the screen. The program supports BMP, JPG, TIFF, PNG, and GIF formats, with user-selected color depth and quality settings. It also includes a zooming tool, a screen ruler, and a color picker as well as system-wide hotkeys and preset selection sizes: *http://www.snapfiles.com/get/mwsnap.html*.

- Pearl Crescent Page Saver captures an image (PNG) of a complete web page. This is a plug-in for Firefox and the basic version is free: *http:// pearlcrescent.com/products/pagesaver/*.

- Safari Snapshooter saves an instant picture of any web page to your desktop. After you create an account at *http://www.talkingletter.com*, a free copy of *The Snapshooter* is sent to you by email: *http://safarid. com/index.php?page_id=256*.

- Snagit by TechSmith Corporation is a static screen capture tool with nice editing features and can be bundled with Camtasia: *http://www. techsmith.com.*

- Skitch is a free web service (beta) to upload pictures from cameras, capture screenshots, add captions and text: *http://skitch.com/.*

- WebSnapshot allows you to enter the URL and press snap. Or drag and drop it from your browser. Click on the thumbnails to save: *http://myspyder.net/tools/websnapshot/.*

Screencasting tools, including screencasting help, open source tools, and commercial software

This section includes resources to help record screens and create screencasts. These tools offer more than just taking a snapshot of a static page (as represented above). Some of the products below are part of learning management systems, but most can be obtained independently. A general resource with examples is available at: *http://lib20.pbworks. com/w/page/16753986/resources-screencasting.* This site also has a section with tips, tools, ideas, and resources for screencasting. Joe Ganci produced an article called "Seven top authoring tools" providing a comparison of their features at: *http://www.learningsolutionsmag.com/ articles/768/?utm_campaign=lsmag&utm_medium=email&utm_ source=lsm-news.* The following PDF provides the guidelines used to create the Camtasia tutorials at the University of Illinois Libraries: *http:// www.library.illinois.edu/diglit/camtasia.pdf.*

Screencasting help

- Screen capture, screencasting, and software demo tools: *http://c4lpt. co.uk/Directory/Tools/capture.html.*

- Free recording/hosting comparison: *http://www.notess.com/screencasting/ 2008/04/07/free-recordinghosting-comparison/#more-72.* Greg Notess created the same screencast demo using five different free screencasting tools: uTIPu, Webinaria, FreeScreenCast's Screencast Recorder, Jing, and Screencast-O-Matic (April 2008).

- Screencasting primer: *http://beth.typepad.com/beths_blog/2007/03/screencasting_p.html*. Lots of tips and tricks for producing great screencasts.

- Twelve screencasting tools for creating video tutorials: *http://mashable.com/2008/02/21/screencasting-video-tutorials/*. Some additional free and commercial software options for screencasting.

- Screencasting set-up for Macs: *http://css-tricks.com/screencasting-setup/*.

Open source (free) screencasting tools (for additional options see the LibGuide: http://uiuc.libguides.com/content.php?pid=646 38&sid=477617)

- BSR Screen Recorder: *http://www.thesilver.net/ from bsrsoft*. Captures video, sound, pictures, or anything on a screen. Features 2D and 3D zooming during recording. Allows for up to 15 minutes' free recording. Uses Avi editor.

- CamStudio: *http://camstudio.org/*. Free version of Camtasia. Records screen and audio activity and turns the AVI files into streaming Flash videos. Limited editing.

- Capture Fox: *https://addons.mozilla.org/en-US/firefox/addon/8090*. Handy add-on for Firefox that will record anything on your computer screen (browser or desktop apps). Choice of recording quality and frames-per-second. Recording is saved to your computer. Must upload to a video site to share.

- Jing: *http://www.jingproject.com/*. TechSmith. Free hosting and sharing for Windows and Mac. Limited bandwidth. Useful for on-the-fly screencasting for reference chat services. Includes hosting on *Screencast.com*. For examples of Jing tutorials (hosted on *Screencast.com*) see Houston Community College Libraries: *http://library.hccs.edu/learn_how/tutorials.php*.

- Screencast-O-Matic: *http://screencastomatic.com/*. Create your screencast online. Java-based tool lets you capture screen actions, records and exports .mov file. See examples (and tips) produced by the Collins Hill High School Media Center at: *http://www.chhsmediacenter.com/tutorials.html*.

- Screenr: *http://www.screenr.com/*. Creates a format that can be viewed natively on the iPhone. Designed to work directly with Twitter.

- Wink: *http://www.debugmode.com/wink/*. Free, open source, capture; screen action; post-capture editing; audio options. For an example see "Optimizing pictures in PowerPoint": *http://www.indeavors.com/resources/ppt1_tut.htm*.

Commercial screencasting tools (for additional options see the LibGuide: http://uiuc.libguides. com/content.php?pid=64638&sid=477617)

- AllCapture from Balesio: *http://www.allcapture.com/eng/index.php*.

- Camtasia Studio from Techsmith Corporation (*http://www.techsmith. com*): *http://www.techsmith.com/camtasia.asp* – a screen recorder and simulation tool. One of the most robust and popular screencasting tools. It also handles PowerPoint, video, and audio and can be used for lecture capture. Techsmith also offers Snagit for static screen capture, and Jing: *http://www.techsmith.com/jing/* – a free web-based screen capture tool. Camtasia and Snagit are also available as part of Lectora Inspire. For examples of Camtasia tutorials see the University of Illinois tutorials at: *http://www.library.illinois.edu/learn/tutorials/*

  – Camtasia for Mac: *http://www.techsmith.com/camtasiamac/*. Mac version of Techsmith's Camtasia product, includes editing.

- Captivate from Adobe: *http://www.adobe.com/products/captivate/*. Another robust and popular screencasting tool. For examples see University of Washington University Libraries: *http://guides.lib. washington.edu/howdoi*.

- iShowU. For Mac recording and editing options and audio features: *http://www.shinywhitebox.com/home/home.html*.

- LECTURNITY (imc AG): *http://www.im-c.com/en/products/professional-authoring/product-overview/product-overview/* and *http://www.im-c.com/en/products/presentation-recording/#anchormain*.

- Morae from TechSmith. In addition to capturing audio, screen activity, and keyboard/mouse input, Morae is a good tool for usability studies to discover patterns and calculations and graphs' data: *http://www.techsmith.com/morae.html*.

- Qarbon ViewletBuilder: *http://www.qarbon.com/presentation-software/viewletbuilder/?os=win*. Also offers ViewletACE: a test and assessment tool; ViewletCam: a screen recorder for software simulations; and Composica.

- Examples from Washington State University: *http://www.wsulibs. wsu.edu/electric/search/category_results.asp?loc=tutorials&cat=Instructional+Viewlets.*

- ScreenFlow offers lots of features, including editing. For Mac: *http:// www.varasoftware.com/.*

- SWiSH Max is an advanced Flash creation tool, offering drawing tools, scripting, and Flash video: *www.swishzone.com/.*

- Wondershare DemoCreator is similar to Wink and captures screenshots and mouse movement on the screen: *http://www.sameshow.com/buy/ demo-creator-giveaway-buy.html.*

Screencasting for mobile devices

- Screenchomp (developed by Techsmith, also known for Camtasia). For more information see: *http://www.techsmith.com/labs.html.* Free download from iTunes: *http://itunes.apple.com/us/app/screenchomp/ id442415881?mt=8.*

- Educreations. For more information see: *http://www.educreations. com/.* Free download from iTunes: *http://itunes.apple.com/us/app/ educreations-interactive-whiteboard/id478617061?mt=8.*

Both the above apps are free and allow the user to draw and write freeform on the iPad screen as you might do with a tablet PC. The ease of use of these two apps makes screencasting a possibility for the iPad. It would be very easy to turn out a quick screencast for a class. Limitations include a lack of options for exporting video. Screenchomp only exports to Facebook, and Educreations only connects with Facebook or its own third-party video hosting service.

General software for creating learning objects

- Adobe Acrobat Connect Professional Presenter. Formerly Macromedia Breeze Presenter, it is a PowerPoint converter designed to work specifically with Acrobat Connect Professional (see Virtual Classroom). Adobe obtained this and the following products as a result of its purchase of Macromedia in 2005: *http://www.adobe.com/products/ presenter/.*

- Adobe AIR. A runtime that lets developers use proven web technologies to build rich Internet applications that run outside the browser on multiple operating systems in order to provide performance support to learners, who can be either online or offline: *http://www.adobe.com/products/air*.

- Adobe Captivate is primarily a screen application capture tool (screencasting) but its capabilities have been extended so that it is now a pretty complete and popular authoring tool: *http://www.adobe.com/products/captivate*.

- Adobe Contribute. For website and blog content management: *http://www.adobe.com/products/contribute/*.

- Adobe Director. For the development of games and multimedia applications: *http://www.adobe.com/products/director/*.

- Adobe Dreamweaver is a widely used website creation tool which can be used for course authoring as well as with the CourseBuilder extension particularly: *http://www.adobe.com/products/dreamweaver*.

- Adobe e-learning suite. The suite includes Flash, Captivate, Dreamweaver, Photoshop, Acrobat Pro, Presenter, Soundbooth, Bridge CS5, and Device Central CS5: *http://www.adobe.com/products/elearningsuite/*.

- Adobe Flash. The almost universal animation/video plug-in which can be used for course authoring in the hands of a skilled programmer: *http://www.adobe.com/products/flash/*. Two examples are: University of Glasgow Study Skills Tutorial at: *http://www.lib.gla.ac.uk/Training/tilt/studyskills.shtml*; and Acadia University Library: Plagiarism at: *http://library.acadiau.ca/tutorials/plagiarism/*.

- Adobe RoboHelp for building help systems: *http://www.adobe.com/products/robohelp*.

- Apple iLife. iLife is a suite of applications that can be used to create digital content, such as pictures, movies, music, and web pages. Some use it to create e-learning. It is available only for Mac OSX: *http://www.apple.com/ilife/*.

- Brainshark converts any kind of document (video, PowerPoint, etc.) to web-friendly, SCORM, and mobile formats. Allows adding voice recordings to each. Tests can be created. Mybrainshark is available free: *http://www.brainshark.com*.

- Breakthrough Performance Tech Performance Drilling. A verbal performance simulator and avatar creator for rapid course authoring: *http://www.bptresults.com/*.

- Cogentys Flash authoring tool is part of their LMS. It includes PowerPoint to Flash conversion and quiz and survey creation. Cogentys also offers eLearningTV (*http://www.elearningtv.net/*) with monthly video updates and discussions: *http://www.cogentys.com*.

- Knowledge Direct (Digitec Inc.). Part of the Knowledge Direct Learning Management System. Includes PowerPoint conversion, games, test questions, and audio: *http://www.knowledgedirectweb.com*.

- HTML5. A new standard for structuring web content. It incorporates multimedia features that have been previously dependent on third-party browser plug-ins such as Adobe Flash and Microsoft Silverlight: *http://www.w3.org/TR/html5/*, *http://www.html5rocks.com/*.

- Mindflash. A collaborative authoring tool for e-learning with a portal for delivery. Conversion from PowerPoint, video, Word, or PDF files. Also offers online quiz creation: *http://www.mindflash.com*.

- NYCircuits ScreenBook Maker. A tool for creating visual tutorials for computer training. They also offer the Joomla CMS: *http://www.nycircuits.com*.

- One True Media. A free tool that can combine video, audio, music, images, and texts into one synchronized learning object: *http://www.onetruemedia.com/*.

- Raptivity provides a pre-built library of rapidly-customizable interaction models. There are software templates with over 245 learning interactive templates to allow for the user to customize games, simulations, brainteasers, interactive diagrams, virtual worlds, and more to your course within minutes. The content published by Raptivity is a single Flash file so it fits right into hundreds of e-learning tools and can be used anywhere: *http://www.raptivity.com/elearning-product/*.

- Snap! by Lectora is a flash interaction builder. Very inexpensive. PowerPoint to Flash converter (with templates) with YouTube and video narration capabilities. Quizzes and surveys can be added and results captured and sent to a custom database: *http://rapid-e-learning.trivantis.com/*.

- Trivantis Lectora Publisher. Can publish to HTML5 for mobile learning. Also offers Lectora Inspire which includes TechSmith Camtasia, Snagit, Flypaper, and Snap!: *http://www.trivantis.com*.

- UBC MLOAT (University of British Columbia Multimedia Learning Object Authoring Tool) is a free tool that can combine video, audio, images, and texts into one synchronized learning object. Offered along with several other tools: *http://www.learningtools.arts.ubc.ca/mloat.htm.*

- Wildform Flair is a general authoring tool that allows users to create Flash and video presentations, convert PowerPoint to Flash, create quizzes, etc. Also offers Flix for Flash video and Wild FX for Flash text animation: *http://www.wildform.com.*

- William Horton Consulting Templates. Offers e-learning and PowerPoint templates: *http://www.horton.com/productintro.aspx.*

- Wondershare Rapid E-Learning Suite includes PPT2 Flash for PowerPoint conversion, QuizCreator, DemoCreator, and WebVideo Author: *http://www.sameshow.com.*

- Zenler Studio. This is a beta release of a "Game-based e-learning course development tool." It includes PowerPoint conversion and quiz creation features: *http://www.zenler.com.*

PowerPoint/Flash conversion

PowerPoint is a tool that is widely used by educators and librarians. It is very common for tutorials to be built using PowerPoint and then converted to Flash. Camtasia and Captivate provide easy uploading of PowerPoint presentations which then can be converted to Flash. However, there are many other resources available (many that are open source) that can convert these files to Flash. A list of PowerPoint to Flash conversion tools is available at: *http://www.masternewmedia. org/2004/04/14/powerpoint_to_flash_conversion_tools.htm.* Here are some examples (for additional examples see this LibGuide: *http://uiuc. libguides.com/aecontent.php?pid=64638&sid=2925263*):

- Cisco WebEx Presentation Studio is a hosted (SaaS) PowerPoint, video, etc., converter. You can create multimedia presentations with video, PowerPoint slides, and audio: *http://www.webex.com.*

- DigitalOfficePro PowerFlashPoint offers a PowerPoint to Flash converter and PowerQuizPoint for creating quizzes: *http://www. digitalofficepro.com.*

- FlashDemo FlashPoint offers a PowerPoint converter and FlashDemo Studio for screen capture: *http://www.flashdemo.net.*

- Flypaper provides a Flash conversion and digital signage tool. It is also available as part of Trivantis Lectora Inspire: *http://www. flypaper.com.*

- iSpring Pro is a PowerPoint to Flash converter. Also available is iSpring Presenter, QuizMaker, and SDK: *http://www.ispringsolutions. com.*

- LecShare Pro is a tool that provides for conversion of PowerPoint presentations with audio to QuickTime movies, accessible HTML, MPEG-4 files (video podcasts), and/or Microsoft Word documents: *http://www.lecshare.com.*

- Open Office is an open source office suite which converts PowerPoint to Flash and MS Word documents to PDF: *http://www.openoffice. org.*

- PresentationPro PowerCONVERTER and OnlinePRESENTER. These are PowerPoint plug-ins: *http://www.presentationpro.com/.*

- Speechi Pro is a PowerPoint converter in several versions with additional features like audio, quiz, and SCORM modules and whiteboard support: *http://www.speechi.net/us.*

- SWiSH Max4 is a PowerPoint to Flash converter with Flash editing tools. Also available is SWiSH Video 3 for the conversion of video to Flash: *http://www.swishzone.com.*

- Trivantis Snap! A PowerPoint converter with YouTube and video narration capabilities. Snap! Empower enables the creation of Flash animations: *http://www.trivantis.com/snap/e-learning-software-for-PowerPoint-Presentations.*

- Wondershare PPT Flash Professional is a PowerPoint to Flash converter: *http://www.sameshow.com.*

Images (image sites, image capturing and editing tools)

Image sites

- Creative Commons search: provides the ability to search different websites (like Google Images, Flickr, and Wikimedia Commons) for Creative Commons works. Enter your search query, then click on the database you wish to search: *http://search.creativecommons.org/.*

- Flickr is a free photo- and video-sharing website. You can upload images from your desktop, email, or camera phone. Manage and share image/collections using privacy controls: *http://www.flickr.com/*.

- Flickr Creative Commons provides images that have been given special permission to be used in a variety of settings: *http://www.flickr.com/creativecommons/*.

- morgueFile: this site allows you to search easily for free images to use in a presentation. Use the search filter to find photos based on keyword, category, size, color, and more: *http://www.morguefile.com/*.

- Office.com Images. Microsoft Office has collected a series of royalty-free clip art and photos for use in presentations: *http://office.microsoft.com/en-us/images/*.

- iStockphoto has photos, illustrations, video, etc., available for purchase: *http://www.istockphoto.com/*.

- Photos 8 is a source for copyright-friendly photos and desktop wallpapers: *http://photos8.com/*.

- Picasa is Google's free image manager and editor that quickly modifies digital images: *http://picasa.google.com/*.

- Picnik (free and to-pay versions) is another great photo editing tool. The free version allows you to crop, rotate, resize, and make other style edits. It allows you to pull your photos from various web albums like Flickr, Facebook, and Picasa too: *http://www.picnik.com/*.

- Pics4Learning is a source for copyright-friendly images selected specifically for teachers and students, arranged by topic: *http://pics4learning.com/*.

- stock.xchng is a site that hosts free images uploaded by contributors. You can upload your own images as well: *http://www.sxc.hu/*.

- World Images Kiosk: search for images for academics' projects, grouped by subject: *http://worldimages.sjsu.edu/*.

- Wylio is an image search site that only displays Creative Commons licensed images, and automatically creates citation information: *http://www.wylio.com*.

Image capture and editing tools

- Adobe Fireworks: *http://www.adobe.com/products/fireworks.html*.

- Adobe Photoshop (not free) is the image editing software used by most web and desktop publishing professionals the world over. While learning Photoshop can be a daunting task, adeptness with the program allows users to enhance and/or alter digital images in a seemingly infinite number of ways: *http://www.adobe.com/products/ photoshop/main.html* and *http://success.adobe.com/en/na/sem/ products/photoshopfamily.html?sdid=IBFJQ&skwcid=TC|22179|ado be%20photoshop||S|e|7383519382.*

- GIMP is one open source alternative to Photoshop: *http://www.gimp. org/.*

- iPhoto is part of Apple's iLife software that comes installed on all new Macs, or can be bought separately. iPhoto is an excellent way to manage and present your digital image collection. In addition to its simple interface and powerful options for publishing/sharing your photos, it includes robust image editing tools: *http://www.apple.com/ ilife/iphoto/.*

- IrfanView is a free (for personal and educational use) graphics viewer for Windows: *http://www.irfanview.ca/.*

- Picasa is a software download from Google that helps you organize, edit, and share your photos. It's free, and easy to use: *http://picasa. google.com.*

- Photofiltre is a free image editor: *http://photofiltre.en.softonic.com/.*

- Snagit (not free). This is a robust screen capture software to capture all or parts of screens and edit, including a feature to add captions: *http://www.techsmith.com/screen-capture.asp.*

- XnView is a free utility that can be used for viewing and converting graphics files. You may wish to use XnView to add images to your course website, or to create custom icons for your site: *http://www. xnview.com/.*

Audio

Recording

- Audacity: an excellent, open source and free audio editor that is often of better quality than the built-in recorders used in screencasting and videos: *http://audacity.sourceforge.net/.*

- Juice (from *http://www.chhsmediacenter.com/jaycut.html* Podnova Windows Library) is a free podcast receiver and syncing tool for Windows: *http://windows.podnova.com/software/7803.htm*.

- NanoGong is a voice recording tool that can be added to Moodle or a website: *http://gong.ust.hk/nanogong/*.

- OPTX ScreenWatch Producer (OPTX International) is software for recording lectures: *http://www.screenwatch.com/*.

- Podbean.com is a podcasting tool: *http://podbean.com/*.

- ReadSpeaker is a tool for getting a spoken version of online content: *http://www.readspeaker.com*.

- Tuval Speech-Over. Adds voice-over narration to PowerPoint presentations: *http://www.speechover.com*.

Music

- Free Music Archive. Choose from high-quality music files, searchable by genre to use in multimedia projects: *http://freemusicarchive.org/*.

- Incompetech. Royalty free music: *http://incompetech.com/m/c/royalty-free/*.

- Rumblefish. A website where you can search for and purchase licenses for audio files for use in published videos: *http://www.rumblefish.com/index.php*.

- ccMixter. Free, copyright-free music: *http://www.ccmixter.org/*.

Sound effects

- A1 Free Sound Effects. Download sound effects files for free: *http://www.a1freesoundeffects.com/*.

- The Freesound Project. Free Creative Commons licensed sound effects files: *http://www.freesound.org/*.

- Jamendo. Free downloadable music: *http://www.jamendo.com/en/*.

- SoundBible. Sound effects clips. Use the search bar at the right of the screen to see if the site has the sound you are looking for: *http://soundbible.com/*.

Video and software to integrate photos, videos, and audio (video editing and other software)

Video editing

- Apple iLife. iLife is a suite of applications that can be used to create digital content, such as pictures, movies, music, and web pages. Some people use it to create e-learning. It is available only for Mac: *http://www.apple.com/ilife/*. An example of a video created in iMovie from the undergraduate library at the University of Illinois is available at: *http://www.youtube.com/watch?v=rhY0gYKOT8*.

- Final Cut Pro X for Mac. Robust Apple product for video editing and media organization: *http://www.apple.com/finalcutpro/top-features/*.

- Premiere (Adobe). A professional robust video editor. Examples of movies edited with Adobe Premiere at the University of Illinois Libraries are available at: *http://www.library.illinois.edu/diglit/video/index.html*.

- Windows Movie Maker. This is a video editor and media management software program that comes with Windows and allows users to import screenshots, photos, videos, and other media, add narration and captions, and then export as a video. A web page with tips and a video from Collins Hill High School Media Center are at: *http://www.chhsmediacenter.com/moviemaker-tutorials.html*.

Other software to create animated presentations

- One True Media. Free and pro accounts to mix media and use templates, music, transitions, and sound effects to create a mashup video: *http://www.onetruemedia.com/*. Examples at: *http://uiuc.libguides.com/exhibit*. In addition to creating photo exhibits, the images can be uploaded to One True Media and transitions and audio added, such as with the Michael Jackson Exhibit at: *http://uiuc.libguides.com/content.php?pid=192935&sid=1617667*.

- Prezi. Free 100mb and pro version available. Users can import media, pan and zoom, use templates and storylines: *http://prezi.com/index/*. See school examples at: *http://www.chhsmediacenter.com/prezi.html*.

- SWiSH Max4 is a PowerPoint to Flash converter with Flash editing tools. There is also the SWiSH Video 3 for conversion of video to Flash: *http://www.swishzone.com*.

- VoiceThread allows users to create a narrated slide show from photos and images. It is great for digital storytelling, narrating presentation slides, and much more. No software needed: *http://voicethread.com/*.
  - "I Love Databases": sample presentation by Joyce Valenza.
  - "Noodle Bib Tutorial": Susan Geiger, Hayward, CA.
- Xtranorma is a free animated movie making tool: *http://www.xtranormal.com*.
- Zentation provides free and pro accounts to combine video and slides to create presentations. Videos can be posted at Google Video, or PowerPoint slides to Zentation. The video runs right next to your slide: *http://zentation.com/*. An example presentation is available at: *http://zentation.com/viewer/index.php?passcode=epbcSNExIQr*.

Puzzles, games, and activities

- Half-Baked Software Hot Potatoes. Freeware (not open source) for tests and assessments. Also offers Quandary (open source) for creating web-based action mazes – a kind of interactive case-study: *http://hotpot.uvic.ca*.
- Raptivity provides a pre-built library of rapidly-customizable interaction models. There are software templates with over 245 learning interactive templates to allow the user to customize games, simulations, brainteasers, interactive diagrams, virtual worlds, and more to a course within minutes. The content published by Raptivity is a single Flash file so it fits into hundreds of e-learning tools and can be used anywhere: *http://www.raptivity.com/elearning-product*.
- Respondus. This is a test and assessment creation and management tool that is part of the Web CT/Blackboard Learning Management System. Also available is Respondus StudyMate, a stand-alone tool that provides options for the creation of game-like activities and puzzles: *http://www.respondus.com*.
- TrainingPlace.com is an example of a commercial personal learning system based on learning styles research. The system presents different "learning experiences" based on whether they are "transforming, performing, conforming, or resistant" learners (Learner Orientation Theory): *http://trainingplace.com/*.

- Webducate Dragster is a rapid authoring tool to create drag and drop activities using multimedia. Works with Articulate and Wimba. Also offers Accessible Multimedia Player (AMP) and Pollster: *http://www.webducate.net.*

Simulation, scenario, and animation tools

- Adobe Flash Builder is a 3D simulation development tool that is also used for developing cross-platform rich Internet applications and content using the open source Flex framework: *http://www.adobe.com/products/flashbuilder.*
- CodeBaby Studio is for the creation of 3D characters (avatars): *http://codebaby.com.*
- Experience Builders is a role-playing simulation builder: *http://www.experiencebuilders.com.*
- JeLSIM Builder is a free toolkit for producing educational simulations: *http://www.jelsim.org/* and *https://jelsim.dev.java.net/.*
- Knowledge Quest Expert Author and Xstream Media includes software for simulation tools: *http://www.knowledgequest.com.*
- Linden Research Second Life is a 3D animated social networking community with great potential for learning: *http://secondlife.com.*
- NexLearn SimWriter is a social simulation creator: *http://www.nexlearn.com.*
- Proton Media ProtoSphere is a 3D simulation environment: *http://www.protonmedia.com/.*
- Regis Learning Solutions' (RLS) Framework 3.0 is an e-learning development platform that includes assessment tools. They also offer the SimPort simulation platform for simulation development: *http://www.regislearning.com.*
- Right Seat Vox Proxy. Provides an add-in for PowerPoint to create 3D talking animated characters: *http://www.voxproxy.com.*
- Roleplay (based in New Zealand) is a SaaS based tool for designing scenario-based learning. Includes analytics: *http://www.roleplaytraining.com.*
- Snap! Empower by Flypaper interface is a WYSIWYG drag-and-drop Flash interactions builder: *http://rapid-e-learning.trivantis.com/.*

- TelSim NOAH. An animated talking character/avatar for e-learning or web pages: *http://www.noahx.com*.

- Thinking Worlds (Caspian Learning) is a 3D engine and authoring environment which enables designers to create and publish highly immersive simulations like Second Life: *http://www.thinkingworlds.com*.

- Vcom3D Vcommunicator Studio allows users to develop animated characters. The suite includes Gesture Builder and Vcommunicator Mobile: *http://www.vcom3d.com*.

- Worldweaver DX Studio for Windows allows users to develop animated characters, apps, and games with a suite of graphics tools: *http://www.dxstudio.com/*.

Mobile applications

- Adobe PhoneGap. A cross-platform tool for developing mobile apps including e-learning: *http://phonegap.com/*.

- ITC Learning Zirada mLearning Publisher is an authoring tool for mobile learning: *http://www.itclearning.com.au/*.

- Questionmark Perception is state-of-the-art assessment software and includes an iPhone/iPad app: *http://www.questionmark.com*.

- Trivantis Lectora Publisher. Can publish to HTML5 for mobile learning. Also offers Lectora Inspire which includes TechSmith Camtasia, Snagit, Flypaper and Snap!: *http://www.trivantis.com*.

Testing and assessment tools

There are many resources available to help with the creation of quizzes, polls, surveys, tests, and assessments for online learning. Below are a few of these. (For others, see the following LibGuides: *http://uiuc.libguides. com/aecontent.php?pid=64638&sid=2925751* and *http://uiuc.libguides. com/aecontent.php?pid=64638&sid=477624*.)

- Articulate Quizmaker: *http://www.articulate.com*.

- Google Analytics is a free service that allows users to track usage statistics for their websites. It requires creating an account, setting up profiles for the website(s) you want to track, and then adding nine lines of HTML code generated by Google Analytics to each web page you want to track. The code generated by Google Analytics includes references to the remotely hosted JavaScript file (ga.js) used by Google to collect data, the account number, and a reference to the JavaScript function. Most screencast software programs publish tutorials for use on the web as a shockwave flash (.swf) file, with an accompanying HTML and JavaScript file used to render the tutorial in a web browser. Before placing the tutorial online, the published HTML file needs to be edited so that it includes the analytics code: *http://www.google.com/analytics/*.

- Morae by TechSmith has three components: Recorder, Observer, and Manager. The Recorder has a camera built into the monitor to track participants' eye movements, record all clicks, and record all web page changes during the usability testing, as well as a microphone to record the participant's thinking process (using the think-aloud protocol). Participants' information experience during task completion is observed live from a distance using the Observer. An Observer, referred to as a task logger, can use the IP address of the computer on which the recording is taking place and connect directly to the computer. The task logger can watch the participant and hear comments and observations as tasks are being completed. The Observer will gain valuable insights into the thinking process of the participant without being seen by the participant or disrupting the testing process. The Manager is the third and most powerful part of the software. All recordings from the Recorder and all task loggings from the Observer are downloaded and analyzed on the Manager. The analysis consists of tabulating the number of web changes, the number of clicks, and the amount of time spent by a participant on the completion of each task. See *http://tnla.org/associations/5700/files/bakoyemappt.pdf* for a PowerPoint presentation by Fagdéba "Bako" Bakoyéma and Christy Groves on their use of Morae for usability testing. Other functionalities of the Manager include the ability to create video clips to highlight the participant's experience, as well as charts and PowerPoint presentations to share design issues with stakeholders and policy makers: *http://www.techsmith.com/morae.html*.

- Qarbon ViewletBuilder is software to create demonstrations, simulations, live recordings, quizzes, surveys, and highly interactive Flash content. Also available is Viewlet Quiz to create Flash surveys and quizzes: *http://www.qarbon.com*.

- Questionmark Perception offers state-of-the-art assessment software and also has an iPhone/iPad app: *http://www.questionmark.com*.

- Respondus is a test and assessment creation and management tool that integrates well with learning management systems. Also available is StudyMate, an inexpensive tool for creating Flash learning activities that can be used as a stand-alone tool or integrated into learning management systems. Focus on formal education: *http://www.respondus.com*.

- Tanida Quiz Builder creates quizzes in Flash: *http://www.quiz-builder.com*.

- TeraLearn Collaboration and Testing Solution (CTS) is a test and assessment tool. Authoring (including conversion from MS Word, PowerPoint, and Excel) is available as part of the system: *http://www.teralearn.com/*.

- Wondershare Quiz Creator for creating quizzes and surveys: *http://www.sameshow.com*.

Eye tracking software and equipment

Eye tracking software calibrates the computer monitor for the student's eyes and is useful in usability studies to track how the user views a page. The software, along with appropriate hardware, reflects, records, and tracks the student's eye movements.

The following link is to a wiki page that provides a catalog of eye tracking options. It is offered by COGAIN: Communication by Gaze Interactions: *http://www.cogain.org/wiki/Eye_Trackers*.

Software

Open source

- ITU Gaze Tracker is a video-based open source tracker: *http://www.gazegroup.org/downloads/23-gazetracker*. It is hosted through SourceForge: *https://sourceforge.net/projects/gazetrackinglib/*.

- openEyes is an open source, open hardware toolkit for low-cost real-time eye tracking: *http://thirtysixthspan.com/openEyes/software.html*.

- Wiki page for eye trackers: with a section for open source, low cost, and freeware: *http://www.cogain.org/wiki/Eye_Trackers#Open_source_gaze_tracking_and_freeware_eye_tracking*.

Commercial

- Attention Tool by iMotions Eye Tracking Solutions. Offers various products for usability and market research studies: *http://www.imotionsglobal.com/*.

- Nyan2 by Interactive Minds is an all-in-one eye tracking data analysis suite software package for eye tracking studies: *http://www.interactive-minds.com/en/eye-tracking-software*.

Equipment

Many software products provide suggestions for equipment to be used, but the minimum needed is a computer (60–120 hz) with between one and four cameras (can be a binocular system or a monocular system), a monitor, a keyboard, and a mouse. Examples of products are:

- SMI Vision: *http://www.smivision.com/*.

- Tobii Eye Tracker: *http://www.tobii.com/en/eye-tracking-integration/global/products-services/hardware/eye-tracking-academy*.

- Wiki page with many options: *http://www.cogain.org/wiki/Eye_Trackers#Eyetrackers_for_eye_movement_research.2C_analysis_and_evaluation/*.

Sophisticated eye tracking equipment may be available at universities with eye tracking labs that contain software and equipment such as SR Research's EyeLink trackers (the EyeLink II, the EyeLink 1000, and the EyeLink 2K) that can be reserved. See these pages for examples:

- Ball State University: *http://cms.bsu.edu/Academics/Centersand Institutes/CMD/InsightandResearch/Capabilities/EmergingMediaFormand Function/EyeTracking.aspx*.

- Bentley University Design and Usability Center: *http://usability.bentley.edu/eye-tracking*.

- University of Massachusetts Amherst Department of Psychology: *http://www.psych.umass.edu/eyelab/*.

- University of Southern California Neuroscience Program: *http://ilab.usc.edu/itrack/*.

Appendix 1
Survey to librarians: conducted by Lori Mestre, University of Illinois at Urbana-Champaign

Survey to librarians

This anonymous online survey consists of 19 questions (multiple-choice and short answer options). Respondents have many opportunities to provide additional comments to allow them to discuss major aspects of their experiences in developing tutorials and learning objects. The survey takes approximately ten minutes to complete and is submitted electronically. The sections of the survey include: Part I Design considerations (including how to design for multiple constitutencies); Part II Learning style considerations; Part III Assessment of tutorials; and Part IV Background information.

Part I: Design considerations for tutorials

1. Do you state the educational objectives for your tutorials?

    a. Yes

    b. No

    c. Other response (box to fill in)

2. Do your tutorials teach concepts (like process, Boolean operators) or focus on mechanics?

    a. They teach both concepts and mechanics

    b. They focus on a specific task or mechanic

    c. Comment (box to fill in)

3. What technologies do you use when creating your tutorials? Choose all that apply
   a. Camtasia/Captivate/Jing screencasts
   b. Flash
   c. Web pages only
   d. PowerPoint
   e. Video
   f. Other (box to fill in)

4. Do you have a systematic approach to designing tutorials (with guidelines for fonts, colors, sizes, length, captioning, voice, progression)?
   a. Yes, we have established guidelines/standards so all of our tutorials are consistent in look/feel/design/structure
   b. We generally know how we want them all to be, but haven't established guidelines
   c. Not really
   d. Comment (box to fill in)

5. Do you conduct a usability study before releasing your tutorial?
   a. Yes, for every one
   b. We did for the first one, but haven't consistently done that
   c. No
   d. Comment (box to fill in)

6. Who provides feedback on your tutorials or learning objects?
   a. Other colleagues
   b. Colleagues and students
   c. Students
   d. We don't have a systematic process for this
   e. Comment (box to fill in)

7. Do your tutorials or learning objects link out for librarian's help?
   a. Yes, we have a feature that allows students to access our chat or a librarian's email from within the tutorial
   b. No, we only include the librarian's information, the library URL or the Ask a librarian URL, but it's not interactive
   c. Comment (box to fill in)

8. Generally, how long are your tutorials or learning objects?

    a. 1–3 minutes

    b. 3–5 minutes

    c. 5–10 minutes

    d. Longer

    e. Comment (box to fill in)

Part II: Learning style considerations

1. Do you use media for learning through both auditory and visual channels?

    a. Yes, we include both

    b. We include many visuals, but not audio

    c. Our tutorials are text based only

    d. Our tutorials are text based with screenshots or images

    e. Other (box to fill in)

2. Do you incorporate active learning in your tutorials (e.g., where students can't proceed until they complete a task)?

    a. Yes, in every tutorial

    b. Yes, in some tutorials

    c. No

    d. No, but we'd like to if we had the technology and skills to do so

    e. Comment (box to fill in)

3. Do you use simulations or interactive features (or games) for tactile learners?

    a. Yes, we have these in every tutorial

    b. We have these, but embedded within the tutorial. We include pop-ups that allow them to practice

    c. We would love to do this but don't have the skills or software

    d. Other (box to fill in)

4. Do you systematically provide accessible alternatives for your tutorials (alt tags, accessible code, captioning, voice, static page alternatives, etc.)?

    a. Yes, it's a requirement at our institution

    b. Yes, generally, although it's not a requirement

c. We try to adhere to these but might not do it systematically

d. Other (box to fill in)

5. Do you use features to make the tutorials more library personal (live chat embedded, pictures of librarians, feedback boxes)?

a. Yes

b. Somewhat

c. Not yet

d. Please explain (box to fill in)

6. Do you plan your tutorial so that a user can pick and choose what to do next (from within the tutorial)?

a. Yes, we allow students to modify what they are doing even within a tutorial

b. No, there is no option to pick and choose. Each tutorial needs to run from beginning to end

c. Other (box to fill in)

7. Explain how you design and evaluate your tutorials or learning objects for multiple learning styles.

– (box to fill in)

Part III: Assessment of tutorials

1. Do you include quizzes with feedback, and simulations in your tutorials?

a. Yes, we embed these in each tutorial

b. We include a form at the end of each tutorial for feedback

c. We do this in conjunction with our learning management system (e.g., WebCT, ANGEL, Blackboard, Desire2Learn)

d. No, but we would like to

e. Not yet

f. Comment (box to fill in)

2. How else do you assess your tutorials?

– (open box for comment)

Part IV: Background information

1. What type of library are you affilitated with?

   a. Academic library

   b. Public library

   c. School library

   d. Special library

   e. Other

2. Have you had any training in learning styles?

   a. Yes, I've taken coursework

   b. Yes, I've attended workshops

   c. Only by reading and online info

   d. Not really

At the end of the survey, if you would be willing to provide URLs for your tutorials please contact lmestre@illinois.edu with a personal message with the URL.

Thank you for filling out the survey. If you have any questions or would like to follow-up please contact Lori Mestre: lmestre@illinois.edu.

Appendix 2
Learning style tutorial usability questions/script for ERIC, ORR, interactive tutorials (Group A)

Used for Mestre (2010) study

I. Learning style inventory. Each student takes two learning style quizzes (inventories): Vark *http://www.vark-learn.com/english/page.asp?p=questionnaire*; and the Index of Learning Styles (ILS) questionnaire *http://www.engr.ncsu.edu/learningstyles/ilsweb.html*. Results are printed off, but not shown to the individual until after they complete the study.

II. For each tutorial, students will take a pre-test, work through a tutorial, and then do a post-test. During the pre- and post-tests they will talk through what they are doing and why.

III. Students will then go through the tutorial again, this time answering questions as they go through the segments in order to provide a debriefing about the tutorials.

IV. The static web page ERIC tutorial will be done first, then the screencast tutorial of Online Research Resources, and then the interactive tutorial.

Group A: Process during session

I. Introductions and consent form/purpose of study form.
II. Background questions prior to first tutorial:

A. Are you taking or have you taken any online classes (either totally online or certain aspects online)? Yes _____ One _____ Two _____ Three _____ Four _____ Five or more _____ No _____

B. Have you ever used an online tutorial before? Yes _____ No _____ Not sure _____

III. Static tutorial for Group A (ERIC)

A. Which statement best describes your *previous* use of ERIC:

_____ I have never searched ERIC before today.

_____ I have searched ERIC at least once before today but had trouble finding what I needed.

_____ I have searched ERIC more than once before today and was able to find what I needed.

_____ I can successfully use ERIC to search for articles.

B. Today, I'm going to ask you to view a tutorial to help you learn about searching articles using ERIC. After viewing the tutorial you will be asked to do a search and then asked some additional questions. Here's the scenario: you need to find articles about the impact of television violence on children. Your instructor told you to search library databases, rather than just what's freely available on the Internet.

1. Pre-test questions: starting at the library home page (I have this open) show me and tell me how you would get articles on that scenario.

2. View ERIC tutorial (which includes an embedded quiz).

3. Post-test: now – let's go back to the library home page. Remember the scenario: you need to find articles about the impact of television violence on children. Your instructor told you to search ERIC, rather than just what's freely available on the Internet. Tell me and show me how you would find articles for your topic.

4. (They do the process and are reminded to talk through what they are doing as they do it and why, along with any impressions, comments, etc.)

C. Critique of static tutorial. Show tutorial page. Some of these are suggested questions to get responses.

1. Was the purpose of this tutorial clear? Did you know what the expected outcomes should be?

2. Describe your thoughts when viewing this tutorial. Comment on, text, visuals, organization …

3. Comment on the amount of text (explanation used). Was it the right amount, too much, too little?

4. What was your favorite part of the tutorial?

5. What was your least favorite part of the tutorial?

6. Were the images used helpful?

7. Did you read the text as you went along, or just focus on the images?

8. How understandable was the language and terminology used in the tutorial?

9. Comment on the information. Was it clear, understandable? Is there another way that the information could be presented?

10. What were the most troublesome areas you had in terms of understanding?

11. Did you feel at any point that this module was too long or too boring, or did you feel your attention drifting? If so, where?

12. Is there something else that would help make this tutorial more understandable, clearer?

IV. Group A: interactive tutorial (Online Research Resources)

A. Next I'm going to ask you to view a tutorial to help you learn about searching articles using Online Research Resources. Which statement best describes your *previous* use of Online Research Resources:

_____ I have never searched Online Research Resources before today.

_____ I have searched Online Research Resources at least once before today but had trouble finding what I needed.

_____ I have searched Online Research Resources more than once before today and was able to find what I needed.

_____ I can successfully use Online Research Resources to search for articles.

B. You will view a tutorial and be asked to do a search and then asked some additional questions. Here's the scenario: you need to find articles about sports and drugs at the college level. Your instructor told you to search through general library databases, rather than just what's freely available on the Internet. In this case you will *not* use ERIC.

1. View tutorial.

2. Post-test: now – let's go back to the library home page. Remember the scenario: you need to find articles about sports and drugs at the college level. Your instructor told you to search through general library databases, but not ERIC. Tell me and show me how you would find articles for your topic.

3. (They do the process with reminders to talk through the process.)

C. Critique of tutorial. (Show tutorial again.) Some of these are suggested questions to get responses:

1. Was the purpose of this tutorial clear? Did you know what the expected outcomes should be?

2. Describe your thoughts when viewing this tutorial. Comment on, text, visuals, organization …

3. What was your favorite part of the tutorial?

4. What was your least favorite part of the tutorial?

5. Comment on the amount of text (explanation used). Was it the right amount, too much, too little?

6. Were the images used helpful?

7. Did you read the text as you went along, or just focus on the images?

8. How understandable was the language and terminology used in the tutorial?

9. Comment on the information. Was it clear, understandable? Is there another way that the information could be presented?

10. What were the most troublesome areas you had in terms of understanding?

11. Did you feel at any point that this module was too long or too boring, or did you feel your attention drifting? If so, where?

12. Is there something else that would help make this tutorial more understandable, clearer?

13. Which type of tutorial was most helpful for you? Explain how.

14. Now that you've gone through a couple of tutorials, give your views on how you prefer to learn (e.g., by doing as the instructor explains, by hearing/seeing/reading and then doing, or by figuring it out on your own).

15. Do you prefer to have the information presented in a sequential manner or do you prefer to pick and choose the information?

V. Interactive tutorial: present the first few minutes of the tutorial and ask them to talk through what they are doing as they do it – their impressions, the pros and cons, etc.

VI. Demographic questions:

1. What year are you in college (freshman, junior, grad student, etc.)?

2. How old are you?

3. What is your major?

4. What was your identified learning style from both tests that you took?

5. What ethnicity/ethnicities/race do you identify with?

6. What is your native language?

7. What other languages do you converse in?

VII. Give them a summary of their learning style results and do any last debriefs from the session.

VIII. Give them the gift card (and have them fill out the form for this), copies of learning style results, and study information.

Lori Mestre
lmestre@illinois.edu
Head, Undergraduate Library
University of Illinois at Urbana-Champaign
217-244-4171

Appendix 3
Learning style tutorial usability questions/script for ORR, ERIC, interactive tutorials (Group B)

I.   Learning style inventory. Each student takes two learning style quizzes (inventories): Vark *http://www.vark-learn.com/english/page.asp?p=questionnaire*; and the Index of Learning Styles (ILS) questionnaire *http://www.engr.ncsu.edu/learningstyles/ilsweb.html*. Results are printed off, but not shown to the individual until after they complete the study.

II. For each tutorial, students will take a pre-test, work through a tutorial, and then do a post-test. During the pre- and post-tests they will talk through what they are doing and why.

III. Students will then go through the tutorial again, this time answering questions as they go through the segments in order to provide a debriefing about the tutorials.

IV. The static web page Online Research Resources tutorial will be done first, then the screencast tutorial of ERIC, and then the Interactive tutorial.

Group B: Process during session

I. Introductions and consent form/purpose of study form.

II. Background questions prior to first tutorial:

    A. Are you taking or have you taken any online classes (either totally online or certain aspects online)? Yes _____ One _____ Two _____ Three _____ Four _____ Five or more _____ No _____

B.   Have you ever used an online tutorial before? Yes _____ No _____ Not sure _____

III. Static tutorial for Group B (Online Research Resources):

A. Which statement best describes your *previous* use of Online Research Resources.

_____ I have never searched Online Research Resources before today.

_____ I have searched Online Research Resources at least once before today but had trouble finding what I needed.

_____ I have searched Online Research Resources more than once before today and was able to find what I needed.

_____ I can successfully use Online Research Resources to search for articles.

B. Today, I'm going to ask you to go view a tutorial to help you learn about searching articles using Online Research Resources. After viewing the tutorial you will be asked to do a search and then asked some additional questions.

1. Pre-test: you need to find articles about sports and drugs. Your instructor told you to search library databases, rather than just what's freely available on the Internet. You were told to go to the library web page to find this. (I have the screen at the library home page). Tell me and show me how you would find articles for your topic. (They do the process and are reminded to talk through what they are doing as they do it and why, along with any impressions, comments, etc.)

2. View Online Research Resources tutorial.

3. Post-test: now – let's go back to the library home page. Remember the scenario: you need to find articles about sports and drugs. Your instructor told you to search library databases, rather than just what's freely available on the Internet. You were told to go to the library web page to find this. Tell me and show me how you would find articles for your topic. (They do the process and are reminded to talk through what they are doing as they do it and why, along with any impressions, comments, etc.)

C. Critique of interactive tutorial. Show tutorial page. Some of these are suggested questions to get responses:

1. Is the purpose of this tutorial clear? Do you know what the expected outcomes should be?

2. Describe your thoughts when viewing this tutorial. Comment on narration, text, visuals ...

3. Did you think the use of the different modes (text, image, and sound) were helpful?

4. Did you read the text as you went along, or just focus on the narration and images?

5. If you read the text, did you have enough time to read all the screens?

6. How understandable is the language and terminology used in the tutorial?

7. Was the tutorial too fast or slow? Did it move too quickly?

8. Comment on the information. Was it clear, understandable? Is there another way that the information could be presented?

9. What were the most troublesome areas you had in terms of understanding?

10. Did you feel at any point that this module was too long or too boring, or did you feel your attention drifting? If so, where?

11. Is there something else that would help make this tutorial more understandable, clearer?

IV. Group B: Screencast tutorial (ERIC)

A. Next I'm going to ask you to view a tutorial to help you learn about searching articles using ERIC. Which statement best describes your *previous* use of ERIC:

_____ I have never searched ERIC before today.

_____ I have searched ERIC at least once before today but had trouble finding what I needed.

_____ I have searched ERIC more than once before today and was able to find what I needed.

_____ I can successfully use ERIC to search for articles.

B. You will view a tutorial and be asked to do a search and then asked some additional questions. Here's the scenario: you need to find articles about the impact of television violence on children. Your instructor told you to search library databases, rather than just what's freely available on the Internet.

1. Pre-test questions: starting at the library home page (I have this open) show me and tell me how you would get articles on that scenario.

2. View ERIC tutorial (which includes an embedded quiz).

3. Post-test: now – let's go back to the library home page. Remember the scenario: you need to find articles about the impact of television violence on children. Your instructor told you to search ERIC, rather than just what's freely available on the Internet. Tell me and show me how you would find articles for your topic.

4. (They do the process and are reminded to talk through what they are doing as they do it and why, along with any impressions, comments, etc.)

C. Critique of tutorial. (Show tutorial again.) Some of these are suggested questions to get responses:

1. Was the purpose of this tutorial clear? Did you know what the expected outcomes should be?

2. Describe your thoughts when viewing this tutorial. Comment on, text, visuals, organization …

3. What was your favorite part of the tutorial?

4. What was your least favorite part of the tutorial?

5. Comment on the amount of text (explanation used). Was it the right amount, too much, too little?

6. Were the images used helpful?

7. Did you read the text as you went along, or just focus on the images?

8. How understandable was the language and terminology used in the tutorial?

9. Comment on the information. Was it clear, understandable? Is there another way that the information could be presented?

10. What were the most troublesome areas you had in terms of understanding?

11. Did you feel at any point that this module was too long or too boring, or did you feel your attention drifting? If so, where?

12. Is there something else that would help make this tutorial more understandable, clearer?

13. Which type of tutorial was most helpful for you? Explain how.

14. Now that you've gone through a couple of tutorials, give your views on how you prefer to learn (e.g., by doing as the instructor explains, by hearing/seeing/reading and then doing, or by figuring it out on your own).

15. Do you prefer to have the information presented in a sequential manner or do you prefer to pick and choose the information?

V. Interactive tutorial: present the first few minutes of the tutorial and ask them to talk through what they are doing as they do it – their impressions, the pros and cons, etc.

VI. Demographic questions:

1. What year are you in college (freshman, junior, grad student, etc.)?

2. How old are you?

3. What is your major?

4. What was your identified learning style from both tests that you took?

5. What ethnicity/ethnicities/race do you identify with?

6. What is your native language?

7. What other languages do you converse in?

8. Would you prefer to learn this information directly from a teacher or through an online tutorial?

VII. Give them a summary of their learning style results and do any last debriefs from the session.

VIII. Give them the gift card (and have them fill out the form for this), copies of learning style results, and study information.

Lori Mestre
lmestre@illinois.edu
Head, Undergraduate Library
University of Illinois at Urbana-Champaign
217-244-4171

Appendix 4
Guidelines and procedures for creating tutorials in Camtasia

 University of Illinois at Urbana-Champaign

Note: A PDF of the complete guidelines is available at: *http://www. library.illinois.edu/diglit/camtasia.pdf*. The following is the table of contents for the complete document.

The guidelines, including screenshots, were compiled to ensure consistency and professionalism in the style and design of tutorials which are produced at the University of Illinois at Urbana-Champaign.

The sections included are:

Appendix 5
Marketing communication plan

Marketing strategies for online library services need to take a multifaceted approach in order to reach users in as many ways as possible, and collaboration with various groups and departments on campus is an important part of the process. The promotion of online library services can take advantage of high-tech options, but it should also work in the realm of "traditional" publicity as well.

As with most items that need to be promoted, it is good practice to have a communication plan. This plan provides the contact points for disseminating information regarding the tutorial/web page. It can include who to contact within departments, suggested online targets to link to or embed within the web page/tutorial, suggested discussion lists (listservs) for announcing the web page/tutorial, as well as suggested promotional language. There can be a general list of places to where to send the information, as well as specific departments depending upon the content of the tutorial. Library staff, faculty, and student workers need to be alerted to the list of tutorials so that they can point others to the list and potentially refer them to relevant tutorials at the point of need (whether in person or through a virtual reference chat). Table A5.1 is an example of a marketing checklist developed by Mestre to be used to announce a resource. In addition to containing particular places in which to announce the new resource, the checklist also contains sources where the tutorial can be downloaded, linked, or embedded, such as links on Facebook, Twitter, blogs, guides, YouTube, and through repositories. The checklist provides columns for documenting contact information and actions taken.

Table A5.1 Marketing checklist for tutorials

Mode of marketing	Name	Email	Phone	Website	Course management system	Date announcement sent	Date posted
Library electronic resources contact							
Library database contact (for web page info)							
Library help page contact							
Faculty member in …							
Faculty departmental listserv x							
Faculty departmental listserv y							
Faculty course management system z							
Housing media contact							
Listserv x							
Listserv y							
Listserv z							
Campus email distribution system for general notices							
Newsletter editor x							
Newsletter editor y							

Newsletter editor z							
Web page editor x							
Web page editor y							
Web page editor z							
Student listserv a							
Student listserv b							
Student listserv c							
Cultural house x							
Cultural house y							
Cultural house z							
Cultural houses ...							
Distance education coordinator							
Library listserv x							
Library listserv y							
Library listserv z							
Librarian x							
Librarian y							
Librarian z							
Blog x							
Blog y							
Blog z							
RSS feed x							
RSS feed y							
RSS feed z							

(continued)

Table A5.1   Marketing checklist for tutorials *(continued)*

Mode of marketing	Name	Email	Phone	Website	Course management system	Date announcement sent	Date posted
Library Twitter feed							
Twitter feed for ...							
Library Facebook							
Facebook for ...							
Library blog							
Faculty blog							
Student blog							
LibGuide editor x							
LibGuide editor y							
LibGuide editor z							
Institutional repository (download)							
ANTS *http:// liontv.blip.tv/* (to download)							
MERLOT (to download)							
YouTube (to download)							
iTunes U site (to download)							
http:// slideshare.net (to download)							

Appendix 6
Suggestions for multimedia inclusion

Table A6.1 (developed by Mestre) provides some strategies for incorporating instructional multimedia within tutorials to accommodate different learning styles and abilities. These suggestions were derived from the various research studies referred to in this book, and especially from student remarks and observations from the Mestre (2010) study. Table A6.1 could be used as a quick checklist when designing tutorials.

Table A6.1 Suggestions for multimedia inclusion

Instructional technique	Examples
Provide multiple examples of a concept	Use text in conjunction with pictures, diagrams, photos, definitions, contrast, metaphor, visual models. Include additional options for students who want to learn more.
Activities	Make activities easy to complete without help or explanation; and use worked examples for novices. Sequence content logically – start with simple, work up to more complex. Give learners control. Provide multiple opportunities.
Use appropriate multimedia	Remove unnecessary graphics, text, and audio: ■ do not use purely decorative or unrelated graphics; ■ make graphics as simple as possible; ■ use consistent graphics style throughout; ■ show graphics in context (e.g., whole search screen, not just search box).
Highlight salient points to focus on main points	Use voice tone, volume and pitch, body language (if video or photo), expressions, large font, italics, bolded text, icons, arrows, call-out bubbles, and repetition of main points. When using color, check on accessibility for screen readers and color blindness.

(continued)

Table A6.1 Suggestions for multimedia inclusion *(continued)*

Instructional technique	Examples
Provide options from which to "pick and choose"	Include visible navigation, table of contents, chapter markers, and concept headings to allow users to choose relevant sections to view. Branching is also effective for accommodating different learner needs.
Make the experience personal and relevant	Include features that personalize the experience (such as choosing a scenario, or character). Use examples that students will encounter in their daily life. Include interactions or activities that simulate a realistic context.
Present information in multiple formats	Use video, graphs, text, audio, kinesthetic, and reflective exercises. Provide options for students to follow along in a linear approach (step-by-step) or to pick and choose sections. Provide a static web page with screenshots, video clips, and exercises for those who want to scan quickly. Provide a PDF version of a screencast. Convert screencasts to additional files so that they can be downloaded easily to mobile devices.
Provide interactive experiences	Include activities that require the student to do something. These could be questions, multiple-choice questions, spot-checks, fill-in-the-blank responses, trying out a task (e.g., opening a new window), reflecting upon situations, drag and drop exercises, games, etc. Link steps to a broader conceptual framework; show how they fit into larger processes. Include activities that help develop higher levels of learning (evaluation and analysis) as well as lower levels (understanding and applying).
Avoid overload	When bringing in a new element (such as a call-out button to emphasize a point), cease talking. Only introduce one element at a time and provide time for the student to process the new information. Include text within images and put corresponding words and graphics near to each other.
Provide flexible models of skilled performance	Include various exercises, such as multiple-choice options, fill-in-the-blank exercises, pop-up windows to allow students to practice in a live context, and tasks to be completed outside the tutorial. Within the tutorial, provide examples of an expert performing the task (through video clip, Flash, or screencast). Show a before-and-after example.

Provide opportunities to practice with supports	Provide guided practice and scaffolding within a tutorial. Include options to "learn more" or "try it." Provide options for linking back to content for reinforcement. Include options for connecting with live chat support and sending responses to an instructor. Include "help" links within the tutorial and glossaries.
Provide ongoing, relevant feedback	Use frequent checks, such as periodic multiple-choice questions. Include scenarios or simulations that require an action and periodic questions that require a response from the student.

Index

Note: numbers in italic indicate figures or tables